Also by the Dolans

Smart Money: How to Be Your Own Financial Manager
Smart Money: Family Financial Planner

STRAIGHT TALK
on Money

Ken and Daria Dolan's Guide
to Family Money Management

Ken and Daria Dolan

A Fireside Book
Published by SIMON & SCHUSTER
New York   London   Toronto   Sydney   Tokyo   Singapore

FIRESIDE
Rockefeller Center
1230 Avenue of the Americas
New York, New York 10020

First Fireside Edition 1995

FIRESIDE and colophon are registered trademarks
of Simon & Schuster Inc.

Designed by Irving Perkins Associates
Manufactured in the United States of America

5   7   9   10   8   6   4

Library of Congress Cataloging-in-Publication Data is available.
ISBN 0-671-79808-1
0-684-80049-7 (Pbk.)

This publication expresses the opinions and ideas of its authors and is designed to provide useful advice in regard to the subject matter covered. It is sold with the understanding that the authors and publisher are not engaged in rendering legal, accounting, or other professional services. Laws vary from state to state, and if the reader requires expert assistance or legal advice, a competent professional should be consulted.

The authors and publisher specifically disclaim responsibility for any liability, loss, or risk, personal or otherwise, that is incurred as a consequence, directly or indirectly, of the use and application of any of the contents of this book.

This book is dedicated to our daughter, Meredith,
who turned a couple into a real family

Contents

How This Book Can Help You

"Hey, Dolans . . . another book! Why?" That's a good question. We thought we put everything anyone could ever use or need in our first book. But times change, and investment strategies that worked for most families in the '80s may be dead in the water in the '90s.

The 1980s brought American families a lot of economic and financial changes, some good and some bad. Tax law changes in 1986 and 1990 knocked the stuffing out of the best-laid investment plans, and the economic problems and federal budget deficit that still hang over us in the '90s will force more tough solutions onto our shoulders as this decade moves on. In Washington's drive to raise more money to pay the country's bills, we may be faced with even more financial shocks. What will happen to you if your parents' estate is taxed on the amount over $200,000 instead of over $600,000; if the cost of your child's college education keeps rising faster than inflation; if Social Security payments are taxed more; if one of your parents enters a nursing home; or if you're downsized out of your job?

All of these questions are real possibilities in your and your family's future. How will you answer them? Are you working with a financial professional who is able to help you (if he or she has even thought about these problems) or are you dealing with a product-pusher?

We see some disturbing trends among brokers, insurance agents, accountants, bankers, and financial planners—trends that you need to know about so that you can protect yourselves. You have to take a stronger stand and a more "hands-on" position with your family's money because there is advice, good and otherwise, flooding in from every quarter nowadays. Some of this advice is bogus. It's meant to confuse and mislead you. Some of it is given with the best of intentions and is just plain wrong.

So how do you find good, reliable information? (You're not going to like the answer!) You must learn the basics yourself. You can do it. Contrary to what some would have you believe, it's not that difficult. The financial services people aren't any smarter than you are. They've just spent more time at it than you have.

That's why we've written this book. If you follow along with us, you will see that it is possible to talk about money (you see we don't call it "finance"!) in simple, everyday language. You can get a handle on it. In fact, when they take charge of things themselves people consistently do better managing their own money than the professionals do. Wall Street doesn't want you to know this, but both the NAIC (National Association of Investor Corporations), the group that helps regular people organize and set up investor clubs, and the American Association of Individual Investors, which helps educate thousands of investors and would-be investors every year, can provide statistics to support this.

Which leads us to ask you, "If people do better on their own, why would you try to find someone else to do it for you?" Why? Because you've been made to think that you can't handle it yourself. But you can.

We want to let you in on a little secret your broker or financial planner would never want you to know. Before they try to sell a product to you, someone has to make a sales presentation of products to them. They are only the middlemen, at best, funneling products off the shelves of the brokerage firm, mutual fund company, or insurance company into your hands. And since we sat in that middleman position when we worked on Wall Street, we know of what we speak. We listened to a lot of "good news" sales presentations that didn't always hold up on closer scrutiny. But unless your investment adviser has an independent mind, he or she might be parroting back to you a bunch of selective statistics. It's been proven time and time again that you can get statistics to prove just about any case you want to make. Does that do you, the investor, any good? Usually not.

It's also important to understand that investment professionals generally follow the herd. Unless your adviser is the "head bull" who starts the trend and allows you to be the first one at the trough, you could wind up with little or nothing. The most successful investors don't follow the herd and end up reaping the greatest rewards. The hard reality is that your adviser is more than likely a follower if he or she can say, "Everybody's doing this."

The last point we want to make before we get started is that financial advisers are eternal optimists down to their toes. You can't sell any product unless you're excited and upbeat about it. But you know what happens when you're told how great a movie or a book is. The more people talk it up, the more likely you are to be disappointed when you see or read it. "What was all the fuss about?"

It's the same when you're built up to think you've just bought the next great investment by some pumped-up, energetic financial adviser. Even when it generates a reasonable return for you, it's not enough because you were told to expect a lot more. What's even worse about optimistic financial advisers is that when evolving circumstances burst their balloon of optimism (and from time to time this surely does happen), they react very badly, panicking and taking you and your portfolio down with them.

We believe it is critical that you read this book so that you can make your own decisions with confidence. It is crucial to your family's and your financial health because when you're sold an inappropriate investment you are the only one who loses. (The person selling it to you gets paid for both good and bad advice.)

Reading all the information we have brought together in this book can change your life. Our goal is to empower you to take control of your own financial future. Managing your money is *not* brain surgery. In fact, once you learn the basics, you will be able to take charge of every facet of your financial life yourself. You will be able to make intelligent decisions without a lot of expensive and often worthless advice.

Once you've read this book, you'll be able to buy mutual funds confidently without paying big commissions, buy stock at a discount and reinvest the dividends at no charge, tell the IRS, "No," and not be bothered by them again, even wring the best money possible out of a stingy employer.

The way to get the most out of this book is to take it a chapter at a time. Don't feel pressured to read it cover to cover over a weekend. First choose the chapters that are most important to your situation; you can come back and pick up the others later. Just remember, all you need are the basics to get started. Once the foundation is laid, you will be able to build any financial house you like: ranch, Tudor, or Colonial.

And keep in mind that your opinion counts. None of the professionals agree on how to proceed, so why should you worry if someone disagrees with a plan that feels right to you? If you put 100 financial planners, brokers, bankers, and insurance experts in one room, you would get 100 different opinions. So, together, let's make that 101 opinions! Those "experts" don't know you and your specific needs as well as you do yourself. Why should you let them tell you what's best for you and your family?

You will never again have to accept any investment advice that doesn't have your personal stamp on it. You won't have to follow the herd unless you feel it's the right move to make. You will never again have to make an investment decision out of fear or a feeling of inadequacy.

We are not going to weigh you down with a lengthy tome so packed with unnecessary details that you will end up more confused than confident. But this book will give you all the crucial information you need to make the right decisions in every aspect of your financial life.

Today is the beginning of the first day of a new financial life for you and your family. We are in the Information Age. Knowledge is power. Once you've finished reading this book you will be *empowered* with the knowledge to take control of your financial future yourself. You can do it!

Let's get started!

CHAPTER ONE

The Roof over Your Head

How to Buy, Finance, Insure, Refinance, and Sell Your Home

The American dream: being able to own your own home, a secure haven for yourself and your family. It is more than a house, more than an address, and *much more* than a mortgage payment. Yet it seems these days many of us find this dream simply that—a dream. Real estate prices have skyrocketed in the past 20 years, and what our parents took in stride as a regular milestone of life now seems beyond our reach.

Wait a minute! You *can* realize this dream, and make sure your family finances don't become a nightmare in the process. With a little help (that's what we're here for), you can afford a down payment, buy your house at the right price, keep your monthly payments reasonable, get the mortgage that is right for you, and wisely protect your home once you buy it.

In this chapter you'll learn about alternative sources of funding, cutting the fat out of your home owner's insurance premiums, no-money-down strategies, whether or not to use a real estate agent, how to choose between fixed- and adjustable-rate mortgages, minimizing points and other closing costs, and the tax breaks you get as a home owner. You'll also learn the pros and cons of some popular options you've probably heard a lot about lately—things like refinancing, biweekly mortgages, renting with an option to buy, and shared-equity arrangements.

By the end of this chapter, you'll be fully equipped to buy the house of your dreams and keep your costs down to earth.

SHOULD YOU BUY?

The first question you need to address right up front is whether or not to buy at all. Should you buy? Is now a good time? Our belief is that if you find a house you love and you can afford to make the payments on the mortgage, it's *never* a bad time to buy. What can you afford? As a rule of thumb, you should buy a home that will cost no more than 28 percent of your gross income. That means if your income is $50,000 per year, your monthly cost of mortgage payment (principal and interest), insurance, and property taxes combined should be no more than $50,000 ÷ 12 × 0.28, or $1,166.67 per month. Too many people in the mid-1980s were permitted, and in some cases encouraged, to take on housing debt in excess of 35 percent of their gross income ("Don't worry, your salary will increase"—NOT!) and they are running into trouble now. Use the table on pages 16 and 17 to estimate monthly mortgage payments, given the amount of the loan and the current interest rates. Then check with your local real estate agent or county tax assessor on property taxes. Finally, call your insurance agent and get an estimate on home owner's insurance. Add these all up and make sure they do not total more than 28 percent of your total annual income—an absolute maximum would be 30 percent.

If you have a lot of other debt, you must factor that into the equation as well. Most lenders don't like to see you spending more than 36 percent of your gross income on debt payments, including your mortgage. Is it time to buy? That depends on you. Just remember, it's *never* time to buy more than you can afford.

Don't buy your home as an investment—you'll be setting yourself up for disappointment. Don't expect the double-digit-inflation-swept appreciation we saw in the 1980s, when people moved every three years and kept buying bigger, more expensive houses. The 1990s will see much more modest growth, and in some parts of the country no growth—or even depreciation of real estate values. So you can't look at your home as a way to make money. It's a place to live, a place to raise your family, and one of the only ways to borrow money with the interest tax deductible (more on that later). If you sell at a profit—great! But don't let potential gain be the primary reason for selecting a particular home. One that's comfortable for your family at a price that doesn't put undue strain on your budget should be what you're looking for.

Of course, that doesn't mean everyone should rush out and buy a home. For example, if you are moving to a new town or retiring to a new community, we think it often makes good sense to rent for six months or a year before you buy. Get a feel for the neighborhood, see which parts of town you like and where you tend to spend time. Where are your friends, how is the commute to work, what about the schools or libraries or parks? Check out all the amenities and services that are important to you before you sign on the dotted line for a 30-year commitment. Make a decision that fits you and your family, and don't rush into it. Given today's sluggish real estate market, a good deal today will probably be an even better deal tomorrow.

NEGOTIATING THE BEST PRICE

Which brings us to our next subject: getting a good deal on your home purchase. Remember, in many ways buying a home is no different from buying a car—everything is negotiable! A lot of people don't realize how much power they have in the negotiation process. It's fine to say, "I'll pay your asking price if you pay my closing costs," but don't be blinded by the excitement (and strain) of negotiating. Keep your eye on the bottom line, what you're really paying for that house. Is it a competitive price?

Of course, the best way to know whether or not a given house is well priced is to do a lot of comparison shopping. Visit at least a dozen houses in the same neighborhood and compare. Do they all have central air-conditioning? Do they have a driveway, a carport, a garage? Are the windows single-pane or double-pane? Do they have good closet space? Adequate storage space? An attic or basement? How old are the appliances in the kitchen? These are some of the things to compare when you look at houses, above and beyond the number of bedrooms and bathrooms.

Let's run through a quick checklist of possible problem areas to look into before you write a check:

- Has the basement leaked in the past two years? If so, what has the seller done to repair it?
- Has the roof leaked in the past two years? If so, what has the seller done to repair it?
- When were the gutters last cleaned, and what condition are they currently in?

Here's a look at what your monthly mortgage payments would be at various interest rates and mortgage amounts.

Monthly Mortgage Payments

15-year fixed-rate loan (monthly principal and interest payments):

Loan amount	7%	7½%	8%	8½%	9%	9½%	10%	10½%	11%	11½%	12%
$ 20,000	179.77	185.40	191.20	196.95	203.00	209.00	214.93	221.08	227.32	233.64	240.04
25,000	224.70	231.75	239.00	246.18	253.75	261.25	268.66	276.35	284.15	292.05	300.05
30,000	269.64	278.10	286.80	295.42	304.50	313.50	322.39	331.62	340.98	350.46	360.06
35,000	314.59	324.45	334.60	344.66	355.25	365.75	376.12	386.89	397.81	408.87	420.06
40,000	359.53	370.80	382.40	393.90	406.00	418.00	429.85	442.16	454.64	467.28	480.07
45,000	404.47	417.15	430.20	443.13	456.75	470.25	483.58	497.43	511.47	525.69	540.08
50,000	449.41	463.50	478.00	492.37	507.50	522.50	537.31	552.70	568.30	584.10	600.09
55,000	494.36	509.85	525.80	541.61	558.25	574.75	591.04	607.97	625.13	642.51	660.10
60,000	539.30	556.21	573.60	590.84	609.00	627.00	644.77	663.24	681.96	700.92	720.11
65,000	584.24	602.56	621.40	640.08	659.75	679.25	698.50	718.51	738.79	759.33	780.11
70,000	629.18	648.91	669.20	689.32	710.50	731.50	752.23	773.78	795.62	817.74	840.12
75,000	674.12	695.26	717.00	738.56	761.25	783.75	805.96	829.05	852.45	876.15	900.13
80,000	719.06	741.61	764.80	787.79	812.00	836.00	859.69	884.32	909.28	934.56	960.14
100,000	898.83	927.01	956.00	984.74	1,015.00	1,045.00	1,074.61	1,105.40	1,136.60	1,168.19	1,200.17

30-year fixed-rate loan (monthly principal and interest payments):

$ 20,000	133.06	139.84	146.75	153.78	161.00	168.20	175.52	182.95	190.47	198.06	205.73
25,000	166.32	174.80	183.44	192.23	201.25	210.25	219.40	228.69	238.09	247.58	257.16
30,000	199.59	209.76	220.13	230.68	241.50	252.30	263.28	274.43	285.70	297.09	308.59
35,000	232.85	244.72	256.82	269.12	281.75	294.35	307.16	320.16	333.32	346.61	360.02
40,000	266.12	279.68	293.51	307.57	322.00	336.40	351.03	365.90	380.93	396.12	411.45
45,000	299.38	314.64	330.20	346.01	362.25	378.45	394.91	411.64	428.55	445.64	462.88
50,000	332.65	349.60	366.88	384.46	402.50	420.50	438.79	457.37	476.17	495.15	514.31
55,000	365.91	384.56	403.57	422.91	442.75	462.55	482.67	503.11	523.78	544.67	565.74
60,000	399.18	419.53	440.26	461.35	483.00	504.60	526.55	548.85	571.40	594.18	617.17
65,000	432.44	454.49	476.95	499.80	523.25	546.65	570.43	594.59	619.02	643.69	668.60
70,000	465.71	489.45	513.64	538.24	563.50	588.70	614.31	640.32	666.63	693.21	720.03
75,000	498.97	524.41	550.33	576.69	603.75	630.75	658.18	686.06	714.25	742.72	771.46
80,000	532.24	559.37	587.02	615.14	644.00	672.80	702.06	731.80	761.86	792.24	822.90
100,000	665.30	699.21	733.77	768.92	805.00	841.00	877.58	914.74	952.33	990.30	1,028.62

- Has there been any standing water around the driveway or foundation in the past two years?
- Have any windows leaked in the past two years? If so, what has the seller done to repair them?
- How old is the roof?
- How old is the furnace, the air-conditioner, and the water heater?
- When was the fireplace last used?
- Are there any storm doors, storm windows, screen doors, or window screens, other than what are installed currently?
- How much insulation is there in the basement/crawl space and attic?
- What type of floor is under any carpeted areas?

And let us add one more caveat. Don't assign great value to furnishings and finishings. When you finally move in and pull back those drapes, they could be totally rotted through. So if you can get the seller to throw them in because he's too lazy to take them down, that's one thing, but don't pay extra for them. The same goes for appliances. Three weeks after you move in, you could find that you have to replace the dishwasher, a burner blows on the stove, etc.

A good negotiation lets everybody win. You need to discover what the seller needs, not what the seller wants. By asking questions like "How long have you lived here? Why are you selling?" you can get a sense of what it will take to make the seller happy *and* get you a good price.

DOLANS' SAFETY WARNING: Don't sign a deal where you have to wait for the seller to find and buy a house to move to. It could take six months for him to find another house. Meanwhile, you have everything on hold, possibly buyers of your current home who want to move in, possibly interest rate changes—who knows? If you have to wait six months, the value of the house you've made a deal on could even drop.

USING A REAL ESTATE BROKER WHEN YOU BUY

When you're shopping for a home, unless you're dealing directly with sellers, the people you'll see most often are real estate agents. Don't take anything they say as gospel. *They're not working for you.* Most people don't realize that the agent is the *seller's* broker. And a lot of people get taken advantage of by forgetting that.

A real estate agent is not going to point out the warps, the furnace cracks, the rusty pipes. And that means you should always insist on an inspection—even for a brand-new home. Just because a house is new doesn't mean it was constructed the way it was supposed to be.

And *you* hire the inspector. Do not use the real estate agent's inspector—get your own. Licensed inspectors are listed in the Yellow Pages. Does it make sense to spend a couple hundred dollars on a home inspection to protect a $50,000 + investment? You know where we stand on that one!

A real estate agent, even one working for the seller, can give you a lot of information. You can find out the age of the house, what improvements and modifications have been made, and so on. But don't take everything that the agent says as Bible truth.

The best thing to do is to find a way to get into a friendly conversation with the people who are selling the house. Find out things like how long they've been in the house and why they're selling. If you get an answer like, "We lost a job and we have to sell to move someplace else," you probably have considerable leeway in negotiating the price, particularly in a bad market. If the sellers have lived in the house for 30 or 40 years, they probably have their mortgage paid off, so that the entire sale is profit. Again, in that type of situation you may have a little more negotiating room on price and seller financing.

On the other hand, if the sellers say they're moving because the public schools aren't good enough for their kids or the street gets too much through traffic, you may want to reconsider. Even if you don't have school-age children, when you eventually try to sell the house yourself, you may have a difficult time finding a buyer.

You can also use a *buyer's broker,* something most people don't know about. Yes, you'll pay a fee, but you get a professional working on your side, asking the right questions, negotiating the price, and so on. So if you really hate negotiating, or you feel out of your league when buying a home, consider putting a real estate professional on *your* side. A buyer's broker will help you by ensuring that the house is inspected before you buy—that most important element we keep harping on! He or she can also often obtain a copy of the deed, which lists the original price; that can be a real boost for your negotiation strategy.

How are buyer's brokers compensated? There are three different methods: 1) They can take a percentage of the purchase price, 2) they can work for a flat fee, or 3) they can charge by the hour. We recommend either the flat fee or hourly charge. The broker will have less temptation to lead you toward more expensive houses if he is not going to receive a percentage of the sale price.

We'll grant you it's not the easiest thing in the world to find a buyer's broker. There are only a little over 6,000 of them around the country, but if you do some research you can find one. Ask your local board of realtors, insurance agent, or real estate attorney first. If those avenues fail to produce, send $25.00 plus $2.90 postage to P.O. Box 23275, Ventura, CA 93002 (805-643-2337 or 800-729-5147), requesting *Who's Who in Creative Real Estate*, a national directory of more than 1,000 brokers' names and addresses.

SECRETS TO FINDING THE BEST HOUSE BUY

One question few buyers ask is: "How long has this house been on the market?" Yet this is an extremely important consideration! If you find that the house was first listed 18 months earlier and is still for sale, the sellers might be desperate and might drop the price. Also ask at what price the house was initially listed. Check the broker's listing sheets for this information.

Remember, an agent is going to take you to the most recently listed properties. It's just human nature to avoid properties that others have avoided in the past. You can safely assume that almost everything you're being taken to is relatively new to the market. Which means you're probably not going to see the bargains—unless you ask.

If you're looking for a real bargain, what you really want to do is to say, "I want to be taken to your oldest listings." Who is going to be the most anxious to get the heck out? The person who has been sitting there for six months or more.

You will also get a better deal if you make yourself an *attractive buyer*. That means being ready, willing, and able to buy. Shop for mortgage money *before* you go looking at houses. If you've already been preapproved for the mortgage, you come to a seller saying, "We're not going to have a problem getting a mortgage loan. We've got a committed lender. So, real estate agent, we don't need any of your help in finding mortgage money, and we can get this closed in X number of days. We're ready!"

Along the same lines, a first-time buyer may actually be more attractive than someone who already owns a home. If you can come to the seller and say, "I don't have to worry about selling my home before I can buy yours," you may be in a much stronger negotiating position—especially if that house has been on the market for many months.

DOLANS' CREDIT ALERT: It's a great idea to check on your credit and make sure the report is clear and error-free before someone else (like a prospective lender) checks it. You can get a free report once a year from the credit-reporting service TRW. Write to TRW Consumer Assistance, P.O. Box 2350, Chatsworth, CA 91313-2350. Include your full name, current address, addresses for the past five years, Social Security number, and date of birth. Also enclose a copy of something with your current address printed on it, such as your driver's license.

Check your credit a good 60 days before you intend to apply for a loan; that way, if there is a problem, you can clear it up before you apply for the loan.

BUYING HOMES FROM FORECLOSURES

The one silver lining to the horrible banking crisis of the past few years is the fact that home buyers have more opportunity than ever before to pick up bargains by buying foreclosed homes. Chances are quite good that your bank has more real estate in its portfolio than it cares to think about, and you could be just the buyer to take that property off its hands. Call the REO (Real Estate Owned) department of your local bank for foreclosure information.

Every time the Resolution Trust Corporation (RTC) closes another S&L, it picks up a bundle of real estate. The RTC has homes in every state, with the most plentiful supplies in Arizona, Florida, Louisiana, New Jersey, New York, Oklahoma, and Texas. To find out about listings in your area, call 800-782-3006. You'll reach the RTC's Asset Information Program. Tell them what kind of home you're looking for, and they'll mail you a list for free.

The RTC also auctions off homes. To find out about auctions near you, call 800-348-1484. Just remember, auction buyers are almost exclusively cash buyers, so come prepared to write a check.

A MORTGAGE YOU CAN LIVE WITH

Once you've found a house you want to buy, and you've agreed on a price you're comfortable with, you're ready to shop for a great deal on a mortgage.

Just as in shopping for a house, when you're looking for a mortgage, you want to comparison shop. Talk to at least three different lenders and find out the kinds of deals they offer. Our favorite source of information on mortgage rates is HSH Associates in Butler, New Jersey; call 800-UPDATES. HSH Associates canvasses the country every week and compiles many lenders' mortgage rates. For $20.00, they will send you the complete list of mortgage deals in your area for any given week. Instead of your having to call any and all lenders to see what they're offering, you get the entire picture in one up-to-date list. It's a great time and aggravation saver.

When comparing mortgages, you will be faced with a lot of different choices, so let's walk through the various options one by one to help find the package that's best for you.

First, you're going to have to choose between a fixed-rate mortgage and an adjustable-rate mortgage (ARM). In the '80s, people who chose the adjustable rates looked like the smartest ones because we went from extremely high inflation and corresponding interest rates to much lower inflation and interest rates, so their mortgage payments kept going down. But we don't think that will be generally true for the 1990s.

Basically speaking, we prefer fixed-rate mortgages, because you can lock in low interest rates now and never have to worry about seeing your monthly mortgage payment go up—our "no surprises" strategy. We don't believe that people should take great risks with their hard-earned bucks. We like to know what we're getting for our money. We say you should shop for the best mortgage you can get at the time you are going to buy, lock it in, and buy your house.

Generally, when you apply for a mortgage you can lock in an interest rate that stays in effect for 60 days. If you think it will take longer than 60 days to get to settlement, ask for a longer lock-in period up front—*before* you pay the mortgage application fee with the interest rate locked in. Be sure the contract you sign also has a "mortgage contingency clause" based on that rate, otherwise you could lose your deposit if rates rise and you can't close. Don't try to outguess the market by waiting for a better interest rate. It's like trying to buy a stock on the day it trades at its lowest price; it's virtually impossible to do. If the house is fairly priced and the mortgage carries an interest rate that you can afford, don't try to guess. Once you've locked in a rate, you don't have this uncertainty hanging over your head. You know what the number is going to be.

DOLANS' SAFETY TIP: Lock in your rate *in writing,* not over the telephone. You may even be able to get a written agreement that promises that if rates go lower, you'll get the lower rate. Once again, negotiate.

DOLANS' SCAM BUSTER: Since the lock-in period is usually 60 days, unscrupulous lenders could try to slow down the approval process if interest rates are going up, in hopes of going beyond the 60-day period and seeing the lock expire. The only way they are going to approve your loan quickly and rush to settlement is if they are absolutely, totally, 100 percent convinced that rates are going down. If you suspect your lender is up to these kinds of dirty tricks, contact your state banking department.

You know the old saying "The squeaky wheel gets the grease." Once you've chosen your lender, keep after him. Call every few days to inquire if he needs any more paperwork, if he can read your application, and how your loan is proceeding. Left to his own devices, with no gentle prodding from you, it could take longer to get your mortgage approval. So nicely bug the lender periodically.

WHEN DOES AN *ARM* MAKE SENSE?

The only time an adjustable-rate mortgage makes sense is when you know you're only going to live in the house for three years or less. Here's why. Generally speaking, the adjustables are 2 percent lower than the fixed. In year one you're 2 percent ahead of the game. Most ARMs cannot be raised more than 2 percent per year (6 percent for the life of the loan), so even if rates go up to the max, you'll still be even with the fixed rate in year two. If rates continue to go up, you could be 2 percent above the original fixed rate in year three, but that just washes out the advantage you had in year one, and you're net even.

However, if you stay in that house beyond three years, an ARM could turn out to be much more expensive than a fixed rate. And now is not the time to be buying for the short term. A house, generally speaking, is an illiquid asset. You can't assume you will be ready, willing, and able to sell in three years. We feel you're taking a big risk now to go with an adjustable rate.

However, if you do decide to go with an ARM, there are three very important things to remember.

Number one: Opt for a three-year ARM rather than a one-year ARM if you can get one. Rates lately have tended to go in three-year cycles, and if you can get a low three-year rate now, you may be adjusting at the low point in the cycle every time. But you must hit the low in the cycle or you could end up readjusting at the high point every three years.

Number two: Make sure your ARM has a cap on both the incremental raise and the lifetime raise. In other words, you want to be sure that the interest rate can't go up more than a certain amount (no more than 2 percent) each time *and* that it can't go up more than a certain amount (no more than 6 percent) during the entire lifetime of the loan. Be sure you can afford the payments under the worst-case scenario.

Number three: In terms of the interest rate on which your ARM interest rate is based, make sure your ARM is tied into one of our two favorite indexes. Every ARM is tied to a certain public rate, such as the six-month Treasury bill rate or the Federal Funds rate. When it's time to adjust your mortgage, the bank adds a predetermined amount to this rate, maybe 4 percent, to come up with your new rate.

The two indexes we like are the six-month Treasury bill interest rate (which is released by the Federal Reserve on the first business day of each week) and the 11th District Cost of Funds (which is released on the last business day of each month). The 11th District is generally better but harder to find. You can call the Federal Home Loan Bank in San Francisco, at 415-616-2600, for the current rate. We like these two because they tend to be less volatile.

To summarize, an ARM can give you a lower monthly payment in the early years, but it may well cost you more money (and peace of mind) down the road.

WHAT ABOUT 15-YEAR MORTGAGES?

In general, we prefer fixed- over adjustable-rate mortgages, and we prefer *30-year* fixed-rate mortgages, for one reason only: Your monthly payment will be lower. With discipline, you can always pay it off much sooner by prepaying principal, but you're not committed to do that.

There's been a lot of publicity lately about 15-year mortgages. You'll get a lower interest rate on the 15-year mortgage, but your monthly payments will be higher because you're paying off your loan twice as fast. There's certainly nothing wrong with paying it off in less than 30 years. But our point is: Keep it flexible. Take the 30-year, and you still have the option of prepaying it if you want. But if you don't want to prepay—or you get into a situation where you *can't* make those extra payments—you don't have to and can just continue with your regular payments.

Some home buyers may qualify for Veterans Administration (VA) loans. We say that if you can survive all the paperwork, you may find a good rate there. But you have to have a lot of patience to deal with VA-approved lenders. The VA will approve financing up to 100% of the appraised value of the home or the purchase price, whichever is less. Usually lenders will allow loans to a maximum amount of $184,000 on a VA-guaranteed loan. VA loans have now been expanded to include reservists and members of the National Guard who have served for six years or more, so don't assume your type of service doesn't count. Check with your local Department of Veterans Affairs office for more detailed information, or call the national office, at 800-827-1000.

New rules will also help home buyers obtain Federal Housing Administration (FHA) loans. You can now borrow up to 100 percent of closing costs, the FHA maximum has now risen to $151,725, and your interest can now be as low as 3 percent on the first $25,000, 5 percent on the next $120,000, and 10 percent on anything above $125,000. You'll also have to pay a 3.8 percent fee for FHA insurance, plus an annual mortgage interest premium of 0.5 percent. Call 202-708-2676 for more information.

One more warning about mortgages: Remember we said not to use the real estate agent's inspector? Don't necessarily take any "easy financing" he may recommend either. He could have cut a sweetheart deal with the lender that doesn't get *you* the best deal in town.

REDUCING POINTS AND CLOSING COSTS

We are often asked how to compare one loan with a higher rate but fewer points to another loan with a lower rate but more points. We have a very easy rule of thumb to help you make that comparison.

First, let's be clear on our terminology. Points are an up-front fee charged by the lender; they are part of your cost in taking out the loan. One point is simply 1 percent of the amount *financed*. That means if you buy a $100,000 house and you make a down payment of $10,000, you are financing $90,000, and 1 point would be $900.

How do you compare a 7 percent mortgage with 2 points to an 8 percent mortgage with no points? Simple. Just count every point as an eighth of a percent added to your mortgage interest rate. Using our example above, if you are offered a 7 percent mortgage with 2 points, 2 points equal two-eighths (or one-quarter), so effectively you have a 7¼ percent mortgage. That still beats 8 percent with no points, so it's worth paying the points.

Banks are notorious for saying, "We'll give you 7.875 (7⅞ percent) interest and 2 points or 8.125 (8⅛ percent) interest with no points." And people will say, "Oh, I can save money. I'll go with the no points." But they are being offered the exact same deal!

What if you don't have the cash up front to pay the points? Sometimes you can negotiate with the seller to raise the selling price of the house by the cost of the points, and then have the seller pay the points. What you're really doing is folding the points into your mortgage. That way, you can still get the lower interest rate, if that indeed turns out to be the better deal. For example, let's say you agreed to buy the home for $140,000, with points that will cost $3,000. Ask the seller to bump the price to $143,000. Then have him pay the points with the extra $3,000. He receives the $140,000 he was asking for, and you get to pay the points over the life of the loan.

As for closing costs, you should assume they'll run between 5 and 7 percent of the amount financed. This is another possible area of negotiation with the seller. He may be willing to pay for some of the closing costs in order to sell the house. Here are the basic closing costs you'll encounter:

2–5 points (2 percent–5 percent of the amount financed)

$1,000–$3,000 for title search, title insurance, and certificate of occupancy

$750–$1,000 for attorney's fees

$500–$750 for property appraisal (the cost of the bank's appraiser to estimate the value of the home) and application fees (the cost of applying the loan)

$500 for legal fees to the bank

$300–$500 for an engineering inspection

$100–$300 for termite inspection
$100 for recording fees
$300–$500 for the survey

If you are buying a house that was only recently purchased and is now being resold, you may be able to skip the survey and the appraisal. Two particularly helpful books on the subject are *The Common Sense Mortgage* (1993 edition), by Peter G. Miller (Harper Perennial, $10.00) and *Successful Real Estate Negotiation,* by Peter G. Miller and Douglas M. Bregman (Harper Perennial, $8.95).

HOW MUCH SHOULD YOU FINANCE?

Many people wonder, should I finance the maximum amount? Is it in my best interest to put down as little (or as much) as possible? Generally speaking, you should only mortgage what is comfortable for you and your family. And that goes back to our 28 percent rule. Your mortgage payments should not be more than 28 percent of your annual gross income.

Don't be blinded by the tax deductibility of your interest payment. Don't get us wrong, we *love* tax-deductible interest! But you can tax-deduct yourself right into the poor house! Remember, your net tax savings at best has been 31 cents for every interest dollar, though under President Clinton this could rise.

What we're really saying is that just because mortgage interest is tax deductible, that doesn't mean you don't have to pay it. And you can't wait until your taxes are filed to pay it. You have to make a payment every single month.

When you're shopping for a lender, pick the one with whom you'd prefer to do business. If it's not the best deal you've been offered, maybe you can get him to sweeten it. Try saying, "I can do better over there. But I've been your client for X number of years. Don't you want to keep me? Because I've decided that whoever gives me a mortgage also gets my personal accounts." You *can* negotiate with some lenders. It doesn't matter if it's a traditional lender or a mortgage broker or a mortgage banker. You want the lender who is going to give you and your family the *best deal today.*

A lender may turn around and sell your mortgage to somebody else once the closing is over, especially if it's a small bank or mortgage company. There's not much you can do about it, and it's not usually a problem, but to protect yourself, ask how it would affect you, if at all? How could you get stuck? Are there any "due on sale" clauses? (That means you would have to repay the entire mortgage.) Basically, you want to make sure that even if the loan is sold, your terms won't change.

DOLANS' SCAM BUSTER: If you get a mortgage bill from a strange company saying that your loan has been sold, *confirm that fact before you send any money*. Your original lender should also inform you that your loan has been sold. If you haven't heard from your original lender, check it out!

Most lenders begin foreclosures after a 90-day period of non-payment. We've heard some nasty stories about people paying a "new lender" only to find out the whole thing is a scam. They got notices from the real lender saying they were being fore-closed on while three months of their mortgage payments were probably headed for Tahiti.

DOLANS' SAFETY WARNING: Don't get caught in the middle of the loan process only to see your bank go belly-up. Yes, you're negotiat-ing and you're getting the best deal, but you don't want the best deal if it's from an unsafe bank.

You may be saying, "What do I care if it's unsafe? It's giving *me* money!" But if you are in the middle of the loan process and that bank goes under, it will probably take your loan fees with it, and you could be out thousands of dollars without a mort-gage. If you're using a bank, savings and loan, or credit union, check their safety. It's easy to do. A company called Veribanc checks the balance sheets of all three types of institutions quar-terly; for $10.00 for the first inquiry and $5.00 for each additional institution, Veribanc will tell you whether or not the lender is in good financial shape. Call 800-44-BANKS.

OUR TWO FAVORITE NO-MONEY-DOWN STRATEGIES

First-time buyer's lament: What if you really have no money to put down, but you can afford the monthly mortgage payments? Our two favorite little-or-no-money-down strategies are *rent with an option to buy* and *shared-equity arrangements*.

Renting with an option to buy is a great deal for you. You get to try out the house before you buy it. And if you decide it really *is* what you thought you wanted, you've already built up some equity. You can usually apply 25 to 50 percent of the money you've paid in rent toward the purchase price. That's why this strategy is far more beneficial for the would-be buyer than it is for the seller. Once people start living in a place, they realize what is wrong with it. Seventy percent of such lease options never materialize into a sale.

The seller also has to be careful of the installment sale rule. Of course, the renter wants as much of his rent payments as possible to count toward purchase. But if too much of the rent is applied toward purchase, the IRS may consider it an installment sale. That wouldn't hurt the person renting with an option to buy, but it could be a real big tax problem for the seller.

The other strategy for buyers who can't come up with a down payment is to get your parents (or other relative) to make a shared-equity arrangement with you. They make the down payment; you make the mortgage payments. You qualify for the mortgage on your income, and you get the mortgage-interest tax deductions. Your parents retain 50 percent ownership in the property and get a whole slew of real estate investment tax write-offs. With their kids living there, they also have good partners for their investment! Some years down the road, you can either pay them back with 50 percent of the appreciated price of the property (or as negotiated) and become the sole owner, or when the property is sold you split the profits 50–50.

We must say we prefer equity sharing with parents or other relatives over dealing with total strangers, particularly during difficult economic times. If family members have been intelligent about their finances to date, we don't think they are all of a sudden going to get stupid and put up money on an asset that's not worth it. And they don't want to see their kids in a tough situation. They have just as much interest in their kids getting a good deal as themselves. For more information on both strategies, and others, we like Martin Shenkman's book *How to Buy a House with Little (or No) Money Down* (Wiley & Sons, $12.95, paperback).

CUTTING THE COSTS OF OWNING YOUR HOME

We've talked so far about getting a good deal when you buy your home. We'd also like to share with you some tips on good deals after you buy.

One of the most popular trends these days is the biweekly mortgage. Basically, instead of paying mortgage interest 12 times a year, you divide your monthly payment in half and pay that amount (which is ½₄ of your annual mortgage interest payment) every two weeks. You thereby make 13 months' worth of payments in 12 months. Great idea—as long as your money goes to the right place! Stop and think for a moment. If you're making a thirteenth payment, that payment is applied to both principal and interest. Wouldn't you save more if you just made principal payments? Certainly.

Unfortunately, in a properly structured biweekly mortgage that thirteenth payment is, in fact, applied to both principal and interest. But that's still a good deal because just one extra month's payment per year can cut a 30-year mortgage down to a 21-year mortgage—and save you many thousands of dollars in interest payments. But the fact is that many biweekly mortgage payment programs are biweeklies *in name only*. Often your two biweekly payments are held until the end of any given month, so that in reality you are still making 12 monthly payments. A true biweekly mortgage is hard to find.

DOLANS' SCAM BUSTER: Watch out for the so-called prepayment companies that charge you a fee to do what you could easily do yourself. They may not really be making biweekly payments for you. They may keep the money in the bank, make your monthly payments, and pocket that thirteenth payment for themselves, or—worse yet—they may take your money and leave town! Always deal directly with the lender in making any prepayment arrangement.

We think the discipline of prepaying principal only each month along with your regular monthly mortgage payment is the best way to go. According to our friend Marc Eisenson, who's written a great book on prepaying your mortgage called *The Banker's Secret*, it doesn't take much to turn your 30-year loan into a 15-year loan—and save many thousands of dollars by doing so. For example, says Marc, if you have a 30-year $100,000 mortgage at 10 percent, you can cut your mortgage from 30 to 15 years by prepaying principal at the rate of $197.03 per month, and you'll save $122,481 in interest payments over the life of the loan. If your $100,000 mortgage is at 9 percent, you prepay $209.64 per month to cut your mortgage term from 30 to 15 years and save $107,086 in interest. And if your mortgage is at 8 percent, you prepay $221.89 per month to cut your mortgage from 30 to 15 years and save $92,133 in interest. To purchase a copy of *The Banker's Secret* ($14.95) write to Good Advice Press, Box 78, Elizaville, NY 12523 or call 800-255-0899.

Now let's show you what only $25 a month prepayment of principal can do for you. Suppose you have a $100,000 mortgage at 10 percent. You can prepay just $25 per month and save more than $36,000 over the life of the loan. The reason? By prepaying principal you are, in fact, reducing the life of the loan, and hence the number of interest payments. See below for savings at other rates of interest and prepayment amounts:

Monthly Prepayment of Principal

	$25	*$50*	*$100*	*$200*
$100,000 MORTGAGE @	INTEREST PAYMENTS SAVED WITH			
10%	$36,657	$60,322	$90,496	$123,176
9%	$29,441	$49,434	$75,785	$105,108
8%	$23,337	$39,906	$62,456	$ 88,260

SAVING MONEY ON HOME OWNER'S INSURANCE

We've discovered that most home owners are overpaying for their home owner's insurance. Yes, you want to protect your home and property. But remember, even if the house burns to the ground, the land isn't going anywhere; the foundation and underground pipes aren't going anywhere. So don't insure 100 percent. Eighty percent of the value should do it. "Eighty percent of what," you ask? Not the market value of the property. What a prospective buyer might be willing to pay to buy your home has nothing to do with the amount of insurance you need. You want to insure for *replacement cost*—what it would cost to rebuild your house if it burned down or blew away. That generally is a different and may be a smaller amount. Your insurance agent should be able to give you a good idea of the cost per square foot of construction. If your agent isn't sure or guesstimates a number, call a couple of local builders and ask their construction costs or hire an appraiser.

Inside the house, make sure you insure for the *replacement value*, not current value, of your furnishings and appliances. That 10-year-old TV may not be worth more than $50, but you sure will have to spend more than $50 to replace it! Use the inventory listing on page 33 to create a worksheet for the household items you'll want to insure.

We'll talk more about smart insurance shopping in Chapter Two, but let us leave you happy home owners with a few more money-saving tips:

- Buy your home owner's, auto, and umbrella insurance policies from the same insurance company. Most offer multiple-policy discounts.
- Raise your deductible to $500 or even $1,000. Remember, you're insuring against disaster, not modest damage or petty theft.
- Check with the insurer on longtime-policy-holder discounts. If you've been a customer in good standing for many years with no claims, you may be eligible for a discount.
- Make sure you have smoke detectors on all floors. This qualifies you for a discount (and if no one in your household smokes, you often get another discount for that, too).

A book we recommend is *How to Get Your Money's Worth in Home and Auto Insurance,* by Barbara Taylor (McGraw-Hill, $12.95).

TOO LATE TO REFINANCE?

It seems as if almost all the people we talked to in 1992 refinanced their homes. Is it too late? We'd say that if interest rates are 2 percent or more below your current mortgage rate, and you're still early on in the mortgage (in the first 10 years), it makes sense to consider refinancing and locking in a fixed rate. If you can get a mortgage with lower costs, then even a smaller spread in interest rates can be worthwhile.

In addition, it always makes sense to refinance if you have an adjustable-rate mortgage and you suddenly realize you're going to be staying in the house longer than you thought you would. Even if you have to ratchet up a little bit to a higher rate, you know darn well the next adjustment is going to be higher still. Get it locked in so there are no surprises.

The only time it may not make sense to refinance is when you know you are not going to stay in the home for more than two years. The payback period on most refinancing deals is about three years (meaning that what you save on monthly payments will make up for your refinanc-

Inventory of Household Items

Accessories
Beds
Bookcases
Books
Bowls
Buffet
Cabinets
Canned goods/supplies
Carpentry tools/supplies
Carpets/rugs
Cedar chest
Chairs
China
China cabinet
Clocks
Clothes hamper
Clothing
Coffee tables
Curtains/drapes
Cutlery
Desk
Dishes
Dishwasher
Disposal unit
Dressers
Dressing table
Dryer
Electrical appliances
End tables
Floor covering
Food/supplies
Freezer
Furniture
Garden tools/supplies
Glassware
Ladders/step stools
Lamps/fixtures
Lawn mower
Linens

Luggage/trunks
Mattresses
Mirrors
Musical instruments
Night tables
Ornamental lawn items
Outdoor cooking
  equipment
Outdoor games
Pet supplies
Plants/planters
Pots/pans
Radio/stereo
Records/tapes
Refrigerator
Scale
Serving table/cart
Sewing machine
Shower curtains
Shovels
Silverware
Small appliances
Snow blower
Sofas
Sports equipment
Spreaders
Sprinklers/hoses
Step stool
Stove
Tables
Television/VCR
Toilet articles
Toys
Umbrella
Utensils
Wall hangings
Washer
Wheelbarrow
Workbench

ing costs only after two to three years). This depends, of course, on how much you lower your monthly payments and how much you pay to refinance.

Refinancing usually costs about 4 percent of the loan amount (a lot of dollars!), which covers points, appraisal fee, title insurance, loan application fees, and other minor charges. You can easily do the calculation yourself. Take the difference in monthly payments and divide that into the refinancing cost. For example, if you will save $200 per month and refinancing costs $5,000, you will be ahead of the game after 25 ($5,000 ÷ 200) months. If you'll be selling before 25 months are up, it doesn't make sense to refinance now.

Dolan Refinancing Calculator

First determine roughly how much you will save each month (bottom line of table). Follow that amount up the column until your finger is at the line for your refinancing costs. This is the number of months it will take for the refinancing to pay off. For example, refinancing costs of $5,000 with a monthly mortgage payment savings of $150 per month will take 34 months to pay off.

Refinancing cost	Months to pay off								
$7,000	140	94	70	56	47	40	35	32	28
6,000	120	80	60	48	40	35	30	27	24
5,000	100	67	50	40	34	29	25	23	20
4,000	80	54	40	32	27	23	20	18	16
3,000	60	40	30	24	20	18	15	14	12
2,000	40	27	20	16	14	12	10	9	8
1,000	20	14	10	8	7	6	5	5	4
THE AMOUNT YOU SAVE PER MONTH:	$50	$75	$100	$125	$150	$175	$200	$225	$250

DOLANS' SCAM BUSTER: Watch out for "settlement-day ambushes." A little known loophole (little-known to borrowers, that is) in the "truth in lending" laws allows lenders to change the fees and charges of a refinancing at the last minute—just when you are least willing and apt to back out! So make sure you tell a potential lender that you know about the loophole (which Congress, by the way, is trying to close) and that you expect him to be as forthcoming and candid about all costs associated with your refinancing deal as he would be if this was an original mortgage.

DOLANS' TAX ALERT: One more caveat on refinancing: When you lower your mortgage payments, you lower your tax deductions as well! Don't forget to recalculate your withholding (on your W-4 at work) to reflect this difference. A reliable rule of thumb: If refinancing your mortgage saves you $2,000 or more per year in interest payments, you'll probably have to reduce the number of exemptions claimed on your W-4 form.

DID YOUR ADJUSTABLE-RATE MORTGAGE MISADJUST?

One of the greatest feelings in this low-interest-rate environment is to have your adjustable-rate mortgage adjust downward. But you may be shocked to find out how many ARMs are adjusted incorrectly. And— surprise, surprise!—the mistake is usually in the bank's favor. Our friend John Geddes, former bank regulator and president of Consumer Loan Advocates (CLA), told us that of the 9,000 ARMs his firm checked in 1991, almost 50 percent had errors—and 77 percent of those errors represented overcharges. The average overcharge to borrowers was $1,588! Most errors occur because the lender used the wrong index in recalculating the monthly payments, or used the right index from the wrong week or month.

Mortgage Monitor, Inc., another mortgage checkup service, reports that not only are ARM miscalculations costing home owners up to $8 billion extra each year, but that billions of dollars of overcharges also exist with mortgage escrow accounts.

CLA's Geddes says that even if you have already refinanced or otherwise closed out a loan, you can still discover and collect on a mistake, if you do so within three years of the mistake. If you are negotiating to refinance your loan, for example, a past error can be a powerful negotiating chip.

You can discover a faulty recalculation yourself, but it takes a lot of checking and number crunching. Two useful resources to guide you are CLA's *ARM AID* (book plus video, $39.95; call 708-615-0024) and

Mortgage Monitor, Inc.'s booklet *Cash in Your Mortgage: Consumer Guide to Recovering Mortgage Overcharges* ($11.95; call 800-283-4887).

If you'd rather have a professional check your ARM for mistakes, contact CLA or Mortgage Monitor for information on their mortgage audit services.

THE TAX BENEFITS OF HOME OWNERSHIP

As a home owner, each year you may deduct the money you spend on property taxes, as well as the interest on your mortgage. You can also deduct permanent improvements when you sell. That doesn't mean you can put in new rugs and paint the walls and count that. You have to materially improve the home—say add a room or finish off the basement. Material improvements raise your cost basis (what you originally paid for the house), which reduces taxable profit when you sell.

When you do sell your primary residence, you have two years to buy a home of equal or greater value in order to defer taxation on your profits or capital gains. If you do roll over your gain and meet that requirement, you owe no current taxes. But if you sell and you don't make a profit, you can't deduct the loss. However, there is a strategy that can be used to convert a loss on a home into a tax deduction, and we'll discuss it in Chapter Twelve.

There is also a once-in-a-lifetime $125,000 exclusion for a primary residence. You must be 55 or older and have lived in the house three of the past five years, and neither you nor your spouse can ever have taken the exclusion before. This rule is once per couple. If you were married to somebody else who was entitled to the exclusion and took it while you were married, you kill it for yourself and your new spouse. The exclusion allows you to pocket $125,000 in gain without paying taxes on the gain. More gain than that, you may pay on the excess.

You should use this exclusion very carefully, because once it's gone, it's gone. For example, if you buy another house of close to the same value as the one you sold, don't use the exclusion. Save it for when you don't buy another home, or for when you buy a home that is much less expensive than the one you're selling. Remember, the *maximum* exclusion is $125,000. If you use it for a $5,000 gain, you've used it. It's gone.

But for anyone entitled to the $125,000 once-in-a-lifetime exclusion, we have even more good news. Let's suppose you purchased your home many years ago and even if you include all the material improvements made through the years, you still can't get the cost basis any higher than $65,000. Let's also suppose that you're about to sell this house for $265,000. You're facing taxes on a $200,000 capital gain. You can save taxes on $125,000 with the once-in-a-lifetime exclusion. But what about the remaining $75,000 of profit? If you purchase a new primary residence for $75,000 or more (good news!), you can start the tax deferral of capital gains all over again.

The deferral of capital gains on the resale of a house can be very tricky, however. You buy a home for $100,000, sell it for $150,000, and then buy a home for $200,000 . . . and so on. But the piper has to be paid sometime. At some point in time you will probably want to take advantage of the $125,000 exclusion and buy a smaller home, maybe in retirement. And when you do buy a less expensive home than the one you sold—or sell a home and don't buy another one at all—the IRS looks back at the capital gains you've deferred over time. We call this the *cost-basis trap*. The IRS is tracking this with computers, so it's getting easier and easier as time goes on for them to catch up with you.

For more information, call the IRS, at 800-829-FORM, and ask for IRS Publication #523, *Tax Information on Selling Your Home*.

ARE YOU OVERPAYING ON PROPERTY TAXES?

Most of us feel our property taxes are too high, no matter what they are, but the fact is that many errors are made on property assessments that result in overtaxation. For example, with home prices worth less today than five years ago in many regions of the country, you may be paying taxes on more than your property is currently worth. Check it out! Call your county assessor's office and find out when your property was last assessed and for how much. Then find out when the most recent assessment in your neighborhood was made, and what the value was (it's public information). You can quickly estimate whether your assessment seems fair.

Another source of error is in improper surveys, old land documents, and mistaken county records. For example, if you applied for a permit to add a garage or a swimming pool but never built one, you could easily be paying taxes on improvements you never made! It's worth a visit to the county assessor's office.

One shortcut we like: Use a real estate assessment pro. Look in the Yellow Pages under Property Tax or Real Estate Specialist, and hire an expert to track down your assessment and lobby to get it reduced. He'll do the legwork, and will be more likely than you to find some hidden tax relief. He will charge you a fee, but once you've reduced your assessment, you can benefit from it for years.

If you are a do-it-yourselfer, there's a great little book on cutting your property taxes called *The Homeowner's Property Tax Relief Kit* by Lawrence J. and Vincent P. Czaplyski published by McGraw-Hill, Inc., for $29.95; call 800-233-1128.

You may also be eligible for a slew of property tax exemptions you've never even heard of, from veterans' exemptions to senior citizen breaks—so speak up! Call your local tax assessor's office and request a list of local exemptions, along with the rules and requirements for applying for them.

THE PROS AND CONS OF HOME-EQUITY LOANS

Your home may be your single greatest asset, so we believe you should carefully guard it. That means don't borrow against it by taking out a home-equity loan or second mortgage unless you can afford to pay the money back. You should borrow only for college funding purposes, medical expenses that you cannot pay, to buy a car, and for important home improvements that maintain or increase the value of your home. Don't borrow on your home because you've always wanted to own a Rolls-Royce when you really can only afford a Chevy Nova.

And you should never, never, in our opinion, borrow on your house to fund a business venture. It is just too risky.

Also, you should be aware that there are limits to how much interest you can deduct on your home-equity loan. While you can deduct the interest on a mortgage up to $1 million (assuming other requirements are met), you can deduct home-equity interest only up to $100,000.

Does it make more sense to set up a line of credit or to get a second mortgage? If you're going to need the money all in one fell swoop, take out a second mortgage. (For example, you get a tuition bill for $25,000 or a medical bill and you don't have the money to pay for it.) But if it's a situation where you'll need the money gradually, such as for making home improvements or tuition installment payments, establish a home-equity line of credit. Even though you don't know what the interest rate will be when you use your line of credit, you also won't have to start paying the money back until you actually take it out.

Most home-equity loans are adjustable-rate loans. If you can find one offering a fixed rate, that's always our preference.

> DOLANS' SAFETY WARNING: Don't take an interest-only balloon payment home-equity loan. Yes, your payments will be lower, but what happens when the balloon comes due and you don't have the money? You may not be able to refinance the loan. And if you don't have the cash to come up with the entire balance due . . . well, you know what happens to your home. It's gone.

SELLING YOUR HOME IN A BUYER'S MARKET

How do you sell your home when everyone is selling and few are buying? Make sure a prospective buyer *remembers* your house. Provide a floor plan. Have two or three snapshots people can take away with them.

There are some basic rules of thumb to help lift your house above the crowd in a crowded market. First and foremost: Make a good first impression. "Curb appeal" (how the house looks from the street, as prospective buyers drive up) is very important. Drive around the block and drive up to your house yourself. What strikes you first? Does the paint look fresh? Are the shutters on straight? Is the front door attractive? Can you see through any windows? If so, does the interior look inviting? Is the driveway in good shape? The lawn healthy? The bushes trimmed? The flowers blooming? Landscaping counts for a lot, so don't hesitate to mulch the flower beds and reseed that worn patch of grass.

The same rule applies to the inside of your house. Does the paint look clean and fresh? Are the carpets clean and the floors polished? The light fixtures dusted? The bathroom mirrors spotless? Basic cosmetic touch-ups count for much more than they cost! Clean out the clutter, too. The less stuff you have inside, the bigger your inside looks! If you must, store extraneous furniture. Finally, it may sound corny, but bake a pie before somebody comes to look at your house. Bake cookies. Put out apple cider or stewed spices. Those great smells really add a homey feeling.

A listener recently called with an idea that helped sell her home—she changed many of the doorknobs! Old doorknobs may show lots of wear; new ones demonstrate a certain freshness and the owner's care of the home.

Beyond appearances, your house will sell better if you price it right and use an agent to market it professionally. For added exposure, you can even list the home with a national relocation service. Most of the large national real estate chains like Century 21 and ERA have relocation services.

You may wish to consider helping out the buyer with financing or closing costs, as long as you heed our safety warnings below. You might also think about offering a home warranty, which guarantees that if any major system or appliance (roof, furnace, fridge) breaks down or needs repair in the first year, you'll foot the bill. If you know your house is in good shape, this is a low-risk way to make your home more attractive to potential buyers—that little extra buyer's "peace of mind"!

DOLANS' SAFETY WARNING: Beware of owner (you) financing, in which you become the "bank." If you must, at least be sure to check out the buyer's financial health and track record. Also, beware of letting a buyer assume *your* loan. If he fails to pay, you and your credit rating are on the hook! We prefer to see the buyer get his own mortgage, rather than assume yours. It's much safer.

THE DANGERS OF SELLING YOUR HOUSE YOURSELF

With real estate agents taking 6 to 7 percent of the sale price right off the top, many folks are thinking about selling their homes themselves. After all, a 6 percent commission may be all the profit there is! But we're of the opinion that trying to sell your home yourself is *not* a great idea in a tough market like this.

There are a couple of reasons: First and foremost is the element of safety. It's sad to say, but when you have strangers coming through your home, you really have no way of knowing they're not there to rob you, or "spec" your house for a burglary after you've gone to work the next day. They may call and ask, "When are you home? When can I see the house? When aren't you home?" A real estate professional will prescreen people, not just for safety, but also for your convenience. You won't be wasting your time on tire kickers or people who may just stop in, saying, "Gee, I was driving by and I saw the sign. Would you mind if I just look around?" And, of course, the kids' clothes are all over and the washing machine just backed up.

Let the real estate people do their job, particularly in a tough market. You protect yourself and you don't have to entertain everybody who feels like walking through your home. In fact, you don't even have to be there. Best of all, you'll have some warning before people come to look at your house.

For more help, see *How to Sell Your House in a Buyer's Market* by Martin Shenkman (John Wiley & Sons).

AVOID THESE MISTAKES AND YOU'LL BE A WINNER

We've given you a lot of advice on shopping for the best deal in town, from home prices, to mortgages, to insurance. We'd like to close this chapter by sharing with you some of the most common mistakes home buyers make. If you can avoid these mistakes, you'll be a winner in the home buying game!

Mistake #1: Buying more than you can afford.

Mistake #2: Buying the first house you see without comparison shopping.

Mistake #3: Shopping with your heart and not with your pocketbook, which often leads to not negotiating the best price because you just want the house so badly. Did you calculate how much house you can really afford using the chart on pages 16 and 17? *Be honest!*

Mistake #4: Compromising on a house just because it's all you can afford, but you're not really happy with it. Or buying a house that you're not thrilled with, assuming that you're going to make certain changes you may not be able to afford.

Mistake #5: Moving into a new area and buying before you really know whether you want to stay.

Mistake #6: Buying your home as an investment.

Mistake #7: Buying a new home before you've sold the old one.

Mistake #8: Not having a professional and independent inspection.

Mistake #9: Not shopping for the best mortgage deal you can find.

Mistake #10: Waiting for the "perfect" moment to buy.

Yes, buying a home, particularly your first home, can be quite a financial challenge, to say nothing of the emotional and physical demands. But if you approach your decision wisely and come well prepared to get the very best deal out there, you can own a house you'll be proud to call home, at a price you and your family can afford.

CHAPTER TWO

Get the Most Out of Every Dollar You Spend

How to Budget, Dig Yourself Out of Debt, Repair Damaged Credit, and Other Spending and Saving Strategies

Most of us work hard Monday through Friday (sometimes even on the weekends!)—on the job, in the office, on the road, or at home. We put in long hours, hurry through lunch, battle the rush-hour traffic, and collapse on the sofa at the end of the day. ("Hey, Dad, want to play Nintendo?") So how come we don't have more to show for it? "Where has all the money gone at the end of the month—and why isn't more of it (or any of it) in our savings account?" That's one of the most common questions we get on our radio and TV shows.

If this sounds familiar, you're not alone. In fact, people who earn a decent living and still have trouble making ends meet are probably in the majority. But you *can* save some of that hard-earned money, no matter how much you make, by adopting a healthier attitude toward managing your finances and by following a few tried-and-true tips for making your dollars go further—and make your life better in the process!

Our feeling is that you don't have to scrimp in order to save. You just have to be a smart spender and a careful shopper. That's what this chapter is all about—getting the most for every dollar you spend, and not spending one extra dollar when you don't have to. We'll also let you in on a few of our own recipes for well-rounded family finances.

FIGURE OUT WHERE IT'S GOING

Let's face it, most people have no idea where all their money goes. You sometimes spend that $100 you withdrew from the bank so fast you can't imagine where it went. So the first thing you have to do is find out where you're spending your hard-earned income.

We've tried a lot of different ways to monitor spending, but the only way to really know where your money is going is to keep a log of every last nickel and dime you spend. That means every day for an entire month. It sounds tedious, but it really works. And the good news is, once you figure out where you're spending your money, it's surprisingly easy to spend less—and save more.

We know it's no fun to write down every expense. It's almost as bad as those diets Ken hates (well, he hates *all* diets, but the ones he hates the most), where you have to write down everything you eat. But the key is discipline. You have to stick to your guns and keep a log—and then use it to see where you're going astray and to help you design a monthly budget that works (more on that in a minute).

A lot of people we talk to on our radio show resist the idea of writing down their expenses and developing a monthly budget. We hate to say it, but we do say it on the air every day, so here it comes: We've all got to realize that just because we are living, walking, and breathing does not mean we are entitled—immediately—to everything our hearts desire. It's a lesson we're trying to teach our daughter Meredith, and one worth repeating to all consumers! It's a psychological rather than a financial issue, and to a degree the decade of the '80s helped foster a habit of overspending and a reliance on easy credit without any consideration of where the money is coming from or how it can be paid back!

As we like to say, you can only wear one pair of shoes at a time.

Enough with the lecture—because we also believe that you can make your paycheck go a whole lot further than it probably is going now just by shopping wisely and spending intelligently. You don't have to reuse plastic baggies (like a woman we know in Vermont does); you don't have to drive your car until it dies (like Daria's father does). You simply have to know the underlying value of what you're buying, and how to get the very best value for every dollar you spend.

We have found that the best way to start is to find the holes in your paycheck bucket. On pages 46 and 47 we provide a worksheet for you to use to help keep track of your expenses. First, fill in the lines for those bills you pay once a month (or less often). Then make a copy for every day of the month, and sit down every night before you go to bed and fill out your daily expenses. It will get easier every day, it sure will help, and it might even be fun. Lord knows it will be fun to have more money in your pocket at the end of the month than you do now.

CUTTING YOUR CREDIT CARD COSTS DOWN TO SIZE

Once you have a better picture of where your money is going, chances are you'll be able to spot some easily "pluggable" holes right away. Our experience has shown that there are two major ways to cut costs (and we love both!): 1) Stop overpaying on necessities, and 2) stop buying luxuries you'll never miss.

Let's attack the necessities first. What are they? Your mortgage, repair and upkeep of your home, utilities like electricity and telephone, insurance, food and clothing. Your credit cards. Your credit cards, although not absolute necessities, have become a habit as well as a convenience. If you carry a balance from month to month on one or more cards, then we must list credit cards under necessities, because it's absolutely necessary that you send in a payment every month!

One of the most likely places most Americans are overpaying today is on their credit cards. When the bank is paying you 3 percent interest on your savings or your money market account, why in the world would you pay 18 percent, 21 percent, or higher interest on your credit card? Who do they think they are?! You can probably save hundreds of dollars, maybe thousands of dollars, every year by reducing your credit card interest payments.

Of course, the best way to reduce your credit card interest payments is to pay off your card balances. But let's say you don't have the money to pay off those cards in full. Fine. Don't worry. You can still slash your payments dramatically by using a credit card with a lower interest rate. Our favorite source of information on low-interest-rate credit cards is Bankcard Holders of America (800-327-7300). Say the Dolans told you to call, and they'll help you find the lowest-interest-rate cards for a charge of $4.00.

DOLANS' SMART MONEY TIP: If you pay off your balance every month, look for a card with a long grace period. That's the time between

Budget Worksheet

	Daily	Monthly
HOME		
Housing (rent or mortgage)	$ ____	$ _____
Natural gas/oil	$ ____	$ _____
Electric	$ ____	$ _____
Telephone	$ ____	$ _____
Water/sewer/trash	$ ____	$ _____
Cable TV	$ ____	$ _____
INSURANCE		
Life	$ ____	$ _____
Auto	$ ____	$ _____
Home	$ ____	$ _____
Health	$ ____	$ _____
FOOD/ENTERTAINMENT		
Groceries	$ ____	$ _____
Meals outside of home	$ ____	$ _____
Movies/theater/sports	$ ____	$ _____
TRANSPORTATION		
Auto (gasoline)	$ ____	$ _____
Auto (maintenance/repairs)	$ ____	$ _____
Public (subway, bus)	$ ____	$ _____
Taxis	$ ____	$ _____
Parking fees	$ ____	$ _____
INSTALLMENT DEBT		
Car payments	$ ____	$ _____
Student loans	$ ____	$ _____
Credit cards	$ ____	$ _____
OTHER		
Vacation	$ ____	$ _____
Education, child care	$ ____	$ _____

Budget Worksheet (*continued*)

	Daily	Monthly
OTHER		
Unreimbursed medical	$ _____	$ _____
Gifts, contributions	$ _____	$ _____
Clothing	$ _____	$ _____
Alimony, child support	$ _____	$ _____
Spending money	$ _____	$ _____
Unreimbursed business expenses	$ _____	$ _____
Retirement plan (IRA, 401(k))	$ _____	$ _____
Savings/investing	$ _____	$ _____
Miscellaneous	$ _____	$ _____

when you charge something and when the interest rate clock starts ticking. But if you carry a balance from month to month, you want the lowest interest rate, period. Unfortunately, if you carry a balance, the grace period doesn't apply—even to new purchases. Does that surprise you? We're sorry to burst your bubble, but when you carry a balance on a card, the issuer does not give you a grace period on anything—including new purchases. You've forfeited your right to it. So every new purchase added to the old balance immediately gets calculated with interest.

Now, we're not against credit cards; in fact, they can be very useful. We're just against overpaying for the privilege! We are against the debt-mania that has possessed so many Americans in the past decade. For instance, the average American has 11 credit cards! You really need only two or three. As we'll discuss later in this chapter, too many cards can be hazardous to your financial health, so start getting rid of your most expensive cards today. Begin with your department store credit cards. They charge outrageous interest rates, and most department stores now accept Visa and MasterCard, anyway. Even Sears, which formerly took only its own card and Discover, has been forced to accept others.

DOLANS' SCAM BUSTER: Credit card companies used to require that you pay a minimum of 5 percent of your outstanding balance each month. These days, most cards require only 2 percent or 3 percent. Thanks for nothing! The less you pay per month, the longer it will take you to pay off that balance—and the more interest you'll wind up paying the credit card company. Don't you get the impression that some companies don't want you ever to pay off the balance?

Here's another gift we'd just as soon refuse: the skip-a-month offer. The issuer tells you that you can skip one payment each year. Again, thanks, but no thanks. You might be skipping a payment, but the interest payment clock never stops ticking. Skip a month's payment and you end up paying another month's worth of interest.

Do they think that we're *stupid?*

OVERPAYING ON NECESSITIES

We'll talk about getting and keeping good credit in a minute, but let's take a quick run through some other necessities you may be overpaying for. How about food? Do you go to the supermarket every day? When you're hungry? Without a list? These are no-nos! Try going once a week, with a list, *after* you've eaten. You'll shop smarter, plan better, and get more for your money. Also, there are many supermarket products you can buy in bulk and save a basketful of cash: diapers, popcorn, cooking oil, pet food, cat litter, toilet paper, paper towels, soft drinks, shampoo, soap, dry pasta, and more. We never pass up a good deal! Here's another grocery store tip: Look up and look down. The most expensive, name-brand products are almost always at eye level in the market, with the better deals often found up above and down below. A little stretching and bending never hurts your figure or your wallet!

Insurance is another big area of overpaying. The first thing to check is your deductible. Raise it. Go for $250, $500, even $1,000 on your home owner's and automobile policies. Your monthly payments will drop significantly, and you'll still be covered in case of disaster. Furthermore, there are some bells and whistles insurance agents love to sell that are a complete waste of money. Check your policy for any of these money-suckers:

- Accidental death coverage
- Specific illness coverage

- Life insurance for children
- Credit card life insurance
- Mortgage life insurance
- Insurance deductible insurance
- Maternity benefits insurance
- Extra coverage for automobile-related death

If you find any of these, cancel them immediately and start putting that money to better use for your own financial well-being and your family's enjoyment.

In Chapter One we cover many places to save money on your home, but we'd like to remind you of two prime areas of potential overpayment: property taxes and improperly adjusted mortgages. See Chapter One for ways to save money in both areas.

Did you know that you are most likely overpaying on your heating and electricity? Maybe you've got leaky doors and windows that you haven't weather-stripped, or windows that should be replaced. Don't be penny wise and pound foolish! Windows and doors cost money to replace, but in the long run you'll save more on your heating and air-conditioning costs than you'll spend on weatherizing.

What about your electric bill? Are you leaving lights on all over the house? Leaving the door open when the air-conditioning is on? Or closing the door and cranking up the A/C when a nice fresh breeze would do the trick? Try turning down your thermostat by just one degree—it will cut your energy use by about 3 percent!

And do you really need the wattage you've got in some of your lamps? Have you tried those high-efficiency bulbs?

A listener's local utility company (God love them!) provided this list of seven ways to cut your electric bills:

- Caulk and weather-strip around windows, doors, and exhaust fans.
- Insulate your electric water heater.
- Insulate hot water pipes and ducts that pass through unheated areas.
- Clean your forced-air heating system filter.
- Have your heat pump inspected to make sure it's operating efficiently.
- Thaw frozen foods in your refrigerator—it will cut cooking time by 35 percent.

- Turn off the oven 15 minutes early and let the built-up heat finish the cooking.

Are you jumping in your car five times a day doing errands when you could have made a list and done them all at once? That's another way to save. And if you'd like to find out, once and for all, if you have the best equipment and both local and long-distance phone service, we recommend *The Phone Book,* by Carl Oppedahl and the editors of Consumer Reports books ($15.95).

There are hundreds and hundreds of other ways to save a little here and a little there, without cramping your style or comfort. Just a few minutes of honest thought should turn up other money savers.

LUXURIES YOU'LL NEVER MISS

Now let's move on to our second area of smarter spending: luxuries. Do you have three movie channels on your cable TV bill every month, rather than just one? C'mon, do you really need more than one? How many movies have you watched lately? How about that new VCR with automatic hocus-pocus programming? Not only does your old VCR work just fine, but it will probably take you two years to figure out how to work the newfangled machine, assuming that you have mastered the one you now own.

On the other hand, if your VCR or camera breaks, nowadays it may be cheaper to buy a new one than to fix the old one. We hate to replace rather than fix, but the bottom line is the bottom line. With technology changing rapidly, often you really can buy for less.

Maybe you're a taxi taker. That's a luxury you'll never miss if there's good public transportation in your area. How about the bus? The subway? A nice walk? Try it and you might like it! And you sure will save a bundle of change—just leave for work a few minutes early.

Take five minutes to go through the coupons in your Sunday paper. Here's the way to use coupons: Clip only the ones you know you'll use—products you regularly buy, name brands you can't substitute. Don't buy products you wouldn't ordinarily buy just because you've got a coupon. That's not going to save you money! In fact, in many cases you can do better with the regular price on a less expensive brand. But if you will buy only one brand of peanut butter, why not get a discount when it's offered?

BILL-PAYING SECRETS

In addition to spending less without getting less, here are some bill-paying secrets we'd like to share that might help make your monthly finances take on a healthier glow.

First, an important thing to remember is that when a bill has a due date, that does not mean you can mail on that day and avoid a penalty for late payment. It's not like your tax return. Your payment must be *in their possession* on that day. Postmarks do not count in the real world. So if you are consistently sending in your mortgage payment on the first, when it is *due* on the first, you could be incurring late charges. If you are not incurring late charges, you may be damaging your credit record. You will be shown as a slow payer, which will in turn escalate your borrowing costs because your credit is not $A+$.

What you want to do is to pay your bills as close to the due date as possible while still making sure they're received on time. That's tough to do nowadays, because you can't always trust the mail. You don't want to pay the day you receive the bill, because you lose the float. A good rule of thumb: Mail your bills a week before the due date. You will have picked up, in some cases, as much as 25 days worth of interest (while the money has been sitting in your bank account rather than theirs) and still be considered an on-time payer.

There are also some bills you *shouldn't* pay—such as offers from credit card companies that say, "For $25 a year we'll protect your credit card if it's stolen." Don't pay a bill that you don't recognize. Don't pay a bill for something you've never ordered, and don't feel compelled to put a contribution in an envelope because you've been sent some cards or address labels. In fact, if you get a mail-order box of goodies from a fruit-by-mail company (for the sake of example) that you never ordered, they are yours to keep, by law, without paying.

Another smart bill-paying tip is to use credit cards for certain large purchases. In case there is a problem later with a product or service—or you never receive a product or service—and it shows up on your credit card, you've got the credit card company on your side, at least at the start of the dispute (with a reminder and some gentle prodding from you).

We had a call the other day from a fellow who had used his credit card to order the first of a series of animal video tapes from a well-known company. He decided he didn't want the rest of the series, but they just kept sending him tapes and billing his credit card. It's called a negative option; if you don't stop them, tapes will keep coming. This guy sent back the tapes, yet they still kept billing him. We told him he was lucky the purchase was on his credit card, because he could send the credit card company the certified receipts of return postage, along with copies of his letters canceling the purchase, and the credit card company would help carry on the battle for him.

THREE STEPS TO RESOLVING A CREDIT DISPUTE

If you have a dispute with a merchant or business about a bill you have charged to your credit card, here are the three basic steps to take to resolve that dispute, get the merchant off your back, and maintain a lily-white credit history.

1. Contact the merchant. It's only fair—give the merchant a chance to refund your money or satisfy your complaint before you appeal to a higher authority. We strongly recommend a complaint *in writing*. But let him know you will indeed pursue ''legal action'' if you do not get satisfaction! Very often just the sincere threat of complaining to the Better Business Bureau or the local chamber of commerce will act as a swift kick in the pants to a reluctant merchant. (It's always a good idea to write down exactly what you expected from the product or service and why it failed to meet your expectations *before* you call or write to the merchant.)

DOLANS' SMART MONEY TIP: Don't accept a store credit unless that's really what you want. If you'll never buy there again, demand your money back.

2. If the merchant won't resolve the dispute to *your* satisfaction (not his!), contact your credit card company. Write a letter informing them that you dispute the charge, and why. Don't wait too long to complain. Gerri Detweiler, Executive Director of Bankcard Holders of America, told us that you must by law notify the credit card company of a dispute within 60 days of first seeing the charge on your bill. The credit card

company must then go back to the merchant and reverse the charge (called a "charge back") within 30 days.

In most cases, that's the end of the story. Businesses need good credit card relations just as much as they need good customer relations, and most are unwilling to wrestle with a credit card company.

3. However, in some cases the business with which you have the dispute will tough it out. It will take on you *and* the credit card company. If that happens, your next step is to bury them all in paper. Contact the Better Business Bureau, the local chamber of commerce, the Federal Trade Commission, your state attorney general's consumer protection office, and the relevant trade association or complaint resolution organization. Here's a starter list:

Airlines: U.S. Department of Transportation Office of Consumer Affairs (202-366-2220)

Automobiles: Automotive Consumer Protection (703-821-7144)

Banks: State banking authorities (in your state capital); the Federal Deposit Insurance Corporation consumer hotline (800-934-3342); for national banks, Comptroller of the Currency (202-622-2000)

Contractors: Your state licensing board

Doctors: Your state medical examining board

Electronics (TV, VCR, PCs, etc.): Electronic Industries Association (202-457-4977)

Funeral services: Funeral Service Consumer Arbitration Program (800-662-7666)

Insurance: National Insurance Consumer Hotline (800-942-4242)

Land sales (interstate): U.S. Department of Housing and Urban Development, Interstate Land Sales Registration Division (202-708-0502)

Lawyers: Local chapter of the American Bar Association or your state bar association

Mail fraud: Postal Inspection Service, U.S. Postal Service (800-654-8896)

Major appliances: Major Appliance Consumer Action Panel (800-621-0477)

Real estate: Your state board of realtors

Travel: American Society of Travel Agents (703-739-2782)

Utility bills: Your local public service commission

If all else fails and you decide to take a company or individual to Small Claims Court, you may want to buy *Everybody's Guide to Small Claims Court* by Ralph Warner (Nolo Press, $14.95; 415-549-1976).

PROTECTING YOUR HARD-EARNED CASH

Another great way to keep your budget on track is to *buy* rather than to *be sold* an item. This means resisting sales pitches over the phone and cutting down on impulse buying. Easier said than done, right? Well, here are a few practical tips. Don't take a lot of cash, credit cards, or even checks with you when you shop. If you need a coat, a pair of shoes, even a loaf of bread, carry only the amount of money you need. Don't have $300 on hand when you're going to buy a handkerchief or three credit cards for a pair of socks. Only take along what you need. As the saying goes, ''You can't spend what you don't have!''

You should never be rushed into buying anything. But if there is something that you absolutely know you are going to need and you find an incredibly good deal, don't pass it up. Just make sure you read all the fine print and know exactly what you're getting before buying.

DOLANS' SCAM BUSTER: We all get those great phone calls that start, "You have just won a fabulous, expense-paid vacation for two . . ." Watch out, there's usually a catch. Maybe you're willing to sit through a three-hour sales presentation on time shares once you get to your "dream destination." But that's not the worst of it. Some of these calls are pure scams. Never give your credit card number out over the phone to someone who has called you. If you don't recognize the name of the person or organization but the offer interests you, ask for details in writing before you make any sort of commitment or give out any personal information. If it's a "free" trip, contact the airlines and hotels participating to make sure the deal is on the up-and-up.

The unfortunate fact of life is most of the "deals" you're offered out of the blue over the phone and through the mail are at best bogus and sometimes downright fraudulent. If you have not entered a contest or sweepstakes, take it from us, you haven't won anything!

DIGGING YOURSELF OUT OF DEBT

For many of us, unhappily, the problem is not "How do I avoid getting in debt?" It's "How do I dig myself out? Where do I start?"

Step One: Transfer your credit card debt to a lower-interest-rate card. You can make the same payment you were making on the higher-interest-rate card, but now you're putting more against the principal, which means you can pay it off and get out of debt faster. For a list of low-interest-rate credit cards and their brochure entitled *How to Qualify for a Low-Interest-Rate Credit Card,* call Bankcard Holders of America, at 800-553-8025. The list costs only $4.00; the brochure, $5.00.

Step Two: Stop ringing up new charges. We know how hard that can be, but it will be worth it in the long run. If you have to, put your two or three cards (remember, you don't need 10 or 15) in your bottom drawer and not in your wallet or purse. That way, you have to pay with a check or cash when you shop.

Step Three: If you're really in debt and your credit rating is shot, maybe you can't get that new lower-interest-rate credit card. Then it's time for a visit to a nonprofit credit counselor. To find one in your area, call the Consumer Credit Counseling Service (CCCS), at 800-388-CCCS. They have more than 700 nonprofit offices in the United States. As long as your consumer loans don't outweigh your annual salary *and* you're working, a counselor will sit down with you and help work out a payment schedule to dig you out from under—and teach you how to budget, too.

Here's another tactic. If you've got some extra cash on hand for emergencies, pay off the debt rather than investing it. There is not a single investment today that (without taking extreme risk) will pay you the rate of interest you're paying on your credit card debt.

For more tips on dealing with creditors and paring down your debt, we like William Kent Brunette's *Conquer Your Debt* (Prentice Hall) and *The Ultimate Credit Handbook,* by Gerri Detweiler (Plume).

THE CREDIT LINE TRAP

By the way, maybe you think having a lot of cards makes sense because they represent lines of credit. They're all paid off, you say, but they are there if you need them, right? Not so fast. When potential lenders pull your credit report and see that you could conceivably extend yourself another $15,000 or $20,000, they will reduce the amount you can borrow by that. In other words, if you have five credit cards with a $5,000 line of credit on each, in the eyes of a potential lender you could charge $25,000. And that's $25,000 less that a bank will be willing to lend you when you apply for a mortgage, a car loan, whatever.

KEEPING GOOD CREDIT AND REPAIRING DAMAGED CREDIT

As for getting and keeping good credit, let's start by dispelling a myth.

Some people think the only way to get a credit record is to carry a balance on their credit card. Absolutely false! Pay off your balance every month, and your credit record will be stellar. In fact, your entire financial picture will be much healthier if you pay off your credit card balances each month.

But even into the most stellar credit life, some rain must fall. Mistakes can occur on your credit history, no matter how careful you've been. And if you find a mistake on your credit report, it can take up to 90 days to get it fixed. So we think it's a good idea to check your credit report once a year, and certainly before you're going to borrow money.

TRW will send you a credit report once a year for free. Requests must be made in writing to TRW Consumer Assistance, P.O. Box 2350, Chatsworth, CA 91313-2350. Allow at least two weeks for delivery.

Include the following information in your request:

- Full name, including middle initial and any indicator of generation, such as Jr., Sr., II, or III.
- Current address, including ZIP code.
- Previous addresses, including ZIP codes, if you've moved in the past five years.
- Social Security number.
- Spouse's first name.
- Photocopy of a document, such as a billing statement or driver's license, that links your name with the address to which the report is to be sent. This is to guard against the possibility of someone requesting a copy of another person's report.

Under federal law, you may also obtain a free credit report from an agency if you are denied credit on the basis of information from that agency.

The other two credit bureaus charge $8.00 to $20.00: Equifax (800-685-1111) and Trans Union (in the East, 215-569-4582; Midwest, 502-584-0121; West, 714-738-3800).

When you receive your credit report, check all account numbers, balances, past-due amounts, and current-status descriptions. Be on the lookout for *duplicate records* of the same account on a single report and *accounts that are not yours*.

If you find a mistake, under federal law you have 30 days to respond. Write to the credit bureau that sent you the report and tell them what you think is wrong on the report and why. They then have 60 days to verify it or delete it from your report. Suppose they check it out and inform you that they've verified it, and they're leaving it on your report. Inform the bureau that you want to include the word "disputed" next to that item on your report. According to the Fair Credit Reporting Act (FCRA), they must comply. FCRA also says that you are allowed to write an explanation of 100 words or less about any disputed item on your report—and that the credit bureau must include that explanation on any copy of your report they send out. So let your reason be heard.

However, it's important that you understand two things as they relate to the insertion of 100 words or less.

1. Its primary purpose is to allow you to explain your side of a specific billing dispute with a merchant or other disputed items, such as a lost mortgage payment, not why your credit history may have been spotty.

2. No matter what the reason for having your explanation inserted in your credit record, a human being may never have the chance to read it because many credit reports are scanned by computers! You may be a victim of the high-tech information age!

Another reason to check your credit report is that all credit information older than seven years (10 years for bankruptcy) must be removed from your credit report by law. You want to be sure your report has been purged of old information.

What should you do if you already have bad credit or no credit? Reestablish your credit. Almost anybody can get a gasoline credit card. Almost anybody can get a card from a local department store. So try for those first. If you get a gasoline card, charge a tank of gas and pay it off. Get a department store card, charge a pair of socks and pay it off. Buy a sweater, buy a pair of cuff links, and go through the process to show that you can pay again.

If you find it impossible to get either of those two types of credit cards, then look into a secured credit card from a bank. This is a credit card that is "secured" by money you deposit in the bank. A secured card issuer asks you to deposit $500 or more into an interest-bearing account (it will pay a *modest* rate of return). The amount you deposit then becomes your line of credit, the maximum amount you can charge on the credit card. As long as you make your payments on time, you will establish a good credit history if you're just starting out, or you will add good credit information in front of the old, bad credit news. Continued timely payments will soon lead to a return of the money you left on deposit (with interest) and an unsecured card.

By the way, there is no way anyone can tell you are using a secured card. It looks just like any Visa or MasterCard.

The nonprofit group Bankcard Holders of America can help you find the best secured credit card deals. Their list is available for $4.00 by calling (800) 327-7300.

If you have had a "sketchy" credit history, it's also important to tell a prospective lender that there is some bad news on your credit report from the past. If you say in advance, "When you pull up my report, here's what you are going to see, and here's the reason for it," it tends to reduce the shock, and in many cases it gets you the money you need.

DOLANS' SCAM BUSTER: No one, for any amount of money, can take accurate bad credit information off your report. One of our listeners sent us an ad from a local paper in which an outfit intimated it could remove any bad credit information from your report, accurate or not. Yet in the contract it said, "If there is material evidence that this is correct, we cannot remove it." Of course, you have to send $250 to get the contract, and this little beauty is buried in the fine print. So don't believe it when someone says he can remove something bad but accurate from your credit report. If it's inaccurate, you can get it removed yourself. You don't need to pay to have it done.

LIFE AFTER BANKRUPTCY

It seems as if bankruptcy these days is being viewed by too many people—including bankruptcy lawyers—as the way to end all financial troubles. But we can't emphasize strongly enough that bankruptcy is not the easy answer to every financial problem. We call bankruptcy "financial euthanasia."

Bankruptcy is a good way to kill a lot of your future credit life. Even though you can get credit cards again, bankruptcy has an insidious way of rearing its head for the rest of your life.

Here are the facts:

- You'll be discriminated against in trying to rebuild credit.
- For 9 out of the 10 years the bankruptcy is on your credit record, you will be unable to get unsecured credit.
- You will have to answer "Yes" for the rest of your life to the question, "Have you ever filed for bankruptcy?" or risk big penalties.
- Although the bankruptcy is removed from your credit record after 10 years, proof of it will remain on file for 25 years in a regional bankruptcy warehouse.
- Psychologically, you will feel the stigma of failure for many years to come.
- Even if you move out of the area in which your bankruptcy occurred (90 percent of people do), it stays on your credit report wherever you go.

Bankruptcy stays on your record for 10 years. But the fallout from it stays with you for life.

Still, there are some cases when bankruptcy is the only way out, especially if you are not working, or if your bills (say from an uninsured medical disaster) are completely overwhelming you and your creditors are unwilling to work out a repayment plan you can handle. Many times a self-employed person whose business fails has no choice but to file for bankruptcy. And, by the way, we hate to follow bad news with worse, but you should be aware that you can file for bankruptcy only once every seven years.

Once you decide to file (or at least to explore the possibility), contact a bankruptcy attorney (no shortage of these, nowadays). He will have you fill out a bankruptcy form, and then he'll take it from there. You'll have to make a court appearance, but the entire process could be completed within three to six months.

There are generally two types of bankruptcy available for consumers: Chapter 7 and Chapter 13, both named for the bankruptcy code numbers that identify them.

Chapter 7 is a "straight bankruptcy." The court oversees the sale of your assets, and any monies realized from the sale are distributed among your creditors. When the Chapter 7 procedure is completed, all your debts are gone, even if the creditors only received a fraction of what was due them.

Chapter 13 bankruptcy is very different. Also known as a "wage earner's bankruptcy," it includes a repayment plan that usually stretches over a three-year period. The repayment schedule attempts to repay the entire amount due your creditors, avoiding a forced sale of assets. To file for Chapter 13 you must have regular employment and secured indebtedness that cannot be more than $300,000. Unsecured indebtedness cannot exceed $100,000.

Understand that filing for bankruptcy does not wipe out all your debts. With Chapter 7 you'll still be liable for:

- Credit card charges made within 20 days of filing
- Personal loans and installment purchases made within 40 days of filing
- Alimony and child support
- Certain back taxes
- Money owed as reparation for intentional harm you caused someone
- Debts resulting from fraud

With a Chapter 13, you'll still be liable for:

- Alimony and child support
- Long-term debts that were not fully repaid during the repayment schedule

It's also important to understand that if you are thinking of filing for bankruptcy only to keep the bank from foreclosing on your house, the odds are against you. If your financial troubles haven't cleared up within the year, statistics show you'll still end up losing your home. So don't let some fancy attorney talk you into bankruptcy just to save your house.

But if bankruptcy is your only alternative, consider doing it. Once you get your creditors off your back, you'll be able to start planning and thinking more clearly about the future. A great book on bankruptcy, both avoiding it and surviving it, is *The Jacoby & Meyers Guide to Personal Bankruptcy*, by Gail J. Koff, Esq. (Henry Holt & Co.).

START PUTTING AWAY A LITTLE AT A TIME

Let's assume you've been careful not to get into a financial sand trap. You pay your bills on time, you make a good living, your credit cards are under control. So how come you don't have anything left at the end of the month? Probably because you have not made a conscious effort to save.

The best way to increase your savings: Start saving. Easy for us to say, you think. Here's how. When you're buying something for 79 cents, don't dig through your change purse and find 79 cents. Break a dollar. Do this with all your purchases. Then, as your pocket or purse starts to get heavy with accumulated change, or every night when you get home from work, take your change out and put it in a coin jar. As soon as it's filled up, roll it, take it to the bank and deposit it in your savings account. You can't get rich on $57 a month, but it's more than a lot of people save. It's a start.

Next, along with your other bills, pay yourself every month. When you write your checks for the electric bill, gas bill, phone bill, etc., write one to your savings account, too. Maybe it's 10 percent of your monthly take-home income. If you can do more, do more. What you're gradually building up to is a six-month nest egg. That means you want to have enough money in the bank to pay your absolute necessities for six months. Add up your monthly mortgage, insurance premiums, car payments, food, utilities, and minimum payments on credit cards. Multiply by six. Scary, isn't it? But this is your goal.

Since this is your emergency nest egg, the money should be kept in a money-market mutual fund, which is completely liquid and pays interest anywhere from ½ to 2 percent higher than bank savings and money market accounts, or your credit union savings account, which is also usually a better deal than your bank. Like a bank, money market mutual funds will even give you check-writing privileges should an emergency arise. Most have single-check minimums of $100.

After you've saved that liquid emergency nest egg, then you need to assess your goals. Short-term goals need short-term investments. That means six-month, one-year, three-year, maybe five-year CDs or Treasury bills or notes. Stock and bond mutual funds are not short-term investments. You don't put your $25,000 into a stock or bond mutual fund because you may want to buy a house at the end of the year. You can't rely on the stock or bond market going up in the short term. Money you won't need for at least five years can be invested in equity funds or other alternatives. We'll talk more about all these investment options in Chapter Four.

Here's one final money-saving tip. Use your Automated Teller Machine sparingly. Not only are you often charged a fee to get your own money out of the bank (good grief!), but you also tend to spend more carefully when you discipline yourself to go to the well less frequently. The best trick is to go only once a week.

We'd like to end this chapter by asking you to take a pledge. Raise your right hand. Higher. A little higher. OK, now promise us *and* yourself that you will place as high a priority on *keeping* your hard-earned money as you do on earning it in the first place. It's really easier than it sounds. It just means spending more carefully and shopping more wisely. Follow the tips in this chapter and you will find you still have a little bit left in the bank at the end of the month. You and your family will be better off—and no one deserves it more!

CHAPTER THREE

Get the Most from Your Bank

How to Pick a Safe Bank and the Services That Are Right for You

Almost every family uses a bank or savings and loan institution, probably without thinking much about it. But as a smart consumer you should shop just as carefully for a bank as for a car or a home. And right at the top of your shopping list should be written in big, bold letters: SAFETY. Why? Just ask those of your friends who had trouble at the hundreds of institutions that have failed recently. Safety is the very first thing you should demand from any bank you do business with, be it for personal checking, business accounts, mortgages, or car loans. You want to know your bank is stable and secure.

How can you tell? First, make sure the bank, S&L, or credit union is federally insured. For banks and S&Ls, that means FDIC-insured (insured by the Federal Deposit Insurance Corporation); for credit unions, it means insured by the NCUA (National Credit Union Administration). Coverage by these agencies certainly does not guarantee that the institution itself is safe, but it does help reassure you that, up to certain account limits, your money is safe in case the bank or credit union goes under.

DOLANS' SAFETY WARNING: Remember, you are insured only up to a maximum of $100,000 in any bank. That includes all your different accounts—CDs, money markets, savings, and checking (individual and joint)—in all the various branches of that bank.

There are actually ways to insure a lot more than just $100,000. In fact, a family of four could insure as much as $1.4 million by using a combination of individual accounts, joint accounts, and testamentary trust accounts. Your Individual Retirement Account and Keogh Plan, if you have self-employment income, also qualify for their own $100,000 insurance provision. However, this IRA/Keogh coverage is likely to change soon. But even if your accounts are all covered, you still want to use a safe bank. To learn that your bank has been taken over is nerve-racking, even when there's nothing to worry about.

SAFETY THAT REALLY COUNTS

Beyond federal insurance, there is a great deal more you want to find out about a bank's safety before you agree to do business there. One of the simplest ways to judge safety is to use one or two very good rating services. We recommend Veribanc (800-44-BANKS) and Weiss Research (800-289-9222). For just $10.00 for the first institution and $5.00 for each successive one, Veribanc will give you a verbal report and follow it up with a written one. Weiss Research charges $15.00 per institution for its safety reports.

For further reading, we recommend the book *Is Your Money Safe?* by Warren Heller (Berkeley). It explains what happens when your bank fails, the traps in FDIC insurance, problems for borrowers when a bank fails, and insights into coming trends for the consumer in banking.

If you tend to be a do-it-yourselfer or you're from Missouri (the Show-Me State), you might prefer to do your own checkup on your bank's financial health. Here are the three most important areas to look at:

- *Profitability.* Does the bank or institution operate at a profit every quarter? You want a bank that is making money, not losing it.
- *Balance sheet.* Does the bank have strong book value? You want a bank whose net worth, when divided by total assets, is at least 5 percent.
- *Problem loans.* These used to be in foreign loans to Third World countries, but now they crop up in the bank's real estate portfolio. You want a bank that has set aside sufficient loan loss reserves to cover problem loans.

All these figures are in the bank's Consolidated Annual Statement, which should be available right at the bank; if you don't see a copy, ask one of the tellers. Some banks will also give you their Quarterly Call Report, which is the financial report that banks and savings and loans are required by law to file with the government every 90 days. In it, banks must adhere to strict federal guidelines, so the information is likely to be the "cold, hard facts," as opposed to the Annual Report, where banks make their numbers look good.

WHAT TYPE OF BANK IS RIGHT FOR YOU?

There was a time when small neighborhood S&Ls or community banks were the right choice for most families. We could bank with someone we knew; we could get a loan more easily; we could feel like a member of the bank's family. And we could usually get a better rate on a loan at a savings and loan. But nowadays, with the latest rash of mergers and takeovers, the distinction between a local S&L or community bank, a large commercial bank, and a credit union has blurred. In fact, since some of the S&Ls can't even afford to make loans anymore, you often have no choice but to borrow from a bank or credit union.

Do depositors get treated better at S&Ls and community banks than at commercial banks? Is a commercial bank more interested in a commercial account? We don't think so anymore. In any case, "better" is a relative term. Better in terms of service? Better in terms of people? A bank with a smaller client base may leave you with fewer mistakes on your statements.

If you run a small business and need detailed runs of every payment and deposit, you're going to want a commercial bank, not a small savings and loan. On the other hand, studies have shown that the lowest checking and savings account fees come from smaller, local savings and loans and community banks.

It's a real trade-off. It comes down to finding the bank where you're most comfortable and get exactly the services you need for the most reasonable price. Just don't trade comfort for safety. As a matter of fact, safety can have a direct impact on service. How? Well, the first step a bank in trouble often takes is to reduce its payroll. It maintains fewer branches, and fewer managers and tellers at the branches that do exist, making for longer waiting and probably less time and attention devoted to you. Also expect higher fees on regular services like using your ATM card, writing checks, minimum balance charges, and so on.

GOOD SERVICE, GOOD PRICES

There are two keys to getting good service *and* good prices from a bank or S&L: 1) Comparison shop, and 2) develop a relationship with your banker.

In the past 10 years, banks' typical account fees have exploded, rising by as much as 650 percent. Commercial banks collected over $13 billion in fees from checking and savings accounts in 1991. So it pays to shop around!

Make a list of the services and features that are important to you. And take a good look at your past banking activities. How many times do you use the Automated Teller Machine (ATM) in a month? Do you like to bank in person? Do you write a lot of checks? Establish your own banking profile and then compile a wish list, which might include:

- A full-service checking account with clear statements, no fees for checks written, and interest paid on a certain minimum balance (the lower, the better)
- Direct deposit of your paycheck or Social Security check
- ATMs with no fees for withdrawing money
- Convenient branch locations and hours (but be aware that the banks with the most branches also tend to charge the highest fees)
- Full-service business accounts with payroll, lines of credit, clear reports, and statements
- High-interest savings accounts
- Competitive CD rates
- Short ''hold'' periods for deposited checks. Federal law now limits holds on local checks to three business days and on out-of-town checks to six business days. Three to six days is a lot better than the two weeks many banks used to ''hold'' your deposits— earning interest for the bank every day, of course. But since 90 percent of the money deposited by check in your account has cleared within the first 48 hours, this improvement is still a pretty lousy deal.

Once you've figured out what you want, then put on your walking shoes and visit three or four *safe* banks and S&Ls in your neighborhood.

Take a look at the lines at the tellers' windows. With a pad and pencil, sit down with a customer service representative at each bank, and go through your wish list. Say you are just gathering information and will not make a decision on where to bank today. Write down all the details, rules, and fees, and then sit down in the quiet of your own home and compare.

Once you have found the bank that comes closest to meeting your needs, then go back and talk with the same representative you met with originally. Tell him or her you want to bank there, but you can get X at the bank down the street for less, or Y included in your checking account across the street. You may indeed be able to get the bank of your choice to match a competitor's service or fee in order to get your business.

WHEN DO YOU NOT WANT TO EARN INTEREST?

Watch out for NOW accounts—checking accounts that pay interest but require a higher minimum balance. For most of us, the service fees will wind up costing us more than the interest we earn. Even if the fee is waived when you keep a minimum balance, it's our belief that the interest paid on NOW accounts isn't good enough to outweigh the amount you need to keep there. Non-interest-bearing accounts are generally a better deal. Consider: The minimum balance for a regular non-interest checking account is $1,500; for an account paying interest it is $2,500 to $5,000. Only you can judge which minimum balance you can comfortably maintain. But if you're unsure about the higher amount, don't believe the interest will make up the difference. Remember: On many accounts, in the months when you dip below the minimum you earn *no* interest. So watch out!

TIME IS MONEY

It seems that whenever we're not short of cash, we're short of *time*. So what service banks are focusing on these days is *quickness*—reducing the time you spend standing in line, visiting the teller, or visiting the bank altogether. You can save time with a few simple tricks:

- *Avoid the bank as much as possible.* Have your paycheck, Social Security check, and other regular income automatically deposited in your bank account. Not only will you save time, but you'll earn a few more extra days' interest by getting the money deposited more quickly.

- *Avoid bank "rush hours."* They typically occur on Mondays and Fridays at lunchtime, and on popular paydays like the first and fifteenth day of the month.
- *Avoid ATM "rush hours"* on your way to and from work (and lunch hours when everyone else is using them, too!)

DOLANS' SAFETY WARNING: While you're at it, avoid ATMs after dark, especially in low-traffic streets or neighborhoods. Don't make yourself a target for robbery!

HOW MUCH SHOULD YOU PAY IN FEES?

As with anything else, you want to pay as little as you can without sacrificing service or safety. Here's a rundown of acceptable fees for some popular services. If this is what your bank is charging, it's reasonable:

- Monthly service charge: $2.50–$5.00. If you're getting hit up for $10.00 or $12.00 a month, take your money elsewhere.
- Minimum balance penalties: $3.00–$8.00. Again, if this fee is more than $10.00 a month, you can do better.
- ATM fee: No charge from a branch of your bank, up to $1.00 for another bank. We don't mind paying for using another bank, but—hey—don't charge me for getting my own money out of my own bank!
- Bounced check charge: $7.00–$15.00. (The national average is $25.00.) Again, the best way to avoid this loss is to avoid doing it. Don't write a check unless you mean it!
- Canceled checks returned: No charge to $5.00 per month.

Having your canceled checks returned to you is a must. Some banks charge for this, others don't. Either way, you want your checks back. They are an irreplaceable piece of evidence in any dispute or mistake that arises—not to mention their importance if you are ever audited by the IRS. Paying taxes, equity sharing agreements, repaying loans, selling or refinancing a home, verifying a purchase—if any of these transactions sound familiar, get your canceled checks.

It actually can be risky not to get your checks returned to you automatically. Many banks nowadays will send you a list of the checks you have written, but not the canceled checks themselves, which they may keep for three months or so before they toss them out with the trash. A listed check, or a barely legible Xerox copy of your check, should you need it, may not be good enough in resolving a dispute. If a bank reduces your service charge for sending you a list of checks, it may also charge you a fee for producing or reproducing a check you need. Having your canceled checks returned to you is worth the fee.

> DOLANS' SMART MONEY TIP: Don't get talked into overdraft protection as a solution to long "hold" periods for deposited checks. It's just not the same! You want your deposited money available quickly, not a loan from the bank to cover withdrawals of money that's rightfully yours! And who collects interest on that overdraft loan? Your friendly banker, of course. We're not against overdraft protection to cover a cash flow pinch and avoid the cost and embarrassment of bounced checks, but pay off that overdraft promptly—the interest is never cheap!

THE IMPORTANCE OF DEVELOPING A RELATIONSHIP

Establishing a personal relationship with your banker is a very important step in getting good service from your bank. You want to have someone to call when you have a question, someone to see when you have a problem, and someone to speak on your behalf when you need special attention. You can't establish this kind of relationship through a teller's window. You want to sit down and talk with an officer or a junior officer directly. Even if he or she is not the loan officer, when you need a loan, your personal contact can take you into the loan officer's inner sanctum and provide a personal introduction.

It may take a little time to cultivate a personal relationship, but it's worth it in the end. It will come in very handy sooner or later!

BE ON THE LOOK-OUT FOR THESE BANKING ERRORS

No matter how good your bank is, you still have to be alert to possible mistakes on your statements. Some of the most common are debiting the account incorrectly, unauthorized service charges, and miscalculations of your adjustable-rate mortgage (see Chapter One).

If you find a mistake on your statement, or suspect a mistake has been made in your account, a personal visit to your banker is always more effective than a phone call. Even if he or she has to call the "main office" or another department, you can sit in on the phone call. Your banker has a lot more motivation to solve the problem if you are sitting right there.

If you can't make a personal visit, call the customer service department. If you really get the runaround, see the branch manager. And if that isn't helping either, you may want to threaten to go to your state's banking department. Here's a list!!

State Banking Departments

Alabama
Mr. Zack Thompson
Superintendent of Banks
101 South Union Street
Montgomery, AL 36130
(205) 242-3452

Alaska
Mr. Willis F. Kirkpatrick
Director of Banking, Securities
   and Corporations
P.O. Box D
Juneau, AK 99811-0800
(907) 465-2521

Arizona
Mr. William H. Rivoir
Superintendent of Banks
3225 North Central, Suite 815
Phoenix, AZ 85012
(602) 255-4421
(800) 544-0708

Arkansas
Mr. Bill J. Ford
Bank Commissioner

Tower Building
323 Center Street, Suite 500
Little Rock, AR 72201-2613
(501) 324-9019

California
Mr. James E. Gilleran
Superintendent of Banks
111 Pine Street, Suite 1100
San Francisco, CA
   94111-5613
(415) 557-3535
(800) 622-0620

Colorado
Ms. Barbara M. A. Walker
State Bank Commissioner
Division of Banking
First West Plaza, Suite 650
303 West Colfax
Denver, CO 80204
(303) 866-6440

Connecticut
Mr. Ralph Shulansky
Banking Commissioner

44 Capitol Avenue
Hartford, CT 06106
(203) 566-4560
(800) 842-2220

Delaware
Mr. Keith H. Ellif
State Bank Commissioner
Suite 210
555 E. Loockerman Street
Dover, DE 19901
(302) 739-4235

District of Columbia
Ms. Fè Morales Marks
Acting Superintendent of Banking and Financial Institutions
Suite 1003
1250 I Street, N.W.
Washington, DC 20005
(202) 727-1563

Florida
Mr. Gerald Lewis
State Comptroller
State Capitol Building
Tallahassee, FL 32399-0350
(904) 488-0286
(800) 848-3792

Georgia
Mr. Edward D. Dunn
Commissioner
Banking and Finance
Suite 200
2990 Brandywine Road
Atlanta, GA 30341-5565
(404) 986-1633
(800) 932-6246

Guam
Mr. Joaquin Blaz
Director
Department of Revenue and
    Taxation
P.O. Box 2796
Agana, GU 96910
011 (671) 734-2942

Hawaii
Mr. Clifford Higa
Commissioner
Financial Institutions
P.O. Box 2054
Honolulu, HI 96805
(808) 586-2820

Idaho
Mr. Belton J. Patty
Director
Department of Finance
2nd Floor
700 West State Street
Boise, ID 83720-2700
(208) 334-3319

Illinois
Mr. Bob Piel
Commissioner of Banks and Trust
    Companies
Room 100
117 South Fifth Street
Springfield, IL 62701
(217) 785-2837
(800) 634-5452
(Credit card rate information
    only)

Indiana
Mr. Charles W. Phillips
Director

Department of Financial Institutions
Room 1024
Indiana State Office Building
Indianapolis, IN 46204-2294
(317) 232-3955
(800) 382-4880

Iowa
Mr. Robert R. Rigler
Superintendent of Banking
200 East Grand, Suite 300
Des Moines, IA 50309
(515) 281-4014

Kansas
Mr. Frank D. Dunnick
State Bank Commissioner
700 Jackson Street, Suite 300
Topeka, KS 66603-3714
(913) 296-2266

Kentucky
Mr. Edward B. Hatchett, Jr.
Commissioner, Department of
   Financial Institutions
911 Leawood Drive
Frankfort, KY 40601
(502) 564-3390

Louisiana
Mr. A. Bridger Eglin
Commissioner
Financial Institutions
P.O. Box 94095
Baton Rouge, LA 70804
(504) 925-4660

Maine
Mr. H. Donald DeMatteis
Superintendent of Banking
State House Station #36
Augusta, ME 04333-0036
(207) 582-8713

Maryland
Ms. Margie H. Muller
Bank Commissioner
13th Floor
501 St. Paul Place
Baltimore, MD 21202
(301) 333-6262
(800) 492-7521

Massachusetts
Mr. Michael C. Hanson
Commissioner of Banks
100 Cambridge Street
Boston, MA 02202
(617) 727-3120

Michigan
Mr. Russell Kropschot
Acting Commissioner
Financial Institutions Bureau
P.O. Box 30224
Lansing, MI 48909
(517) 373-3460

Minnesota
Mr. James G. Miller
Deputy Commissioner of Commerce
133 East 7th Street
St. Paul, MN 55101
(612) 296-2135

Mississippi
Mr. Thomas L. Wright
Commissioner
Department of Banking and Consumer Finance
P.O. Box 23729
Jackson, MS 39225
(601) 359-1031
(800) 826-2499

Missouri
Mr. Earl L. Manning
Commissioner of Finance
P.O. Box 716
Jefferson City, MO 65102
(314) 751-3242

Montana
Mr. Donald W. Hutchinson
Commissioner
Financial Institutions
Room 50
1520 East Sixth Avenue
Helena, MT 59620-0542
(406) 444-2091

Nebraska
Mr. James A. Hansen
Director of Banking and Finance
301 Centennial Mall, South
Lincoln, NE 68509
(402) 471-2171

Nevada
Mr. L. Scott Walshaw
Commissioner
Financial Institutions
406 East Second Street
Carson City, NV 89710
(702) 687-4260

New Hampshire
Mr. A. Roland Roberge
Bank Commissioner
169 Manchester Street
Concord, NH 03301
(603) 271-3561

New Jersey
Mr. Jeff Connor
Commissioner of Banking
20 West State Street CN-040
Trenton, NJ 08625
(609) 292-3421

New Mexico
Mr. Kenneth J. Carson, Jr.
Director
Financial Institutions Division
P.O. Box 25101
Santa Fe, NM 87504
(505) 827-7100

New York
Ms. Jill M. Considine
Superintendent of Banks
Two Rector Street
New York, NY 10006-1894
(212) 618-6642
(800) 522-3330
(General consumer information)
(800) 832-1838
(Community Reinvestment Unit)

North Carolina
Mr. William T. Graham
Commissioner of Banks
P.O. Box 29512
Raleigh, NC 27626-0512
(919) 733-3016

North Dakota
Mr. Gary D. Preszler
Commissioner of Banking and Financial Institutions
600 East Boulevard, 13th Floor
Bismarck, ND 58505
(701) 224-2256

Ohio
Mr. John L. Burns
Acting Superintendent of Banks
21st Floor
77 South High Street
Columbus, OH 43266-0549
(614) 466-2932

Oklahoma
Mr. Wayne Osborn
Bank Commissioner
2nd Floor
4100 North Lincoln Boulevard
Oklahoma City, OK 73105
(405) 521-2783

Oregon
Mr. Cecil R. Monroe
Administrator
Division of Finance and Corporate Securities
21 Labor and Industries Building
Salem, OR 97310
(503) 378-4140

Pennsylvania
Ms. Sarah W. Hargrove
Secretary of Banking
333 Market Street, 16th Floor
Harrisburg, PA 17101
(717) 787-6991
(800) PA-BANKS

Puerto Rico
Mr. Angel L. Rosas
Commissioner of Banking
G.P.O. Box 70324
San Juan, PR 00936
(809) 781-0545

Rhode Island
Mr. Edward D. Pare, Jr.
Acting Associate Director and Superintendent of Banking and Securities
Suite 231
233 Richmond Street
Providence, RI 02903-4231
(401) 277-2405
(401) 277-2223 (TDD)

South Carolina
Mr. Robert C. Cleveland
Commissioner of Banking
1015 Sumter Street, Room 309
Columbia, SC 29201
(803) 734-2001

South Dakota
Mr. Richard A. Duncan
Director of Banking
State Capitol Building
500 East Capitol Avenue
Pierre, SD 57501-5070
(605) 773-3421

Tennessee
Mr. Talmadge Gilley
Commissioner
Financial Institutions
4th Floor

John Sevier Building
Nashville, TN 37243-0705
(615) 741-2236

Texas
Mr. Kenneth W. Littlefield
Banking Commissioner
2601 North Lamar
Austin, TX 78705
(512) 479-1200

Utah
Mr. George Sutton
Commissioner
Financial Institutions
P.O. Box 89
Salt Lake City, UT 84110
(801) 538-8830

Vermont
Mr. Jeffrey Johnson
Commissioner
Banking and Insurance
120 State Street
Montpelier, VT 05620-3101
(802) 828-3301

Virgin Islands
Mr. Derek M. Hodge
Lieutenant Governor
Chairman of the Banking
    Board
Kongens Garde 18
St. Thomas, VI 00802
(809) 774-2991

Virginia
Mr. Sidney A. Bailey
Commissioner

Financial Institutions
P.O. Box 2-AE
Richmond, VA 23205
(804) 786-3657
(800) 552-7945

Washington
Mr. Thomas H. Oldfield
Supervisor of Banking
P.O. Box 9032
Olympia, WA 98504
(206) 753-6520

West Virginia
Mr. James H. Paige III
Commissioner of Banking
Building 3, Room 311
State Capitol Complex
Charleston, WV 25305
(304) 348-2294
(800) 642-9056

Wisconsin
Mr. Toby Sherry
Commissioner of Banking
131 West Wilson, 8th Floor
Madison, WI 53703
(608) 266-1621
(800) 452-3328

Wyoming
Ms. Sue E. Mecca
Manager
Division of Banking
3rd Floor East
Herschler Building
Cheyenne, WY 82002
(307) 777-6600

HIGH YIELDS FROM YOUR BANK

These days, lots of us are crying into our coffee when we see the painfully low interest rates we're getting on our savings accounts, CDs, and money market accounts. But let's remember that we use a bank to have easy access to our money—not to make a killing. That's why it really doesn't make sense to have more than three months' worth of expenses in your checking account, and six months' worth in a savings account.

We've abandoned savings accounts entirely in favor of money market mutual funds. Not money market accounts from the bank—these typically pay lower interest rates and often have inferior service to boot! Go with a large, no-load mutual fund's money market fund.

As for CDs, there's certainly nothing wrong with locking in an interest rate for a fixed period of time, having your money federally insured, and rolling over that money when it comes due. (But there may be better "safe" choices for high earners than CDs—we'll talk about them in the next chapter.) Just be sure you're banking with a safe institution, and that you have not exceeded the $100,000 FDIC coverage limit with your CDs and other accounts combined.

To get the highest CD rate, you may want to cross state lines and deposit with a higher-yielding bank. Our friend Bob Heady runs a publication in Florida called *100 Highest Yields* (407-327-7717) that monitors CD rates nationwide and can tell you where the highest CD rates can be found. They also carry the Veribanc safety ratings. The cost is $34.00 for an eight-week trial subscription. But check with the bank *before* you send your check. Some banks do not accept out-of-state deposits (although *100 Highest Yields* canvasses the nation to find only those institutions that will accept out-of-state money).

DOLANS' SAFETY WARNING: You may want to look for higher-yielding CDs, but you should not chase the *highest-yielding* CDs anymore, for two reasons. First, unusually high CD yields may be a telltale sign of a weak bank desperate for cash. Second, if the bank is taken over, you probably won't continue to get that high yield. Back in the mid-1980s, banks continued to honor the high CD rates for the term of the CD even after they were taken over. But, as the banking system weakened, banks cut a new deal with the feds that permits takeover banks to lower these rates. Normally, you'll get a letter stating the new CD rates, and allowing you to withdraw your money early without penalty or to continue with the new, lower rate.

WHAT YOUR BANK IS NOT

There are certain things you can get cheaper and/or better elsewhere. There's simply no sense ordering checks from your bank, for example. After all, it doesn't print the checks, it just uses the same check printing service you can use. Cut out the middle man and you cut the price. You can order checks directly from Checks in the Mail (800-733-4443), Current, Inc. (800-533-3973), or Image Checks (800-562-8768). You'll pay half the price and get exactly the same checks you'd get from the bank.

Another "product" you don't *have* to get from your bank is a credit card. In Chapter Two, we gave you some pointers on finding the best deal in credit cards. The best credit card may not be from your bank. That really should have no impact on your decision where to bank. However, be sure to check your bank's credit card deal against other credit card offers. You may be surprised.

Because I do my banking here, will I also get the best deal on a mortgage or a car loan? Not necessarily. Not unless you have $6 million in accounts! As for consolidating all your banking activities at one bank, the advantage is simplification. The disadvantage is you may get a better deal on some services by shopping around.

Your bank is a place for your cash, for your everyday money transactions, and it can be a very convenient and helpful supplier of other "banking" services. But your bank should not be, generally speaking, your stockbroker or your insurance agent. There are a number of good reasons why. First, in this age of complicated financial matters, you want a specialist. You wouldn't let a dermatologist set your leg in a cast or deliver your baby. You want a professional stockbroker/financial planner to recommend stocks and help you manage your portfolio. And you want a professional insurance agent to help you analyze and meet your insurance needs. In fact, you may want to use a life insurance expert for your life insurance and estate planning, while you should use a property and casualty expert for home, car, and boat insurance.

The point is to use your bank for what it's best at, and nothing else. You may buy a CD or money market as an investment from your bank, but these are really just glorified savings accounts. For stocks, bonds, annuities, and insurance, it's usually best to go elsewhere. Like you, we're very busy people. It's almost impossible to handle all the daily chores of managing a home, a family, and a career, *and* worry about shuttling around among a whole team of financial consultants. But you worked hard for your money. You deserve expert advice and guidance.

Tell your banker right up front that you're not interested in any other financial services the bank may offer. Also tell him you do not want your name rented or sold to other financial salesmen. Who needs to be bothered with calls and/or letters from people you don't know?

DON'T BUY AN ANNUITY FROM THE BANK

We hate to be negative, but one of the things that really gets our goat is when people are taken advantage of by someone they've come to trust. And we're just outraged over the number of callers we've heard from in the past year or two—especially senior citizen callers—who've told us their banker tried to persuade them to roll over their CD money into an annuity.

The fact is, a CD buyer and an annuity buyer are in the market for very different things and any banker who pretends otherwise is doing you a disservice. In subsequent chapters, we'll explain how an annuity works, whether or not it's appropriate for you and how to choose a good one. But it suffices to say that in most cases, you don't buy an annuity from your bank. Usually, all the bank knows is that you consistently roll over CDs without touching them and that is their sole criterion for selling you an annuity. Furthermore, too many of the bank-sold annuities we've heard about are from very unsafe insurance companies (another no-no).

The same goes for life insurance. Some banks will try to sell you insurance as an investment. Unless they are offering you discounts on term life insurance, you shouldn't buy insurance from your bank, because you are buying it for the wrong reasons. Go to an independent life insurance agent who can analyze your needs and help you shop around for the best product. This also holds true for other insurance your banker offers, such as mortgage insurance and credit card insurance.

THE UNIQUE ADVANTAGES OF A CREDIT UNION

One of your best "banking" options may be to use a credit union for some or all of your needs. Since credit unions operate under somewhat different rules than banks, generally speaking you tend to get better rates of interest on deposits and cheaper rates on loans. Since credit unions are owned by their own members, their job is basically to help their members. The only problem is that not everyone is eligible to belong and not all credit unions are covered by an FDIC-type insurance. You need to find out if the credit union is insured by the National Credit Union Association (NCUA).

Most credit unions are organized by businesses, labor unions, community groups, or churches. If you work at the business or belong to the group, you can join the credit union. But it's possible that you are eligible for a credit union and don't know it. Speak up! Ask your employer—and your spouse's employer—if there is a credit union available to employees. If you can't find one through work, look in the Yellow Pages of your local phone book (under ''Credit Unions'') and see if any of the names relate to any of your activities or avocations.

If you are eligible for a credit union, take advantage of it! Most credit unions have checking accounts (called share draft accounts) that boast lower fees and smaller minimum balances than the average bank. They also have savings accounts, good deals on loans, ATMs, direct deposit, and other popular services. By and large, you'll be well treated and well served. For more information, contact the Credit Union National Association, Box 431, Madison, WI 53701.

GETTING THE MOST OUT OF A BANK TRUST DEPARTMENT

One service you may need from a bank is that of its trust department. We're not great admirers of the investment prowess of many bank trust departments, but consider this scenario: Your father dies and passes on a large and complicated portfolio of stocks and bonds to your mother. Your elderly mother has no experience with investments, and she's getting a little forgetful about paying the electric bill, all of which your father used to handle.

Enter the bank trust department. Once an account has been set up in the bank's trust department (which is not a difficult procedure), the bank can handle the regular monthly bills, the ready availability of cash and the management of your mother's portfolio. If you have a situation anything like this one (and a lot of us do), call a good local estate-planning attorney who sets up trusts and ask for a reference. He or she should be able to recommend a good bank trust department to fit your needs.

Then sit down with the trust department account representative and tell him or her exactly what you want. Set guidelines for the investment portfolio (such as, "Preservation of capital is our first priority," or "As long as we keep ahead of inflation, we'll be happy," or "Don't take any big risks with our portfolio").

That should be a good start. You or someone you appoint should receive a copy of the monthly statement from the trust department to confirm that it is following your instructions and doing a reasonably good job. Too many trust departments hide behind their fiduciary responsibility to the detriment of the portfolio. Some of them are still working on an antiquated 20-stock list of what they can buy for their clients—blue chips that haven't moved in 25 years. Compare fees, too. You shouldn't be paying more than 2 percent annually.

The unfortunate reality of life when it comes to bank trust departments is that the rich get richer and the poor get poorer. If you go to the trust department of one of the five largest private U.S. banks with a $5 million plus portfolio, odds are that you will get much better portfolio performance than if you go to your local bank and trust company. Before you sign on the dotted line, check the trust department's investment track record over at least the past five years for several accounts with similar long-term objectives to the account you are thinking of establishing.

In our view, however, you and your family can always do better by taking control of your own money, even when dealing with a bank. So remember, use banks, savings and loans, and credit unions only for your basic money needs, not for long-range planning and goals. There are better alternatives for those.

One last thought. Don't think for a minute that we are being unduly harsh on our banker friends to the exclusion of others involved in the investment process. The only side we're on when it comes to handling your family's money wisely is yours.

CHAPTER FOUR

Investing During Good Times and Bad

How to Set Your Objectives; Evaluate Government Securities, Bonds, and Bond Funds; Choose the Right Stock or Stock Fund; Buy and Sell Smart; and Diversify Your Portfolio

Most families don't buy investments, they are *sold* investments. And all too often, they are sold investments that are unsuitable for their personal situation and won't help them reach their goals.

Of course, you have to know where you're going before you get on the train. Do you want a local or the Orient Express? Will you have to make a stop here and there? How long do you plan to stay aboard? And what is your final destination? These are questions—about your goals, your time frame, your comfort level, your financial situation—that most people never ask before they invest. They dive in before they're ready, because a stockbroker called them up with a "hot tip," or their bank's "financial consultant" kidnapped them when they were trying to roll over their CD, or they read about a terrific mutual fund in a magazine. They learn the hard way.

STEP ONE: DON'T LEARN THE HARD WAY

Your first investment doesn't have to be a painful lesson in humility, as it is for many first-time investors. Take a deep breath. No rushing allowed here. Your money is a precious commodity, and starting today you're not going to trust it to just anyone. Properly invested, it can work hard for you and your family. It can protect you in the bad times and multiply like bunnies in the good times. But slow down, pardner. A good investment today is almost certainly a good investment tomorrow. So don't be rushed into your decision.

Before you buy anything, you must be sure you understand two things: *What* you're buying and *why* you're buying it.

So where do you begin? Right here!

Be careful of some of the investment courses that are taught in night schools or adult education classes. What's the problem? They are often taught by local stockbrokers and financial planners, who, as you might guess, are not always terribly objective. These courses can be instructive and helpful; just take them with a grain of salt. Approach them as a learning experience, not a shopping spree. If you come away with a better idea of your investment options, not pumped up to buy some new issue or commodity fund (we'll get to investment scams later), then you've done your homework and the course will have been worth the money and effort.

The point is that you want to know what you're buying and why before you commit your money. Remember, investments are the only thing you can order over the phone with absolutely no right to change your mind after you hang up. No 30-day free trials here, no 100 percent money-back guarantee. You buy it, you own it. So before you buy make sure you understand the risks, your ability to sell, your prospects for gains, the time frame involved in your commitment, and, most importantly, what could go wrong.

Did you know most bonds can be paid off early (or "called") and that a 10 percent yield you thought you'd locked into for eight years is suddenly gone? Did you know that most "no-commission" new issues of closed-end funds have a broker's commission built in—and they almost certainly and immediately drop to a discount after they begin trading on a stock exchange? Did you know that most mutual funds will cost you taxes each and every year, even if you never sell a single share or withdraw one red cent from your account? Did you know that zero-coupon Treasury bonds pay no current interest, but Uncle Sam taxes you as if you'd received it anyway?

You get the picture. When someone is trying to sell you a product, he or she is most naturally going to paint the prettiest picture possible. So it's up to you to find out "the rest of the story," as radio personality Paul Harvey always says. Don't learn the hard way. Don't learn from your mistakes. Learn so you don't ever commit the mistakes. Learn *first*.

STEP TWO: SETTING YOUR OBJECTIVES

Once you understand your various options, you're ready to find the investments tailor made for you. To do that, you need to establish—very specifically—how much you can afford to invest, the length of time you can afford to invest, and how much money you want to make. "How much money?" you say. "Hey, Dolans, I want to make as much money as I possibly can!" Unfortunately, nobody ever got rich without taking risks. So you have to balance the risks you are willing to take with the amount of money you want to make, and the pace at which you want (or need) your money to grow.

OK. If the answer to "How much money do I want to make" isn't "As much as possible," how do you set realistic investment objectives? Interestingly enough, it's not all that different from what we probably all did as kids with our allowance from our parents. If your parents gave you 25 cents a week (those were the good old days!) and you wanted to buy a $1 rock-and-roll record, you knew it would take you a while, right? So you either had to save every penny for the next four weeks to get that record, or if you could save only 12 cents a week, it would have taken about eight and a half weeks. If your investment goals are realistic, they are reachable.

There are many investment objectives. Maybe it's to buy a house or new car, to pay for a dream vacation, or to build a retirement nest egg. Whatever your goal, you have to set it firmly in your mind, along with a target date for reaching it. Then you take a look at how much money you have available to invest, and what that means about the growth rate you will need from your investments in order to meet your goals.

Our favorite way to calculate growth is with the famous "Rule of 72." The Rule of 72 says that 72 divided by the rate of growth yield of your investment tells you how long it will take to double your money. For instance, if you buy a long-term bond yielding 8 percent, your money will double in 9 years ($72 \div 8 = 9$), assuming no loss of underlying principal. The Rule of 72 is also useful if you already know how long you have to save, say 12 years, for a college education. In this case, divide 72 by 12 to find the rate of growth yield you will need to double your investment in that amount of time (72 ÷ 12 = 6). Six percent.

Remember, you have to attach a dollar figure to your goal. It's not enough to say, "I want to retire at age fifty-five." This doesn't get you any closer to your goal. You have to say, "I have fifteen years to retirement, and I want to have an income of $40,000 per year when I retire. So, if I live in retirement for twenty years, that means I need $800,000."

Whether your goal is a cabin cruiser, your daughter's wedding, or your own retirement, put a price tag on it. What do you want, when do you want it and how much is it going to cost? And what do you need to save and earn on those savings to obtain your goal?

Maybe you have more than one goal (most of us do). In that case, identify your *immediate* goals, your *intermediate* goals, and your *long-term* goals, with dollar amounts listed for all of them, and the time and rate of growth you need to reach each one.

NO PAIN, NO GAIN?

Suppose you know how much money you want, and how much time you have. You want to double your money in three years. No problem, right? 72 ÷ 3 = 24. Great, you need to make 24 percent per year! This seems like a good place to introduce the concept of risk.

Most callers tell us they want to make a lot of money without taking any risks. Unfortunately, it's not that simple. As the saying goes, "No pain, no gain." And shooting for 24 percent per year will almost certainly involve an enormous amount of risk. At the opposite end of the spectrum, we see far too many people being too conservative, particularly with their retirement money, sticking with 3 percent Treasury bills or money markets. What you should do is figure out how much risk is appropriate for you, and then look at investments in that risk range.

Walk yourself through this process: Ask yourself, "Could I lose 50 percent of this investment and take it in my stride? No. Could I lose 25 percent of it and take it in my stride? Well, maybe." All right, we're getting close. "How about 10 percent? If I invested $10,000 and I got back only $9,000, would I be devastated? No." You can take 10 percent risk.

DOLANS' SMART MONEY TIP: Taking a 10 percent risk means you should probably aim for investments that are likely to give you 10 percent more than the 30-year Treasury Bond yield.

If the long-term T-bond is yielding 8 percent, aim for 8.8 percent. If you feel comfortable with 20 percent risk, aim for a total return of 9.6 percent. (Which, by the way, is the average, long-term return of the stock market.) If you can afford to walk away from a 50 percent loss, shoot for 12 percent. You can look up the 30-year Treasury bond yield in *The Wall Street Journal* any day of the week. This is your benchmark for risk and return.

BUYING TREASURIES WITH CONFIDENCE

If you cannot withstand any risk, your investment of choice should be Treasury securities (bills, notes, bonds) guaranteed by the United States government. Not only do you lock in your interest rate, but you also get Uncle Sam's promise to return your principal at maturity. Remember those "callable" bonds we talked about, where the issuer pays you off early and the interest stops? Well, almost no Treasuries are callable.

DOLANS' SMART MONEY TIP: You can tell if a Treasury is callable by looking it up in the newspaper. If it has two different years noted, it is callable. The vast majority, however, have just one year listed, which is the date of maturity, and are not callable beforehand. In addition, your income from Treasuries is exempt from state and local taxes. (Sorry, Tennessee, your state is the single exception.)

Now, what exactly is a Treasury security? It is a general-purpose security issued by the federal government. Treasury *bills* have maturities of less than 1 year. Treasury *notes* have maturities of 2 to 10 years. And Treasury *bonds* have maturities of over 10 years.

T-bills don't pay interest. You buy them at a discount from their face value, and when they mature you're paid the full face value. The *difference* between what you pay to buy the T-bill and the full face value you receive at maturity is your effective yield. It's like a short-term CD, only guaranteed by the government. The minimum investment is $10,000, and $5,000 increments above that.

When you buy Treasury notes, you are sent an interest check every 6 months until maturity, at which point you are sent back your principal.

Treasury notes are sold in increments of $1,000 or $5,000, depending on their maturity, so most folks can buy them. Say you buy a $1,000 Treasury note yielding 6 percent for 8 years. Every 6 months, you receive a check for $30 ($60 per year), and at the end of 8 years you get your $1,000 back. You have, in effect, made an 8-year loan to the government at 6 percent interest.

Treasury bonds, which have maturities of 10 to 30 years, are sold in $1,000 increments and are issued quarterly by the Department of the Treasury. Like T-notes, T-bonds pay interest twice a year, for the life of the bond, and then you are sent the full face value when the bond matures.

HOW TO BUY TREASURIES DIRECTLY FROM UNCLE SAM

Treasury securities are sold at auction at regular intervals to big investors, but if you want to buy individual T-bills, you too can buy them at auction. Don't panic, it's easier than it sounds. Contact the Treasury Direct program at the Federal Reserve Bank nearest to you. Buying directly from the Treasury cuts out the middleman's commission.

To buy T-bills directly from the government, for no fee, just call one of these major branches of the Federal Reserve Bank and ask for the Treasury Direct package:

Atlanta 404-521-8653	Minneapolis 612-340-2075
Boston 617-973-3800	New York 212-720-6619
Chicago 312-322-5369	Philadelphia 215-574-6680
Cleveland 216-579-2490	Richmond 804-697-8375
Dallas 214-922-6100	St. Louis 314-444-8703
Kansas City 816-881-2000	San Francisco 415-974-2230

You will be sent easy-to-follow instructions and the forms you need to buy at the next auction. You send a certified check for $10,000 for each T-bill you want to buy, and you pay what the big boys pay at the auction. The difference or discount (which represents your effective interest) will be rebated after the auction.

You should probably buy Treasury notes and bonds from a broker. Auctions are held only once a month for certain maturities, and once every three months for other maturities. If what you want is not coming up to auction when you want it, go through a major stockbroker. The commission is tiny, and the government bond desk at most brokerage firms is friendly and consumer-oriented. They'll often bend over backward to get you the best rate and maturity.

For much more information about Treasury securities you may purchase *How to Buy Treasuries Through the Federal Reserve* by writing to the Federal Reserve Bank of Richmond, P.O. Box 27471, Richmond, VA 23261; the price is $4.50.

TREASURIES FOR COLLEGE

You may also have heard about zero-coupon Treasuries, which are U.S. Treasury notes and bonds that don't pay any current income and are sold not by Uncle Sam but by brokerage firms and some banks. Like T-bills, they sell at a deep discount and pay full face value at maturity. For example, a $1,000 10-year Treasury zero might sell for $527, and then pay the full $1,000 at maturity (at the end of 10 years). The $473 difference represents your yield (in this case, 6.5 percent). But zeros are not for families looking for current income, because you don't receive any money until the zero matures.

We like Treasury zeros best for tax-deferred accounts, such as IRAs and Keoghs. The reason is simple. Even though you don't receive yearly interest checks, you are taxed as if you did. You won't receive that $473 for 10 years, but you owe taxes on one-tenth of that amount every year. So the best place to hold them is in a tax-deferred account. In an IRA or Keogh, you don't have to pay those yearly taxes and you get the full benefit of the long-term compounding of your zero.

We also like using Treasury zeros to fund your child's college education, because you know exactly how much you will have, and when. But don't forget the taxes that will come due each year in this situation.

Even though Treasury zeros are guaranteed by Uncle Sam, they carry some risks you need to know about. First of all, they are very vulnerable to interest rate fluctuations. A zero's value goes up (even more than that of interest-paying bonds) when interest rates fall, and its value drops (more) when interest rates rise. Like other bonds, the longer the maturity, the more the value of Treasury zeros will fluctuate relative to rising or falling interest rates. Why? Because you have locked in your rate, and as time passes that rate may not look as attractive as new bonds that are issued paying higher interest.

The other problem with zeros is that they cannot adjust themselves to the ravages of inflation. When inflation comes back (not if, but when), the face value of your zero might not be worth what it was worth when you originally invested. For example, $10,000 today will almost certainly buy more than $10,000 five years from now. So you want to be sure to buy a zero whose yield exceeds what you expect for the rate of inflation. If you expect 4 percent inflation while you're holding that zero (probably a reasonable target for the 1990s), you want it to yield more than 4 percent. Then you've got the guarantee of Uncle Sam, and you keep ahead of inflation.

But you also have to keep an eye on taxes. Even if the zero's return keeps pace with inflation, once you pay the tax man, you could still end up behind the eight ball.

DOLANS' SAFETY WARNING: Beware of brokers who try to sell you zero-coupon bonds by showing you how much money you'll have when they mature. Let's go back to that 6.5 percent example we used a minute ago. Suppose you have $25,000 in your IRA account. The broker suggests buying zeros maturing in 10 years that cost you only $527 today. "We can buy forty-seven ten-year zeros with your $25,000 and turn it into $47,000 in just ten years guaranteed!" Some deal, huh? Maybe not. Don't let the $47,000 cloud your thinking. Remember inflation? Let's assume an annual inflation rate of 5 percent over the next 10 years. Today's $25,000 would have to grow to $40,750 in 10 years just to give you the same buying power when those zeros mature. Factoring in inflation means your investment added only $6,250 in additional money to your retirement account. Not quite as impressive as the original $47,000, is it?

The following chart is provided to show you how much it would cost you to buy a $1,000 zero-coupon bond today. Using the IRA example again, the broker suggests 10-year zeros for your IRA. Look down the first column, marked "Years to Maturity," and find 10 years. Move your finger across the columns to the interest rate yield the broker quotes of 6.5 percent. You find that zeros maturing in 10 years at a current yield of 6.5 percent will cost you $527 for every $1,000 bond.

Years to Maturity	6%	6.5%	7%	7.5%	8%	8.5%	9%	9.5%	10%
30	$170	$147	$127	$110	$ 95	$ 82	$ 71	$ 62	$ 54
25	228	202	179	159	141	125	111	98	87
20	307	278	253	229	208	189	172	156	142
18	345	316	290	266	244	223	205	188	173
16	388	359	333	308	285	264	244	227	210
14	437	408	382	357	333	312	292	273	255
12	492	464	438	413	390	369	348	328	310
10	554	527	503	479	456	435	415	395	377
8	623	599	577	555	534	514	494	476	458

YOUR BEST BOND STRATEGY

As we climb the risk totem pole, we go from Treasury bonds issued by the government to corporate bonds issued by American corporations. They are higher risk, because they do not have the full-faith-and-credit pledge of the U.S. government standing behind them. Remember, only the U.S. government has the right to tax and to print money in order to meet its debts. No corporation can do that. For that added risk, most corporate bonds pay higher interest than government bonds. And the longer the term of the bond, the higher your interest rate—and your risk.

Given this trade-off between risk and yield, the best bond strategy is to *"ladder" your investments*. This means buying bonds of varying maturities—say one-year, three-year, five-year, and ten-year bonds. This way, in case of emergencies, you always have money coming due. If interest rates are going up, you've got money coming due in the short term to reinvest at a better rate. And if rates go down, you've got the long-term higher yield locked in. We also believe you should buy corporate bonds only of the highest rating (AA or AAA). Bonds are rated by Standard and Poor's and Moody's Investor Services (to name just two rating services). Their professional opinion of the corporation's ability to make the promised interest payment and return your principal at maturity is an important tool for determining the safety of your investment.

YIELDS VS. RATES VS. CURRENT YIELD

Time out for a minute. Let's define a few terms you'll probably hear when you try to buy a bond. First, there's **face value.** That's the nominal value of the bond—$1,000, $5,000, $10,000, and so on. When a bond sells at **par**, that means it's selling at face value.

Then there's the **rate** or **coupon yield.** That's the interest rate paid on the face value of the bond, or the interest rate you can lock in when the bond is first issued. Next, there's **current yield.** As interest rates rise and fall, the bond's value rises and falls—and the current yield changes as well. The current yield of the bond can be higher or lower than the coupon yield depending on how much money it costs you to buy the bond. If it costs you more than the face value, your current yield will be lower than the coupon yield, and vice versa.

For example, let's say a $1,000 bond is issued at 6.5 percent interest. The rate is 6.5 percent, the face value is $1,000. If you buy at par, you pay $1,000, and your current yield will be 6.5 percent, or $65 per year. So far, so good. But if you buy the bond at a "premium," you might pay $1,200. You're still getting $65 a year, so your current yield is 65 divided by 1,200, or 5.4 percent.

The most important kind of yield is really **yield to maturity.** This takes into account the current yield *plus* your gain or loss at maturity. In the most recent example, you'll still get only $1,000 when the bond matures, even though you paid $1,200, so you have to figure this $200 loss into the equation. Yield to maturity reflects your *true total return,* if you hold the bond to maturity.

There's one more yield that must also be considered—the **yield to call.** What's a call? That's a nasty little feature that allows the issuer of the bond to pay back your principal earlier than the maturity date. Why do most issuers want their bonds to have call features? It's very simple. If they issued bonds in the early 1980s when interest rates were in double digits, why would they want to keep paying you at 12 percent or 15 percent when they can issue new bonds and pay new investors 7 percent or 8 percent? So they call the bonds, pay you off early, and go back to market with a bond at a much lower yield. It's a cost-saving move for them—and a hardship to you. You get your original investment back earlier than expected at a time when interest rates are lower (that's why they paid you off early!). So the income you can now receive from buying new bonds will be substantially lower. That's why it is always very important that you ask about possible call features *before* buying any bond.

THE CRITICAL DIFFERENCE BETWEEN BONDS AND BOND FUNDS

What about bond mutual funds? Bond funds are diversified portfolios of many bonds that have a professional manager monitoring them at all times. You can spread your risk, get greater diversification, and buy into these funds for a low minimum investment—right? Yes, but there is one crucial difference between individual bonds and bond funds that many financial advisers never talk about: You have no guarantees. Your fund does not mature and pay you back a "face value." The fund managers might quote an "average maturity," but that refers to the average maturity of all the bonds in the fund. Your shares never reach maturity. There is no guarantee of return of principal. Nor do you "lock in" a yield with bond funds. Your yield varies every day, based on the trades within the fund and the closing prices of each bond in the portfolio.

If you're on a fixed income or are a senior citizen, you probably want to know that if you put in $1,000 today and wait until maturity, you're going to get that $1,000 back; you'll also want to know exactly what your interest check will be each year. That's not the case when you buy bond funds. A bond fund conducts itself more as a stock fund than as an individual bond. You are totally at the mercy of how well the portfolio is managed and the direction of interest rates.

DOLANS' SMART MONEY TIP: If you are retired, buy individual bonds, don't buy the funds. For more information, see *The Bond Book*, by Annette Thau (Probus Publishing, $29.95; 800-776-2871).

TAX-FREE INCOME FROM YOUR BONDS

Finally, let's spend a few minutes talking about tax-free, or municipal, bonds. These are bonds issued by a city, county, or state government to finance public works and projects like schools, roads, bridges, or water treatment plants. The important benefit to you is that the income from a municipal bond is *tax free*. Who could hate that?

Before you run out and buy a "muni," however, heed a few smart money tips:

- Munis make the most sense for taxpayers in the highest income tax bracket, where the lower before-tax yield will net you a higher after-tax reward.
- Buy municipal bond *mutual funds* if you have less than $50,000 to invest.
- Don't buy all your munis from one state. At first blush, muni bonds or bond funds from your home state might seem particularly attractive, since your income on those is free from federal *and state* (and sometimes even city) taxes. But the risks are greater here if you put all your eggs in one basket. So spread the wealth—and lower your risks. Fiscal problems in Massachusetts, for example, probably would not affect munis issued in California or Maryland.

If you file as a single taxpayer and your adjusted gross income (AGI) is over $30,000 per year, or if you file jointly with a combined AGI over $40,000, you should investigate whether a municipal bond investment makes tax sense for you.

We have provided the following chart to help you decide. The left column shows tax brackets. Look across the top of the chart until you find the tax-free yield of the investment and then go down that column until you are aligned with your tax bracket on the left. This will show you what a fully taxable investment would have to yield to provide you the same amount of income as the tax-free. If you need help in choosing good tax-free municipal bonds, we recommend an excellent monthly newsletter: *Lynch Municipal Bond Advisory,* 2840 Broadway, #201, New York, NY 10025; $250.00 per year. There is a special introductory offering of $79.00 per year if you mention the Dolans when you write.

STOCKS: THE REAL WAY TO BUILD WEALTH

Return of principal, locked-in rates of return—that sounds good. When you buy a bond, you lend money to the government, municipality, or a company, and you play banker, collecting interest and repayment when

Tax-Free Rate of Return
Equivalent Taxable Yields at Varying Tax Rates

	4.0%	4.5%	5.0%	5.5%	6.0%	6.5%	7.0%	7.5%	8.0%	8.5%	9.0%	9.5%	10.0%
15%	4.71	5.29	5.88	6.47	7.06	7.65	8.24	8.82	9.41	10.00	10.59	11.18	11.76
28%	5.56	6.25	6.94	7.64	8.33	9.03	9.72	10.42	11.11	11.81	12.50	13.19	13.89
31%	5.80	6.52	7.25	7.97	8.70	9.42	10.14	10.87	11.59	12.32	13.04	13.77	14.49
33%	5.97	6.72	7.46	8.21	8.96	9.70	10.45	11.19	11.94	12.69	13.43	14.18	14.93
36%	6.25	7.03	7.81	8.59	9.37	10.16	10.94	11.72	12.50	13.28	14.06	14.84	15.63
40%	6.67	7.50	8.33	9.17	10.00	10.83	11.67	12.50	13.33	14.17	15.00	15.83	16.67

	10.5%	11%	11.5%	12%	12.5%	13%	13.5%	14%	14.5%	15%	15.5%	16%	16.5%
15%	12.35	12.94	13.53	14.12	14.71	15.29	15.88	16.47	17.06	17.65	18.24	18.82	19.41
28%	14.58	15.28	15.97	16.67	17.36	18.06	18.75	19.44	20.14	20.83	21.53	22.22	22.92
31%	15.22	15.94	16.67	17.39	18.12	18.84	19.57	20.29	21.01	21.74	22.46	23.19	23.91
33%	15.67	16.42	17.16	17.91	18.66	19.40	20.15	20.90	21.64	22.39	23.13	23.88	24.63
36%	16.41	17.19	17.97	18.75	19.53	20.31	21.09	21.88	22.66	23.44	24.22	25.00	25.78
40%	17.50	18.33	19.17	20.00	20.83	21.67	22.50	23.33	24.17	25.00	25.83	26.67	27.50

The 10 Top-Performing Tax-Free Municipal Bond Funds Ranked by 10-Year Total Return*

Fund Name and Phone Number	5-Yr. Average Annual Return	10-Yr. Average Annual Return
Vanguard Muni Bond—High Yield 800-523-7731	11.56	11.41
Stein Roe Managed Municipals 800-338-2550	10.09	11.41
United Municipal Bond Fund 800-366-5465	10.38	11.35
Safeco Municipal Bond 800-426-6730	10.88	11.33
Financial Tax-Free Income Shares 800-525-8085	11.46	11.25
Vanguard Muni Bond—Long Term 800-523-7731	11.30	11.11
Eaton Vance Municipal Bond Fund 800-225-6265	9.899	10.80
Fidelity High Yield Municipals 800-544-8888	10.57	10.73
Kemper Municipal Bond 800-621-1048	9.262	10.69
USAA Tax-Exempt—Long Term 800-531-8000	10.73	10.65

* Performance figures courtesy of Schabacker Investment Management, Rockville, Md.
All figures through 5/31/93

the loan is due. But no one ever got rich solely by lending money. Great wealth comes from ownership. Ownership means stocks.

The further you are from retirement (or any other goal you've set for your investment portfolio), the more you should consider stocks as an investment. A balanced portfolio will include both stocks and bonds, but the percentages of each will vary.

DOLANS' SMART MONEY TIP: As a rule of thumb (different circumstances dictate adjustments), use your age to determine the percentage of stocks and bonds in your portfolio. If you are 35, own 35 percent in bonds (and 65 percent in stocks). If you are 55, hold 55 percent in bonds and 45 percent in stocks. Readjust your percentages every five years.

CHOOSING A GOOD STOCK

The logical next question is, "Which stocks?" Choosing a good stock really involves two issues: finding a good company and then paying a good price—which really means you're looking for both quality and value. We believe there are a few key signposts to guide you in your search.

To find a good company, look for a well-run, well-managed company. How can you tell? Consistently increasing sales is one good sign; consistently increasing profits is another; low debt is yet another good sign; return on assets of 10 percent or better is yet another—and all four together are very promising.

You also want to use common sense. Does the company offer a product or service people want? Are its prices competitive? Does it beat out competitors in terms of service, quality, selection, location, etc.? The more you know about the company, the better your chances of picking a winner. In fact, we are big fans of investing in your own particular area of knowledge or expertise. If you run a hardware store, you probably know the best tool companies, the best paint companies, the best lawn care companies. If you're a nurse, you probably know the best drug companies, the best surgical supply companies, the best uniform companies. Anywhere you're likely to have an edge, use it! As Peter Lynch said in his best-selling book *One Up on Wall Street,* invest in a company whose business you understand, and a company that can be run by an idiot, because sooner or later an idiot *will* be running it!

Now we turn to the question of price. Look at the stock itself. How does the **share price** compare with the company's **book value**? Book value is simply the net value of the company, its liquidation value, or what you'd get if you added all the assets and deducted all the liabilities and the company was sold tomorrow. You want to compare the share price to the book value, what the experts call "price-to-book value." And when buying a share of stock you don't want to pay more than two times the book value. In fact, many "value investors" pride themselves on buying companies whose stock price is trading below its book value. Paying less for a company than its break-up value gives the investor an added cushion. Price-to-book value can be found in *Standard and Poor's Stock Guide;* S & P does all the math for you.

The second key number to look at is the famous **P/E ratio,** or price-to-earnings ratio. This is the share price divided by the company's annual earnings per share. If the company has earned $1.50 per share, and the price of the share is $30.00, the P/E is 20 ($30.00 ÷ 1.50 = 20). A good value is a P/E that is around the industry average. By industry, we mean companies in the same business. If the P/E is too much lower it might mean investors are wary of the company; much higher, and you could be overpaying for the stock. The more the P/E varies from the industry average, the more speculative the stock.

Information about P/E ratios can be found in S&P's monthly *Stock Guide* and in the weekly *Value Line Investment Survey*. The "Summary and Index" section presents an up-to-date review of each of the 1700 stocks that Value Line researches. For further information, call 800-833-0046. Most newspaper stock tables also show each stock's P/E ratio on a daily basis.

DOLANS' SMART MONEY TIP: Watch out for inflated earnings *estimates.* It's easy (and tempting) for salesmen to quote appealing P/Es, by using "projected" earnings in their equations. Ask for the P/E based on the last 12 months' earnings ("trailing earnings"), then you'll see the true value.

Another indicator of a stock's growth potential can be found in its dividend history, if it's a dividend-paying stock. And why shouldn't you get paid a little something along the way, while you wait for the stock price to grow? Dividends that have steadily risen over a 10-year period signify corporate health, providing the dividends don't outstrip the company's earnings.

As for those earnings, the company should have shown improvement in earnings in at least five of the last 10 years, and have earned a Standard and Poor's rating of at least an A. A rating of A or better indicates a financially strong company that should be able to ride out economic downturns. A+ is the highest rating.

It's also important to find out how many shares are outstanding in the marketplace. A good number is at least 5 million shares. That will indicate the **liquidity** of a particular stock. Why do you care? Because without it, you may not be able to sell when you want.

All of this information is available for free in a large public library or a stockbroker's office in *Value Line Investment Survey* and *Standard and Poor's Stock Guide*. There is never a good excuse for buying a stock without reviewing this information first. If the stock recommendation comes unsolicited from a broker, don't act on the suggestion until you've asked for and received all of these facts and figures.

If you don't consider this data first, proceed immediately to the craps table at your local gambling casino and throw the dice. You'll have the same chance of doubling (or losing) your money there as you will through buying a stock without researching it first! But it is extremely important to remember that even when you do your homework, there's no guarantee that you'll pick a winner every time. All you're trying to do is tilt the odds in your favor. You won't choose correctly all the time (no one does), but it only takes a couple of good choices to make the pain of the losers disappear.

If you can't answer the following questions (be honest!), you should do more research before plunking down your hard-earned dollars for a stock:

- Have I adequately evaluated a company's prospects for the future?
- Is it a leader in its industry, or does it at least possess the potential to be a leader?
- Do I truly understand the company's product—from first-hand experience or lots of research? (Do you really understand gene-splicing or the very latest computer technology?) Be wary if it's a one-product company!
- Have I been able to find enough information on the company to make me feel comfortable to invest?
- Is it a type of stock that fits in with my overall investment objectives?

The Dow Jones Industrial Average is the oldest and most widely quoted of all the stock market indicators. It is made up of 30 blue chip stocks that together represent 15 to 20 percent of the market value of all stocks that trade on the New York Stock Exchange. Since it is most often quoted on television news and in newspapers, it has unfortunately come to signify "the stock market" to many people. But it's not. The DJIA is only 30 stocks, not an entire market. A much broader, and often better, indicator of overall market direction is the Standard and Poor's 500 Stock Index, which is made up of a combination of New York Stock Exchange–listed companies, some companies listed on the American Stock Exchange, as well as over-the-counter stocks. It is a much better bellwether to follow.

STOCKS OR STOCK FUNDS—WHICH ARE RIGHT FOR YOU?

How do you decide between individual stocks and stock mutual funds? The key is in your ability to diversify. A mutual fund allows you to pool your money with many other investors for greater diversification; it is managed by a professional portfolio manager. If you have enough money to buy six to ten stocks in different sectors of the economy, then you can do your own diversification and you don't need a mutual fund. That doesn't mean you go out and buy IBM, Apple, and Compaq. To diversify, you have to buy stock in *different sectors* of the market.

In fact, in our opinion, your longest-range goal should be to earn the ability to have enough discretionary investment capital to buy individual stocks yourself. Lately there has been a trend to rely 100 percent on stock mutual funds and their portfolio managers. This is the most expensive way to build your fortune. Even a no-load (no-commission) fund charges an annual maintenance fee, which is taken out of the fund's value, lowering your profit.

The other potential problem with stock funds is the portfolio manager's need to succeed every quarter. That often results in too much turnover in the portfolio, which increases costs and encourages "quick hits" rather than a more nurturing buy-and-hold strategy. On the flip side, some funds need to remain fully invested in a bear market, which can be very detrimental to the fund's performance.

So how much money do you need? You should always try to buy 100 shares of a particular stock at a time (a "round lot"), because the commissions are less per share. That means if you are interested in buying $2 stocks, all you'd need is $1,000 or $1,200; you could diversify by buying five or six $2 stocks in different sectors. However, we generally don't like "penny" stocks. We believe that penny stocks (stocks that sell for less than $5 per share) are much too risky for almost all investors. We wouldn't buy them, and we don't believe that you should either. They are usually issued by small, young companies without much of a track record or proven staying power.

A lot of research has shown that stocks in the $20 to $30 range tend to go up faster in price than any others. So, if you wanted to buy 100 shares of a $25 stock, for $2,500, times six different stocks, you'd need about $15,000 to diversify properly. That's just for the stock portion of your portfolio. But if you don't have that kind of money to invest, you should consider buying a stock mutual fund at the appropriate time. Even then, you should own more than one stock fund for proper diversification. Some stock funds are value oriented, some are growth oriented, and some are dividend oriented. For the greatest protection, be sure you diversify across these different investment objectives.

CHOOSING A WINNING STOCK FUND

No matter what the investment objective or management style of the fund, you want to be able to pick a winner. That's easier said than done. But here are some tips.

First, take a look at the fund's overall performance for a five- and ten-year period. Market cycles generally run for five or six years. So their five-year track records should show you the best of the best and the worst of the worst. If the fund hasn't been in existence for a five-year period, then you really don't know what to expect. A one-year track record could be entirely dependent on one particular economic trend or event that is not going to continue or reappear for several years.

But nowadays even a five-year track record can be misleading. On November 1, 1992, stock mutual funds were able to drop from their five-year track records a very important date: October 19, 1987. Suddenly all stock funds looked stronger, with better five-year total return records. Buyer beware! Go back and see how the total return looks with 1987 completely factored into the equation. You should be able to get this information by asking the fund. If it's not forthcoming with the answer, check out a *Weisenberger Directory* in a large public library.

As one of our old friends used to say, "In a stiff wind, even turkeys can fly." If all stocks are going up, then everybody can run a portfolio that goes up in value. The real test is how well funds do in the bad years. How did they fare in 1987? How did they fare in the recession of 1981–1982? How did they fare in the bear market of 1973–1974? That's why it's very important to be able to look back over a longer period of time.

You can find performance records in most major magazines every quarter, including *Forbes, Financial World,* and *Money. Forbes* magazine's "Bear Market" rating is a good general guide to how well a fund did when the market was sour.

Good performance in a bad market is a sign of a good fund manager, the one who is picking stocks, buying and selling, timing the market, outguessing other investors. He also is responsible for protecting your money when times get tough. So you want to make sure that the track record you're looking at was achieved by the person *currently* running the fund. If the good manager has left the fund, all bets are off. Ask how long the current portfolio manager has been running the fund.

Opposite is a sample of a mutual fund listing in *The Wall Street Journal*. The first column (starting at the far left) is the name of the fund; the next column gives the fund's "Investment Objective," be it Growth and Income (G&I), Bond (BND), Growth (GRO), or other. Reading across the page, the next column lists the Net Asset Value (NAV). This is simply the total assets of the fund, divided by the number of shares outstanding. If the fund charges no sales commission, or "load," NAV is also the price per share. You can tell by looking at the next column, labeled Offer Price. If it says NL, or No-Load, the NAV and price per share are the same. If there is a number in the Offer Price column, the number is the price per share, with a commission built in. The next column, NAV Change, is the dollar amount the share price rose or fell the previous day. These are based on close-of-day prices. Next comes the % Return Year-to-Date, which gives the percentage gain (or loss) in the NAV since the beginning of the year. Maximum Initial Charge shows the maximum the fund is allowed to charge buyers, based on the prospectus. Total Expense Ratio shows the total amount of all expenses charged by the fund, per share, including management fees and other expenses. These are typically deducted from the fund automatically, not billed to you separately, and are factored into the fund's total return already.

Although we love stock mutual funds for many investors, there is one type of stock fund we don't like and would not recommend: a sector fund. Sector funds are portfolios that invest in stocks of a single industry, such as financial services, drugs, technology, etc. Sector funds can undergo wild swings in share price because they are looking for high capital appreciation in a very narrow field. If the particular industry the fund invests in falls out of favor with Wall Street, you have nowhere to hide. Mutual funds were created to help you diversify for safety. Sector funds are risky investments for you.

ARE MUTUAL FUNDS CHEAPER THAN STOCKS?

Stock funds are not necessarily cheaper to buy than individual stocks—even no-load mutual funds. If you are buying individual shares of stock,

	Inv. Obj.	NAV	Offer Price	NAV Chg.	%Ret YTD	Max Initl Chrg.	Total Exp Ratio	R
AAL Mutual:								
Bond	BND	10.54	11.07	−0.01	+4.7	−0.2	+11.5	C
CaGr	GRO	15.06	15.81	−0.02	+3.2	+1.6	+8.0	D
MuBd	GLM	10.99	11.54	...	+4.7	+0.4	+11.1	D
AARP Invst:								
CaGr	GRO	33.92	NL	−0.20	+5.7	+5.3	+14.3	B
GInIM	BND	16.03	NL	−0.02	+3.7	+0.1	+9.7	D
GthInc	G&I	31.32	NL	−0.11	+7.2	+1.4	+12.4	C
HQ Bd	BND	16.46	NL	−0.04	+4.9	+0.1	+11.9	C
TxFBd	ISM	18.25	NL	...	+5.7	+0.2	+13.7	A
ABT Funds:								
Emrg	CAP	13.35	14.02	−0.09	+4.4	+12.3	+30.9	A
FL HI	MFL	10.38	10.90	...	+5.8	+0.4		NS ..
FL TF	MFL	11.27	11.83	...	+5.6	+0.5	+12.8	C
Gthln	G&I	11.02	11.57	−0.05	+3.2	+1.5	+9.7	D
Utilln	SEC	13.75	14.44	−0.01	+8.6	+0.1	+20.5	C
Acc Mortgx	BND	12.24	NL	−0.04	+3.8	+0.2	+8.1	E
Acc Sht Intx	BST	12.34	NL	−0.04	+3.2	−0.3	+7.6	C
AHA Funds:								
Balan	S&B	12.76	NL	−0.05	+5.7	+2.1	+11.4	C
Full	BND	10.58	NL	−0.02	+5.2	+0.1	+11.3	C
Lim	BST	10.46	NL	−0.01	+2.3	0.0	+5.6	D
AIM Funds:								
AdiGv p	BST	9.88	10.19	...	+2.0	+0.1	+5.1	D
Chart p	G&I	8.87	9.39	−0.04	+4.0	+1.8	+8.4	D
Const p	CAP	15.60	16.51	−0.15	+4.6	+7.5	+28.0	A
CvYld p	S&B	14.97	15.72	−0.10	+5.9	+3.4	+18.8	A
HiYld p	BHI	5.81	6.10	...	+7.5	+1.1	+13.2	E
IntlE p	ITL	10.50	11.11	+0.03	+17.2	+3.0	+11.1	B
LimM p	BST	10.18	10.28	...	+2.0	−0.3	+5.7	D
Sumit	GRO	9.82	NA	−0.07	+1.9	+4.1	+13.1	C
TF Int	IDM	NA	NA	NA	NA	NA	NA	..
Weing p	GRO	16.62	17.59	−0.12	−4.1	+3.2	+3.1	E
AIM Funds C:								
AgrsvC p	SML	19.83	20.98	−0.15	+7.1	+7.4	+38.5	A
GoScC p	BND	10.28	10.79	−0.01	+3.7	−0.1	+8.9	E
GrthC p	GRO	11.85	12.54	−0.12	−3.5	+5.0	+3.4	E
HYldC p	BHI	9.81	10.30	+0.01	+9.0	+1.4	+17.1	B
IncoC p	BND	8.39	8.81	−0.01	+7.7	+0.5	+15.0	A
MuBC p	GLM	8.47	8.89	...	+5.0	+0.4	+12.3	C
TeCtC p	SSM	10.97	11.52	+0.01	+5.4	+0.6	+12.2	B
UtilC p	SEC	13.99	14.80	...	+7.0	−0.8	+16.2	D
ValuC p	G&I	19.40	20.53	−0.15	+6.4	+3.7	+21.5	A
AMF Funds:								
AdiMtg	BST	9.99	NL	...	+2.0	+0.1	+4.3	D
IntMtg	BND	9.93	NL	−0.01	+4.1	0.0	+10.0	D
IntlLiq	BST	10.88	NL	−0.01	+2.8	−0.5	+7.7	C
MtgSc	BND	11.34	NL	−0.01	+2.7	+0.2	+7.9	E
ASM Fd	G&I	9.67	NL	−0.04	+6.2	+2.4	+3.6	E
ASO Funds:								
Balance	S&B	11.84	12.40	−0.06	+8.6	+1.6	+13.8	B
Bond	BND	11.19	11.72	−0.02	+5.6	−0.3	+12.7	B
Equity	CAP	14.42	15.10	−0.11	+11.3	+3.1	+15.6	C
LtdMat	BST	10.72	10.99	...	+3.4	−0.2	+8.0	B
RegEq	CAP	16.93	17.73	−0.03	+3.2	+5.1	+17.5	B
Acornin	ITL	12.91	12.91	+0.09	+20.8	+3.7		NS ..
AcornF	SML	63.99	63.99	−0.10	+15.7	+8.2	+36.7	A
AdsnCa p	G&I	22.42	23.11	−0.02	+7.5	+1.3	+15.6	B
AdvCapl BalxS	S&B	10.44	NL	−0.03	+1.8	+2.8	+8.3	E
AdvCapl Retxx	BND	10.37	NL	−0.02	+6.8	+0.9		NS ..
Advest Advant:								
Govt	BND	9.65	9.65	−0.03	+7.1k	0.0k	+17.0k	A
Gwth	GRO	16.79	16.79	−0.07	+2.8	+3.0	+11.3	C
HY Bd	BHI	9.43	9.43	...	+7.6k	+3.3k	+19.1k	A
Inco	BND	12.77	12.77	−0.03	+7.0	+0.7	+14.4	A
Spcl	SML	18.24	18.24	−0.04	+4.8	+4.2	+27.8	B
Aetna Funds:								
Aetna	S&B	10.59	NL	−0.03	+4.0	+1.5	+7.6	E
Bondx	BND	10.20	NL	−0.03	+5.3	−0.1	+11.1	C
GrwIncm	G&I	10.71	NL	−0.03	+1.9	+1.8	+8.0	E
IntlGr	ITL	10.19	NL	+0.07	+14.8	+2.3	+7.8	C
Alger Funds:								
Growth	GRO	19.74	19.74	−0.26	+3.0	+6.1	+22.9	A
IncGr	G&I	13.59	13.59	−0.03	+2.6	+2.1	+13.9	B
SmCap	SML	22.64	22.64	−0.23	−3.4	+8.5	+20.7	C
Alliance Cap:								
Allan p	GRO	7.04	7.45	−0.06	+5.4	+5.5	+20.3	A
Balan p	S&B	13.95	14.76	−0.06	+4.1	+1.5	+10.3	D
Canad p	ITL	5.37	5.68	−0.04	+11.2	−1.3	+7.4	C
CpBdA p	BND	13.70	14.12	−0.01	+13.6k	+1.1k	+26.3k	A
CpBdB p	BND	13.70	13.70	−0.01	NS	+1.1k		NS ..
Count p	G&I	19.14	20.25	−0.09	−0.7	+3.4	+6.9	E
GlbSA p	WOR	10.63	11.25	−0.01	+9.8	+5.8	+5.5	E
GovtA p	BND	8.53	8.79	−0.02	+4.8k	+0.3k	+11.9k	C
GovtB p	BND	8.53	8.53	−0.02	+4.5k	+0.2k	+11.2k	C
GrInc p	G&I	2.50	2.65	−0.01	+4.4	+2.5	+9.3	D
GrIncB p	G&I	2.49	2.49	−0.01	+4.2	+2.5	+7.7	E
ICalTA p	ISM	13.82	14.47	−0.01	+5.6k	+0.6k	+13.1k	B
InsMuA p	ISM	10.42	10.91	...	+5.5k	+0.5k	+12.6k	B
IntlA p	ITL	16.57	17.53	+0.06	+19.4	+2.2	+8.1	C
MrtgA p	BND	9.27	9.56	−0.01	+5.3k	+0.2k	+11.7k	C
MrtgB p	BND	9.27	9.27	−0.01	+5.0k	+0.2k	+11.2k	C
MrtgTrA p	BST	9.96	10.27	...	+3.3k	+0.3k	+18.2k	A
MrtgTrB p	BST	9.97	9.97	...	+3.0k	+0.3k	+17.7k	A
MltiG p	SEC	10.18	10.28	−0.03	+4.3k	+1.3k	+4.8k	E
Mltin p	WBD	1.90	1.90	...	+2.1k	+0.3k	+0.3k	E
MMSA p	WBD	8.83	9.10	−0.03	+4.9k	+1.4k	+0.4k	E
MMSB p	WBD	8.83	8.83	−0.03	+4.6k	+1.3k	−1.2k	E
MuCA p	MCA	10.58	11.08	−0.01	+5.5k	+0.7k	+12.4k	C
MuCA B p	MCA	10.57	10.57	−0.01	+5.0k	+0.7k		NS ..
MuNY p	DNY	9.89	10.36	−0.01	+5.4k	+0.3k	+12.8k	D
NflMu p	GLM	10.73	11.24	−0.01	+5.4k	+0.7k	+12.7k	B
NflMuB p	GLM	10.73	10.73	−0.01	+5.1k	+0.7k		NS ..
NEur p	ITL	10.54	11.15	+0.09	+14.6	+2.1	+1.9	D
NAGvA	WBD	10.01	10.32	−0.02	+7.0k	+0.5k	+12.1k	B
NAGvB	WBD	10.01	10.01	−0.02	+6.7k	+0.5k	+11.3k	B
PrGrthA p	GRO	11.12	11.46	−0.11	NA	+5.8		NS ..
PrGrthB p	GRO	11.09	11.09	−0.11	+1.6	+5.8		NS ..
QusrA p	SML	22.34	23.64	−0.11	+5.2	+7.8	+13.1	E
ST MlA p	WBD	9.25	9.54	−0.01	+4.1k	+1.2k	+1.8k	D
ST Mlb p	WBD	9.25	9.25	−0.01	+3.8k	+1.2k	+1.0k	D
Tech p	SEC	30.63	32.41	−0.90	+8.6	+11.6	+33.2	A
Wldin	WBD	1.91	1.91	...	+2.2k	+0.3k	+1.4k	D

you'll pay a broker's commission, but you don't have an annual management fee. With a mutual fund, you may not pay a broker's commission, but you'll pay an annual management and overhead fee. Even if you buy a no-load (no-commission) fund, you'll still pay that management fee. The fee differs from fund to fund. You can find out how much it is by reading the prospectus; it's the item called the "expense ratio." This expense ratio is automatically deducted from the fund, so it's not as noticeable, but you still pay it, one way or the other. After all, mutual funds are not charities. They're in business to make money, too. That's why a bond fund's yield is slightly lower than the comparable bond—because the expense ratio has been deducted.

The fact is that you have to look at all the costs you'll encounter, no matter what type of investment you're buying. In a stock mutual fund, a reasonable expense ratio is 1 percent. That means it will cost you $1 for every $100 you invest. In a bond fund, the expense ratio should be no more than .8 percent, or $.80 for every $100 invested. If your fund is charging more than these amounts, you're overpaying. Remember, the higher the fees, the better the fund's performance must be just to keep up with leaner and meaner funds.

SHOULD YOU PAY A COMMISSION?

We believe you should buy from the person who recommended the investment in the first place. If your broker calls you with an investment idea and you decide to buy, and you never would have found that stock or fund without him, do the right thing and buy from your broker.

On the other hand, if you did the research, you had the idea, you knew what you wanted from the start, don't pay "full boat" commissions. Call around to several discount brokers, and go with the outfit offering the lowest commission. You can find local discount brokers by looking in the Yellow Pages.

There is an advantage to having a relationship with a full-service broker. A good broker can put you into winning stocks ahead of the rest of the crowd. A good broker relies on hundreds of hours of research done by the firm. A good broker is also somebody who can hold your hand or periodically give you a pep talk.

The same goes for mutual funds. If you need somebody to help you make a decision or find an appropriate fund, somebody to check on dividends and interest payments, then go to a broker and buy a load fund. His commission is taken from the load. We're not against load funds. But if you do your own research, know about funds, read *Forbes* or *Money* magazine or an investment newsletter, and feel comfortable making your own decisions, then go with no-loads that you can buy direct.

As for the cost of load vs. no-load funds, someone might say, "Why should I pay 8½ percent, when I can get a no-load fund with no commission?" But how about the annual management fee? The fact of the matter is that over a 10-year period, an 8½ percent load fund with an expense ratio of 1 percent will cost you less than a no-load fund with a 2 percent expense ratio. So do the math before you make a costly assumption. The expense ratio is described in the fund's prospectus. Read it carefully.

If you decide to use a discount broker, see pages 104 to 110 for a comprehensive list of discount brokers, including telephone numbers, estimated commissions charged, minimums, and services, courtesy of an excellent investors'organization, the American Association of Individual Investors (AAII).

TWO SECRETS TO BUYING FOR LESS

If you want to save money in your investing (and who doesn't?), here are our two favorite techniques:

"DRIPs"

Dividend reinvestment plans (DRIPs) are plans offered by many blue chip companies that allow you to automatically reinvest your dividends to buy more stock directly from the company. The plan offers two advantages: first, although you may have to buy your first share of the company through a broker and pay a commission, you avoid paying commissions on any future shares you buy; second, it encourages a regular, steady, long-term approach to investing. Many DRIPs also allow you to buy additional shares (beyond what your dividends will buy) directly from the company, commission free!

DOLANS' SMART MONEY TIP: To get a list of all stocks offering DRIPs, a *great* book on the subject is *Buying Stocks Without a Broker*, by

AAII Guide to Discount Brokerage Firms

Telephone	Brokerage Firm	Commission ($) 100 Shares at $50 per share ($5,000)	500 Shares at $50 per share ($25,000)	1,000 Shares at $5 per share ($5,000)	Minimum ($)	Other Services (see key below)
800-221-5873	Andrew Peck Assoc.	48.00	72.50	90.00	50.00	SIPC; Sweep; NLMF; IRA
800-221-5873	Andrew Peck Assoc. "Savings in Size"**	100.00	100.00	100.00	100.00	SIPC; Sweep; NLMF; IRA
800-328-4076	Arnold Securities	35.75	130.16	69.85	35.00	SIPC; Interest ($2,000+); IRA
800-634-4935	Atlantic Discount Brokerage	60.00	135.00	60.00	40.00	SIPC+; Sweep; NLMF; IRA
800-368-3668	Aufhauser (K.) & Company	24.99	41.99	53.00	24.99	SIPC+; Sweep; NLMF; IRA
800-368-3668	Aufhauser (K.) & Company**	42.00	42.00	42.00	42.00	SIPC+; Sweep; NLMF; IRA
800-262-8739	Aurex Financial Corp.	60.00	60.00	60.00	60.00	SIPC+; Sweep; NLMF; IRA
800-321-1640	Baker & Co.	40.00	80.00	55.00	40.00	SIPC+; Sweep; IRA
800-221-2111	Barry Murphy & Company	32.50	62.50	60.00	25.00	SIPC+; Sweep; NLMF; IRA
800-547-6337	Bidwell & Company	29.00	65.00	62.50	20.00	SIPC; Sweep; NLMF; IRA

Phone	Name					Services
800-776-6061	Brown & Company	28.00	40.00	55.00	28.00	SIPC+; Interest ($1,000+); IRA
800-899-6878	Bruno, Stolze & Company	45.00	130.00	75.00	35.00	SIPC+; Sweep; NLMF; IRA
800-262-5800	Bull & Bear Securities	44.00	124.00	70.40	31.00	SIPC; Sweep; NLMF; IRA
800-621-0392	Burke Christensen & Lewis Securities	34.00	120.00	70.00	34.00	SIPC+; Interest ($1,500+); IRA
800-999-3699	Calvert Securities Corp.	50.00	149.50	80.00	45.00	SIPC; Sweep; NLMF; IRA
800-442-5111	Charles Schwab	55.00	155.00	90.00	39.00	SIPC; Sweep; NLMF; IRA
800-222-0124	CoreStates Securities Corp.	70.00	160.00	70.00	35.00	SIPC; Sweep; NLMF; IRA
813-586-3541	Downstate Discount Brokerage	46.00	118.50	65.00	39.00	SIPC; Interest ($500+); NLMF; IRA
800-544-6565	Fidelity Brokerage Services	54.00	154.50	88.50	38.00	SIPC+; Sweep; NLMF; IRA
800-526-7486	First Institutional Securities Corp.	68.00	137.00	68.00	45.00	SIPC; Sweep; IRA
800-228-3011	First Nat'l Brokerage Services*	31.00	110.00	67.00	31.00	SIPC+; Sweep ($1,000+); NLMF; IRA
800-228-3011	First Nat'l Brokerage Direct Service*	48.00	48.00	48.00	48.00	SIPC+; Sweep ($1,000+); NLMF; IRA

Telephone	Brokerage Firm	Commission ($)			Minimum ($)	Other Services (see key below)
		100 Shares at $50 per share ($5,000)	500 Shares at $50 per share ($25,000)	1,000 Shares at $5 per share ($5,000)		
800-326-4434	First Union Brokerage Services	45.00	140.00	90.00	40.00	SIPC; Sweep; IRA
800-221-8210	Fleet Brokerage Securities	46.20	135.55	67.77	37.00	SIPC+; Sweep; NLMF; IRA
800-729-7585	Freeman Welwood & Co.	45.00	145.00	70.00	34.00	SIPC; Interest ($500+); NLMF; IRA
800-634-8518	Icahn & Co.	50.00	75.00	60.00	40.00	SIPC+; Sweep; IRA
800-247-3396	J. D. Seibert & Company	49.00	140.00	75.00	49.00	SIPC+; Sweep; NLMF; IRA
800-233-3411	Jack White & Company	36.00	48.00	63.00	33.00	SIPC+; Sweep; NLMF; IRA
800-678-2626	Kashner Davidson Securities	50.00	160.00	75.00	45.00	SIPC+; Sweep; NLMF; IRA
800-252-0090	Kennedy, Cabot & Co.	35.00	35.00	50.00	35.00	SIPC+; Sweep; IRA
800-688-3462	Lombard Institutional Brokerage	34.00	34.00	34.00	34.00	SIPC+; Sweep; NLMF; IRA
800-221-3305	Marquette de Bary Co.	42.90	146.43	69.85	20.00	SIPC+; Sweep; IRA
800-366-1500	Marsh Block & Co.	33.24	129.95	33.24	25.00	SIPC+; Sweep; NLMF; IRA
800-223-6642	Max Ule	57.00	195.00	70.00	35.00	SIPC+; Interest ($1,000+); NLMF; IRA

800-872-0711	Muriel Siebert & Co. "Value Rates"	45.00	113.00	57.00	37.50	SIPC+; Sweep; NLMF; IRA
800-872-0711	Muriel Siebert & Co. "Share Rates"**	75.00	75.00	75.00	75.00	SIPC+; Sweep; NLMF; IRA
800-472-7227	New England Investment Enterprises	115.00	325.00	115.00	50.00	SIPC+; Sweep; NLMF; IRA
800-872-6533	Olde Discount Stockbrokers	40.00	100.00	52.50	20.00	SIPC+; Sweep; IRA
800-221-1660	Pace Securities	40.00	75.00	70.00	40.00	SIPC+; Sweep; IRA
800-221-1660	Pace Securities PaceSetter Account**	70.00	70.00	70.00	70.00	SIPC+; Sweep; IRA
800-421-8395	Pacific Brokerage Services	25.00	42.00	53.00	28.00	SIPC+; Sweep; IRA
800-772-4400	People's Securities	40.00	131.00	69.00	38.00	SIPC+; Sweep; NLMF; IRA
800-666-1440	Peremel & Co.	40.00	70.00	100.00	40.00	SIPC+; Sweep; NLMF; IRA
800-247-2752	ProVest	40.00	95.00	145.00	40.00	SIPC; Sweep; IRA
800-221-5220	Quick & Reilly	49.00	119.50	60.50	37.50	SIPC+; Sweep; IRA
800-221-8514	R. F. Lafferty & Co.	50.00	62.50	70.00	50.00	SIPC+; Interest ($2,000); IRA
800-328-8600	Recom Securities	39.00	163.00	75.00	35.00	SIPC+; Sweep; IRA
800-631-1635	Richard Blackman & Co.	43.00	98.00	60.00	25.00	SIPC+; Sweep; NLMF; IRA
800-242-1523	Robert Thomas Securities	60.00	155.00	110.00	35.00	SIPC+; Sweep; NLMF; IRA

Telephone	Brokerage Firm	Commission ($)			Minimum ($)	Other Services (see key below)
		100 Shares at $50 per share ($5,000)	500 Shares at $50 per share ($25,000)	1,000 Shares at $5 per share ($5,000)		
800-676-1848	Rodecker & Co. Investment Brokers	72.50	247.50	132.50	50.00	SIPC+; Sweep; IRA
800-488-5195	Royal Grimm & Davis	40.00	75.00	70.00	30.00	SIPC+; Sweep; IRA
718-448-2900	Russo Securities	50.00	75.00	100.00	50.00	SIPC;Sweep;NLMF;IRA
918-582-0110	S. C. Costa Company	48.00	139.00	76.50	38.00	SIPC; Sweep; IRA
800-283-1950	Scottscale Securities	29.00	55.00	65.00	30.00	SIPC; Interest
800-732-7678	Seaport Securities Corp.	34.00	50.00	80.00	34.00	SIPC+; Sweep; NLMF; IRA
800-327-3156	Securities Research Inc.	45.00	115.00	95.00	35.00	SIPC+; Sweep; NLMF; IRA
800-582-8585	Shareholder Services Corp.	40.00	52.00	67.00	37.00	SIPC+; Sweep; NLMF; IRA
800-221-4242	Shearman, Ralston Inc.	40.00	110.00	105.62	40.00	SIPC+; Sweep; NLMF; IRA
800-327-1536	Shochet Securities	63.00	150.00	95.00	40.00	SIPC+; Sweep; IRA
800-695-4220	Spear Rees & Co.	48.00	145.00	75.50	38.00	SIPC; IRA
	St. Louis Discount Securities*	32.00	64.00	62.40	37.00	SIPC; Interest; IRA
800-421-6563	Stock Mart (The)	35.75	162.70	62.87	30.00	SIPC+; Sweep; IRA
800-225-6196	StockCross*	33.50	67.50	110.00	25.00	SIPC; Sweep ($3,000+); IRA

800-225-7720	T. Rowe Price Discount Brokerage	46.00	134.00	75.00	35.00	SIPC; Sweep; IRA
800-669-4483	Thomas F. White & Co.	65.00	130.00	65.00	35.00	SIPC; Sweep; IRA
800-522-3000	Tradex Brokerage Service	35.00	95.00	75.00	25.00	SIPC+; Sweep ($1,000+); IRA
800-962-5489	Tuttle Securities	65.00	195.00	115.00	40.00	SIPC; Sweep; NLMF; IRA
800-426-8106	Voss & Co.	53.63	162.70	104.78	38.50	SIPC+; Sweep; NLMF; IRA
800-221-7990	Wall Street Discount Corp.	35.00	62.50	60.00	35.00	SIPC+; Interest; IRA
800-934-4410	Waterhouse Securities	35.00	111.74	54.72	35.00	SIPC+; Sweep; NLMF; IRA
800-223-5023	Whitehall Securities Inc.	50.00	62.50	125.00	50.00	SIPC+; Interest ($2,000+); IRA
800-221-3154	York Securities	35.00	70.00	45.00	35.00	SIPC+; Sweep; NLMF; IRA
800-433-5132	Young, Stovall and Company	50.00	136.00	78.00	38.00	SIPC; Sweep; IRA
	Average	**46.85**	**109.32**	**74.44**		
	Highest	**115.00**	**325.00**	**145.00**		
	Lowest	**24.99**	**34.00**	**33.24**		

* Non-market orders are higher

** High volume rates

The commissions represent charges on exchange-listed shares for market orders only. Most firms do not charge different rates for over-the-market stocks, but a few do. Confirm all charges and services with firms before making final decisions.

Key to Other Services

SIPC: Provides insurance for securities and cash in customer accounts up to $500,000 through the Securities Investor Protection Corp.

SIPC+: Provides insurance coverage beyond $500,000, for customer accounts at no extra charge.

Interest: Pays interest on customers' cash balances. Amounts in parentheses, if any, indicate minimum amount above which interest is paid. If a discount firm offers a sweep account, we do not include information on cash balance interest.

Sweep: Automatically invests cash balances in an interest-bearing money market fund until those funds are reinvested. Money market funds usually pay a higher rate of interest than cash balance accounts that simply earn interest.

NLMF: No-load mutual funds can be purchased through the firm. Note that some firms charge for this, others do not. In addition, the number of funds available varies from firm to firm; check with the firm for a listing of available funds.

IRA: Self-directed Individual Retirement Accounts can be set up with the firm. The charge for maintaining an IRA varies among the firms.

Charles Carlson (McGraw-Hill, $16.95). To participate in most DRIPs, you must already own at least one share of the company's stock, registered in *your* name.

Ordinarily, it would be quite expensive to buy that first share at a brokerage firm, but there is an organization called First Share that matches you up with other club members, from whom you can buy an initial share of over 100 stocks without commission. The cost is a $12.00 per year membership fee and $7.50 to locate the share seller. For more information, call First Share at 800-683-0743.

Dollar Cost Averaging

Our other top technique for lowering your investment costs is dollar cost averaging (DCA). DCA is a regular program, usually the purchase of mutual funds, in which you automatically invest a predetermined, fixed amount of money every month or quarter. The amount of money you invest each time is the same, but the number of shares you buy may vary, based on the price of the shares. You could wind up buying more shares at lower prices, if you stick with the strategy.

For example, say you plan to invest $500 per quarter. The first time, the share price is $25, so you buy 20 shares. Three months later, the price is $20, so you buy 25 shares. Three months after that, the price has jumped to $30, so you buy 16.666 shares. The average price during these six months was $25. But because you bought more shares when the price was lower, your average is $24.32—$1500 divided by 61.666 (16.666 + 20 + 25).

And, finally, like DRIPs, DCA programs also boast the benefit of regular, steady, long-term investing—a key to success.

KEEPING YOUR STOCK IN YOUR POSSESSION

When you buy shares of stock or a mutual fund, you'll get a statement from your broker or the mutual fund confirming the transaction. You have five business days to send your check, if you're not using money already in your account, though the SEC is trying to change this to three days.

The shares of stock may be bought in the brokerage firm's name (also known as the ''street name'') or in your name. In the first case, the actual certificates of ownership are sent to the brokerage house; in the second case, they are sent to you. Which is better?

There are two schools of thought on this; Daria subscribes to one, and I (this is Ken talking now) subscribe to the other. It doesn't bother me to have stock in the broker's street name. It's safe, and if you decide to sell you can call up your broker and it will be done immediately, because he has the certificates. Secondly, people sometimes lose things. If you lose a stock certificate, it can be a real bother and expense to have it replaced.

But Ken (this is Daria now), how many calls have we received recently from people who have had trouble transferring their stocks from one brokerage to another when the stocks weren't in their name? And nowadays investors who tend to buy and hold for the long term may suddenly find themselves being billed for "inactive accounts," which can cost $50 or more a year! Many people have found that ownership is worth the added responsibility of safeguarding the certificates.

How to decide? Buy-and-hold investors should request the stock certificates. Traders should leave the certificates in the street name.

SMART SELLING SECRETS

We do agree on when you should sell stocks: when they've reached the price you've set as your target for taking profits. Which, of course, assumes you've set a target. This is a very important point. You not only should have a specific dollar profit goal, you should also set targets for each investment you buy—and decide in advance when you will sell. No tree grows to the sky. Disciplined investors are willing to give up some of a stock's possible further upside move when they've made a satisfactory profit.

You should also sell a stock when your reason for buying it no longer exists: when the stock's earnings are dropping on a consistent basis, when the company is losing its position in its segment of the market, when there's all sorts of good news about the company and the stock refuses to move. You should also sell a stock if it consistently goes down from the day you first bought it. You were wrong and you have to admit it. And, sad to say, sometimes you should sell a stock when everyone on Wall Street is touting it. Wall Street is usually late in telling everyone about a great new company. Wall Street insiders may even be encouraging people to buy so they can start lightening up on their own position—leaving *you* holding the bag.

UTILITIES FOR PAINLESS PROFITS

If we were asked to say which type of stock is most widely owned by individuals, we'd have to say utilities. Look at your own portfolio (if you already invest). Do you own any AT&T? Any electric companies? Perhaps a water company? Utilities can be the best investments when you are a retiree, because they tend to pay good, reliable dividends. But when you are 20 years old, you don't need that dividend. You want to find the next Xerox, the next McDonald's. Or do you? What's wrong with being paid a "little something" while you wait for a stock price to appreciate? Nothing's wrong with that.

20 Utilities That Have Increased Their Dividends Every Year for the Past 30 Years (or More)

Allegheny Power System	Rochester Telephone
ALLTEL Corp.	SCANA Corp.
Atlantic Energy	Southern California Water
Central and Southwest Corporation	Southern Indiana G&E
Consumers Water Company	Southwestern Electric Service
Florida Progress Corporation	TECO Energy Inc.
FPL Group	Texas Utilities Company
IES Industries	UtiliCorp United Inc.
LG&E Energy	Wisconsin Energy Service
Northwest Natural Gas	Wisconsin Public Service

Utilities fare best when interest rates are falling; at such times high dividend rates make them a very attractive investment. But once the rates stop falling, some of the bloom is off the rose because you can get a higher rate of return with another investment. If you wonder when you should sell a utility stock, your best time would be when interest rates are rising, all other factors (earnings, dividends, utility rate climate, etc.) being equal.

Which utilities are best? Again, you want a stock with a solid history of paying dividends every year, and increasing those dividends regularly over the years. We also tend to like electric utilities in states with appointed rate commissions. Generally, you want to avoid the southern states, where commissioners are elected. Nobody is going to get elected on a campaign platform saying, "I'm going to raise your rates." Commissions that are appointed tend to allow rate increases more readily, which may not be good for you if you're a customer, but it can be very good for a stockholder.

You also have to be wary, in our opinion, of utilities that are still developing nuclear power. If you're going to buy shares in such a company, make sure its nuclear power facilities are already on line. It's also comforting to know that, historically, utilities tend to weather bear markets (when stock prices are declining) better than most growth stocks.

**The Top Five Utility Mutual Funds
Ranked by One-Year Total Return***

Fund Name and Phone Number	1-Year Total Return
Rushmore American Gas Index 800-343-3355	26.60
Financial Strategic—Utilities 800-525-8085	26.02
Fidelity Select Utilities 800-544-8888	21.40
ABT Utility Income Fund 800-553-7838	20.95
Fidelity Select Electric Utilities 800-544-8888	20.91

* Performance figures courtesy of Schabacker Investment Management, Rockville, Md.

All figures through 5/31/93

COLLECTIBLES ARE FOR FUN

OK, Dolans, let's have a little fun. What about an investment I can actually enjoy?

Count us in! We love having fun. Just be realistic about what you're getting in return. If you want to go out and buy antique furniture, rare artwork, stamp collections—whatever—more power to you. But do it as a collector, as a true connoisseur of your chosen collectibles. Buy them to *enjoy,* to display, to treasure and pass on to your kids—not to make a killing. The same goes for gems. If you want to buy diamonds or rubies, don't put them in the vault. Wear them. Put them in settings and enjoy them.

Which brings us to gold, which many consider the best hedge against inflation. But first, we'd like to stress that investing in precious metals, in all forms, is extremely speculative and not for the faint of heart. Ask anybody who bought gold in 1980 when it was $810 an ounce.

Gold bullion or gold stocks or mutual funds do make sense for the younger investor *if* he is willing to invest no more than 5 percent of his portfolio, and then just sit tight. We think gold will rise eventually, triggered by inflation and/or the huge overload of government debt we've taken on in the past 15 years. Even deflation can help gold because it can trade as a monetary replacement for shaky currencies.

But who knows when? So, no more than 5 percent of your portfolio in gold.

The least risky way to invest in gold is in bullion. That means the metal itself, either in bars or coins. (But unless you're an expert or do your homework, steer clear of rare coin investments, because generally it's just too hard to get good, reliable information and ratings.) The most risky investments are the mining stocks, and the middle-of-the-road risk is a good managed portfolio in a mutual fund.

You can buy gold bullion through any major bank. You can also go to gold companies, but that's a little riskier because you don't know how solvent they are. You never, *ever* want to buy gold bullion you cannot see. If you live in Chicago and buy it in San Francisco, you'll never know if you got what you paid for. You are best served going to a large, money-center bank that has the clout to give you a decent price and the vault in which to store the bullion, like Citicorp, Chase, Chemical, Bank of America, or Wells Fargo.

While buying bullion may be less risky than the other options, it can end up being more costly because you have to pay storage fees every year. With a buy-and-hold strategy (you're willing to sit tight with gold until it does eventually move again), you may have incurred many years of service fees that will certainly eat into your profit.

Which gold stocks or stock funds should you buy? You want a company that is already producing. Avoid any exploration company that's not yet taking gold out of the ground. At least that way you take *some* (not nearly all) of the maximum risk out of your investment.

INVESTING IN A GLOBAL ECONOMY

A global economy is here to stay, and it is very important that the American family become more globally aware and more globally invested for maximum diversification. That's not to say you should go off half-cocked, buying stocks on the Moscow Stock Exchange or putting Johnny's piggy bank savings into a Swiss bank account. In fact, since a number of world markets are not as highly regulated as ours, you could get badly burned. Which means you should become globally invested in the safest way, namely, with international stock funds (funds that buy stock outside the borders of the United States) and global stock funds (funds that buy *both* foreign and U.S. companies). By investing in global bond funds, it's also possible to try your hand at foreign currency and interest-bearing bonds without having to load up on lots of funny money and take a course at Berlitz.

You notice that in both the stock and bond investments we just mentioned, we said *funds.* Don't buy individual Australian bonds yielding 15 percent and think you're globally invested. You're only taking your global piece of investment pie and putting it in a single (risky) spot. By using funds with good performance records over many years (both stock and bond funds), you will be able to profit without exposing yourself to grave risks. In fact, during the 1980s, when the U.S. stock market saw such great upward moves, other countries' stock markets actually beat our own in annual percentage gains. Those who were invested internationally, as well as domestically, had the best gains.

Even though you'll probably live your life in U.S. dollars, it won't hurt you to yen for some foreign shares. (Sorry about the pun!) Just be sure to buy them through the professionals who know how the rules of the game are played overseas.

PUTTING IT ALL TOGETHER: PORTFOLIOS FOR THE VARIOUS STAGES OF YOUR LIFE

How do you put all the pieces together into a comprehensive strategy that makes sense for *you and your family?* Here are our guidelines, depending on your own particular situation:

PORTFOLIO I: SINGLE INVESTOR, NO DEPENDENTS

33%	Growth mutual funds or individual stocks
50%	Tax-free bonds or bond funds
10%	Money market mutual funds
7%	Employee retirement plan/pension

PORTFOLIO II: YOUNG FAMILY (TWO INCOMES, ONE CHILD)

12%	Growth mutual funds or individual stocks
12%	Growth and income mutual funds or dividend-oriented stocks (like utilities)

50%   Tax-free bonds or bond funds
10%   Money market mutual funds
10%   T-bills and T-notes
 6%   Employee retirement plan/pension

PORTFOLIO III: SINGLE PARENT WITH TWO TEENAGERS

17%   Growth mutual funds or individual stocks
17%   Growth and income mutual funds or dividend-oriented stocks
50%   T-bills and T-notes, individual bonds or bond funds, taxable or
      tax-free
10%   Money market mutual funds
 6%   Employee retirement plan/pension

PORTFOLIO IV: MIDDLE-AGED INVESTOR, NO DEPENDENTS

22%   Growth mutual fund or individual stocks
12%   Growth and income mutual fund or dividend-oriented stocks
50%   T-bills and T-notes, individual bonds or bond funds, taxable or
      tax-free
10%   Money market mutual funds
 6%   Employee retirement plan/pension

PORTFOLIO V: EMPTY NESTERS

 9%   Growth mutual funds or individual stocks
25%   Growth and income mutual funds or dividend-oriented stocks
40%   Individual bonds or bond funds, taxable or tax-free
10%   T-bills or T-notes
10%   Money market mutual funds
 6%   Employee retirement plan/pension

PORTFOLIO VI: RETIREES

 5%   Growth mutual funds or individual stocks
10%   Growth and income mutual funds or dividend-oriented stocks
50%   Individual bonds or bond funds, taxable or tax-free
25%   T-bills, T-notes, CDs
10%   Money market mutual funds

Of course, these are just guidelines. You'll want to custom-tailor your own investment program to meet your family's unique needs and situation. But these thumbnail sketches should get you moving in the right direction!

FIVE MISTAKES YOU NEVER HAVE TO MAKE AGAIN

Because there are so many different investment alternatives, you can see how easy it is to take a wrong turn somewhere along the way. But we're here to tell you that it's just as easy to do things right. The key is to avoid some very simple mistakes. Steer clear of these, and you'll be well on your way to success:

Mistake #1: Diving in before you're ready. Do your homework, understand your options, and don't be rushed into a decision you're not comfortable with!

Mistake #2: Not setting realistic goals (or not setting any at all). Remember, you can't get there without a map! Sit down with a sheet of paper and plot out how much you'll need, and when. Then use our Rule of 72 (page 83) to help set your sights on a needed rate of return.

Mistake #3: Not diversifying. Risky, risky, risky. You know the old saying "Don't put all your eggs in one basket." That's doubly true for your investments. Spread the risk—and your net for scooping up rewards—across different maturities with bonds, different sectors of the economy with stocks, and different management styles among mutual funds.

Mistake #4: Taking too much risk. This often goes hand in hand with unrealistic expectations, "swinging for the fences," if you will. Remember that higher returns almost always involve higher risks. So don't be bamboozled by promises of 300 percent profits. It probably means you'll have to take some heart-stopping risks along the way. All too often that "300" number is in the losing column.

Mistake #5: Overtrading. As we told you, the simplest strategies are often the best. If you choose carefully in the first place, a buy-and-hold strategy can build your wealth impressively over the long term. So don't get seduced by complex switching strategies or timing models. They usually involve a lot of spinning with very little weaving. Save your time and your efforts for yourself and your family. Make your money work harder for you; don't make yourself work harder for your money.

CHAPTER FIVE

Smart Ways to Fund a College Education

How to Save, Invest, and Take Full Advantage of Financial Aid Packages

When our daughter Meredith was born 21 years ago, we never dreamed it would cost upwards of $80,000 to send her to college. That kind of money was virtually unimaginable in those days. Experts now predict that the average private four-year college tuition will top $90,000 by the year 2000—and that's not even including another small fortune for room, board, books, travel, clothes, what have you. Expensive private colleges will probably charge tuitions of $100,000 or more for four years; even state schools will run about $50,000 by then.

If your kids are still running around in diapers, the story gets even worse. Tuition costs are rising about 7 percent a year for private schools, 10 percent a year for public schools. By the year 2010, the average tuition for four years will probably be an eye-popping $200,000. Are you going to be able to afford that? Is anyone?

OK, let's take this one step at a time, before you panic and quit before you begin. When we're talking about this kind of money, it almost takes your breath away. So take a couple of deep breaths and follow along as we show you how you can afford to send your kids to college, whether they're 17 years old now, 7 years old, 7 months old . . . or even younger!

FIVE BEST INVESTMENTS FOR FUNDING COLLEGE

For starters, some parents (and we hope this means you) really will be able to pay for most, if not all, of these towering costs—*if you start planning now*. Commit from today forward to a disciplined, growth-oriented program of continuous saving and compounding, and you'll be surprised at how much money you'll have when Junior is ready for the ivied walls.

How a Single $1,000 Investment Will Grow

Percent*	5 Years	8 Years	10 Years	12 Years	15 Years
3	$1,159	$1,267	$1,344	$1,426	$1,558
4	1,217	1,369	1,480	1,601	1,801
5	1,276	1,478	1,629	1,796	2,079
6	1,338	1,594	1,791	2,012	2,397
8	1,469	1,851	2,159	2,518	3,172
10	1,611	2,144	2,594	3,138	4,177
15	2,011	3,059	4,046	5,350	8,137

How a $1,000 Investment Every Year Will Grow

Percent*	5 Years	8 Years	10 Years	12 Years	15 Years
3	$5,310	$8,890	$11,460	$14,190	$18,600
4	5,420	9,210	12,010	15,030	20,020
5	5,530	9,550	12,580	15,920	21,580
6	5,640	9,900	13,180	16,870	23,280
8	5,870	10,640	14,490	18,980	27,150
10	6,110	11,440	15,940	21,380	31,770
15	6,740	13,730	20,300	29,000	47,580

* Percent annual net rate of return (compounded)

Here are our five favorite ways to invest for college funding:

Growth Stock Mutual Funds

There are a handful of excellent, reliable growth stock mutual funds that can build your wealth faster and more reliably than any other investment we know of. We're talking here about growth funds with solid, long-term track records of a 10 percent average of annual gains. A good place to start your search for strong performers is the *Forbes* Honor Roll, which is published in *Forbes* magazine every September in their annual mutual fund survey issue. Also see *Money* magazine's special Mutual Fund Edition each year in May for reports on some of the best-performing mutual funds.

DOLANS' SMART MONEY TIP: Set up a dollar cost averaging program (see Chapter Four) with the fund of your choice so that you automatically and systematically invest a set amount of money every single month into your "college growth fund." Just call the fund and ask; they'll tell you how to set up a dollar cost averaging plan. In fact, many fund families lower their initial investment amount when you agree to a regular monthly contribution.

EE Savings Bonds

Tried, true, boring—yes. But they work! They're safe and they're "no-brainers." And, best of all, you owe no federal income taxes on the interest when you cash in the bonds if you use them to pay for education costs and your adjusted gross income is under $68,250 (100 percent phaseout at $98,250) filing jointly, or $45,500 (100 percent phaseout at $60,500) filing individually. In other words, your ability to use the savings bonds tax-free for college diminishes as your income rises over these levels, completely vanishing or phasing out at $98,250. (The income level rises each year to keep pace with inflation.)

DOLANS' SAFETY WARNING: Watch out when you cash in your bonds. The interest income could send you over the income threshold for this deduction! Look for other deductions and investment losses to offset the gains so you can still avoid taxes. And remember, these bonds should be in *your* name, not your child's, to avoid the taxes.

Another reason we love the use of EE Savings Bonds for college funding is because you're not stuck with the same interest rate for the entire life of the bond. U.S. savings bonds readjust the interest rate every six months, on May 1 and November 1. When interest rates go up, you get a better rate through the years, and if rates go down, you're guaranteed a return of no less than 4 percent providing you hold the bonds for at least six months. Now 4 percent may not sound like much, but generally the variable rate, over a five-year holding period, has exceeded the floor-rate minimum. Even if your income is too high for the tax-free use of EE bonds, the interest is tax deferred, so no taxes are due until you cash them in or they mature, and even then you pay no state or local taxes.

For more information relating to the tax-free aspects of certain EE U.S. Savings Bonds, contact your nearest savings bond office and request publication SBD-2017R.

Savings Bonds District Offices

Atlanta (Georgia, Florida)
1100 Spring Street, N.W., Room 560
Atlanta, GA 30309
404-347-4895

Birmingham (Alabama, Louisiana, Mississippi, Tennessee)
The 2121 Building, Suite 716
2121 8th Avenue, North
Birmingham, AL 35203
205-731-1202

Boston (New England)
10 Causeway Street, Room 463
Boston, MA 02222-1090
617-565-6100

Chicago (Northern Illinois)
John C. Kluczynski Federal Building
230 S. Dearborn Street, Room 530
Chicago, IL 60604-1594
312-353-6754

Cleveland (Ohio, Kentucky)
1301 Superior Avenue, Room 230
Cleveland, OH 44144
216-522-4012

Dallas (Texas)
Earle Cabell Federal Building and Courthouse
1100 Commerce Street, Room 14C-44
Dallas, TX 75242-9972
214-767-0435

Detroit (Michigan, Indiana)
Patrick V. McNamara Building, Suite 1745
477 Michigan Avenue
Detroit, MI 48226-2577
313-226-7375

Greensboro (North Carolina,
South Carolina)
P.O. Box 1199
Greensboro, NC 27402
919-333-5461

Los Angeles (Arizona, Southern
California, Southern Nevada,
New Mexico)
P.O. Box 84-600
Los Angeles, CA 90073
213-209-6580

Manhattan
26 Federal Plaza, Room 3046
New York, NY 10278
212-264-1368

Minneapolis (Iowa, Minnesota,
Nebraska, North Dakota, South
Dakota, Wisconsin)
Marquette Building, Room 490
400 Marquette Avenue
Minneapolis, MN 55401
612-349-5400

New York (New York State,
except Manhattan)
U.S. Customs House, Room 320
6 World Trade Center
New York, NY 10048
212-264-1155

Pittsburgh (Delaware,
Pennsylvania)
Federal Building, Room 2127
1000 Liberty Avenue
Pittsburgh, PA 15222
412-644-2990

St. Louis (Arkansas, Oklahoma,
Missouri, Kansas, Southern
Illinois)
210 N. Tucker, Room 1111
St. Louis, MO 63101
314-425-5715

San Francisco (Northern
California, Northern Nevada,
Utah)
Alameda Federal Center
620 Central Avenue, Building
2E, Room 107
Alameda, CA 94501
415-273-4477

Seattle (Alaska, Colorado,
Hawaii, Idaho, Oregon,
Montana, Washington,
Wyoming)
121–107th N.E., Suite 123
Bellevue, WA 98004
206-442-4536

Trenton (New Jersey)
Federal Building
402 E. State Street
Trenton, NJ 08608
609-989-2088

Washington, D.C. (District of
Columbia, Maryland, Virginia,
West Virginia)
5550 Friendship Boulevard, Suite
400A
Chevy Chase, MD 20815
301-492-5797

Zero-Coupon Bonds

Zero-coupon bonds pay no current income but give a big payoff at maturity, which makes them perfect for college savings plans. You don't need the income now, but you will need it later, and you know exactly when you're going to need it, too. Our favorites are Treasury zeros, sold and guaranteed by the United States government. They're the safest, and they offer the added bonus of being exempt from state and local income tax. See Chapter Four for more about zeros.

> DOLANS' SAFETY WARNING: The only downside of Treasury zeros is that you owe current federal income tax on the "phantom" interest. That's why they work best in a tax-sheltered plan, like an IRA. But don't lock them into an IRA if you're going to need to pay for Junior's college before you turn 59½ or you'll get socked with penalties for early withdrawal. Zeros in IRAs work best for older parents, whose kids will turn 18 after the parent reaches age 59½.
>
> If your child is 14 or older, consider buying zeros in your child's name. The phantom interest will be taxed at your child's rate, which may mean little or no tax at all. Later on we'll show you the downside of putting assets in your kid's name. But if *you* are going to be paying the tuition out of your own pocket, this tax strategy makes sense.

Prepayment Plans

Colleges, your state, many brokerage firms, and even banks are now offering plans to help you "make the grade" with college money by allowing you to prepay future tuition costs years before your child needs the money. You can either prepay a lump sum or make regular payments into the program. The inducement is either a smaller amount paid today to pay for college many years down the road with one lump sum, or the discipline of regular payments when you lack the discipline to save regularly on your own. But don't forget, if you decide to follow this road, there are some potholes to consider. You have to ask yourself some tough questions before you write your check. If you pay directly to the college, what happens if the college closes before Junior enrolls? If you use a state plan, what happens if your job takes you to another state or Junior wants to go to school out of state? In either plan, what happens if Junior isn't accepted at the school?

In most cases, if your child doesn't attend the state or private school you paid directly all those years ago, you should be able to get back all of your principal and, if you're real lucky, a nominal amount of interest. These are important considerations. It's also important to think of the IRS. Uncle Sam usually expects his cut of the capital appreciation of the money originally invested, in the form of taxes. Investigate carefully before using this strategy.

Investing in Yourself

Don't overlook this opportunity. If you have a young child, maybe the best thing you could do is to invest in improving your own education. By raising your earnings potential, you may be able to use that bigger paycheck to build a bigger nest egg, and faster.

USING INSURANCE TO PAY FOR SCHOOL

It really steams us up to hear about insurance agents who try to sell annuities (or ''investment insurance'') to parents for Junior's college tuition. Unless those parents are going to be at least 59½ years old when Junior enters college, they won't be able to get at that ''college fund'' annuity without paying significant penalties to the IRS. Also, the part of your annuity premium that's paying for a death benefit is wasted in this case—you want the money for your kid's college, not for when you die! Nor do we believe ''borrowing'' your own money from an insurance policy makes sense.

Having said that, however, we do believe you should have a term life insurance policy with a death benefit equal to the amount of what it is going to cost to pay for school. So, in the terrible case when one parent dies before college is paid for, the surviving parent is not drowned in debt. A lot of families run into this bind when one of the parents dies right before the kids start college. They get some insurance money, but not enough to pay for college. Often the surviving parent needs that money to support the kids and keep the household going. And when these families apply for tuition aid, the death benefit received is counted as an asset, so then they don't qualify for aid.

DOLANS' SMART MONEY TIP: Have enough life insurance to pay off whatever debts the family has, *including* projected college costs.

LOTS OF SOURCES OF AID

Even if there are several ways to invest and save for that looming college tuition bill, what if you're just not going to be able to swing it on your own? The fact is that there is a lot of help out there, if you just know where to look.

As a parent, the worst thing you can say is, "We haven't saved enough to pay college bills, but we're not eligible for financial aid because we make too much money!" Not so fast! You can qualify for thousands of dollars in financial assistance, often no matter what your income or net worth. So don't automatically assume you cannot qualify. Furthermore, "aid" comes in many shapes and sizes, from grants and scholarships to low-interest loans and work-study programs. The key to getting the most aid is to understand how the system works and to arrange your finances shrewdly. We're not talking about cheating or lying, not one bit! We're simply talking about sending your kids to college without devastating your finances.

The amount of aid you get is determined by each school, based in large part on a preliminary analysis done by a central processing service such as the College Scholarship Service (CSS) or the American College Testing Program (ACT). You send your completed application to the appropriate processor and it, in turn, sends the analysis to the schools you list on the application. The colleges then further analyze the numbers, put together a package of grants, loans, and work-study opportunities, and send you their offer. What the services, and the schools, are trying to determine is how much of the tuition you can afford to pay, and then how much they're going to offer to make up the difference. They use a complex formula that looks at your income, your assets, your child's income, and your child's assets, as well as some standard assumptions on how much money you need to support your family.

NEW FORMULAS FOR DETERMINING NEED

First, let's talk about how the schools determine whether or not you qualify for need-based financial aid (and how to convince them you need more). Then we'll talk about where to get money if you don't qualify. We have some good-news surprises for you in both areas.

There are two formulas for calculating "need": the federal formula and the CSS formula. "Need," we should explain, is the difference between what the school costs and what it says you can afford to contribute. Be sure to check which formula the school you're applying to utilizes (federal or CSS) when determining eligibility. The federal formula just changed, so even if you thought you knew the rules, think again. You may now qualify for aid. Even families who were turned down previously may now qualify.

The federal formula assumes you can afford to contribute up to 47 percent of your (the parents') annual income after a certain baseline. This baseline is what the federal government has determined you need to support your family after taxes are deducted. The 1993 "income protection allowance" for a family of four with one child in college is $16,180. Right. Who do you know who can support a family of four on $16,180? So much for the "allowance"! The formula then assumes you can contribute up to 5.65 percent of your (the parents') net assets, plus 50 percent of the student's annual net income, plus 35 percent of the student's assets.

Since the financial aid formula assumes 35 percent of the student's assets could be tapped to pay the bill, we recommend that you avoid putting assets in the child's name through the Uniform Gift to Minors Act (UGMA). Why stifle your chances for aid? It may make *tax* sense to get assets out of your name, but it will hurt you when you're looking for money for college aid. Not to mention the fact that once you set up a UGMA, Junior owns that money at 18. If he doesn't want to go to college, he can take the money and run, since he controls the cash.

If you've already set up a UGMA account, stop funding it now and make your child start spending the money before starting college. At least for the first year of college, have him buy his own books, supplies, clothes, car, etc., so that you can reapply for aid in the second year with the student's pockets empty.

In a few rare cases, parents' income and assets don't count. This happens when the student is deemed "independent," and (as you might guess) schools are very reluctant to classify students this way. To be considered independent for federal aid purposes, the student must meet at least one of the following six criteria: (1) be at least 24 years of age as of January 1 of the academic year for which aid is being requested, (2) be a veteran of the U.S. armed forces, (3) be a graduate or professional student, (4) be married, (5) be a ward of the court or have both parents deceased, or (6) have legal dependents other than a spouse.

The big change in the federal formula is that home equity is no longer included as an asset in the formula. That means that when the school is figuring out how much money you have, it doesn't count your home. This is great news. Under the old formula, thousands of families who owned homes did not qualify for aid, and might have had to mortgage the house to the hilt (or sell it outright) in order to send Junior to college. Now home equity is not counted against you. The federal guidelines also no longer look at a farm's net worth if you live and work on a farm. (If you own a farm but you don't live there, that doesn't count; you have to live on the farm.)

While the federal formula is used to determine eligibility for federal student aid programs, many colleges are using another formula developed by the College Scholarship Service called the CSS Institutional Methodology to determine eligibility for institutional aid funds. The CSS methodology still considers home equity but gives colleges the option of capping the home value at a maximum of three times your annual income.

THE MOST IMPORTANT YEAR OF INCOME FOR MAXIMIZING AID

To determine income, the colleges look at the tax year from January to December that includes the last half of the student's junior year in high school and the first half of his senior year. This is called the "base year," and it's most critical for determining how much aid you'll get. One of the biggest mistakes we see people make is not even thinking about financial aid until they've narrowed down the field of schools to which they are interested in applying. At that point, it's pretty late in the game.

You've got to start in your child's junior year. Simply put, the less income you show on your application in that base year, the more aid you'll qualify for. Now, again, please don't think it's in your interest to lie. That's not the way we like to do business, nor will it work, since your numbers are often checked against IRS records. In fact, you may be asked to submit a copy of your tax return.

But there are some perfectly legitimate ways to reduce your reported income. For instance, if you're expecting a bonus from work at the beginning of the base year, ask your employer to consider accelerating payment into the prior year. Avoid cashing in Series EE Savings Bonds in the base year because that will also inflate your interest income. Arrange your withholding so that you don't wind up getting a big state income tax refund in your base year. Also avoid large capital gains in your base year. Since you have to reapply for aid each year, you must try to minimize your discretionary income every year until January of the student's junior year in college.

DOLANS' SMART MONEY TIP: If you need cash in your base year, borrow against your investments rather than selling them (if the sale would generate a capital gain). This has a double advantage: It avoids raising your reported income, and it reduces your reported assets, since these debts are deducted from the value of the investments to determine your net assets.

And remember, the formula looks both at parents' income and at student's income (unless the student is "independent").

Remember, too, that the rules for qualifying for financial aid are even tougher than getting a deduction from the IRS. When you report your income to the IRS, you can deduct contributions made to qualified retirement plans, like a 401(k). You may even be able to deduct your IRA contribution. But when you apply for financial aid, the money you put into a retirement plan that year is still considered income for that year, so it counts against you.

ASSET MANAGEMENT TO GET MORE AID

In addition to income, the aid formula looks at your net assets. To determine net assets, the colleges look at cash, checking accounts, savings accounts, CDs, stocks, bonds, money market accounts, mutual funds, trusts, and ownership interests in businesses. They also look at the real estate you own other than your primary residence or farm. They take the full value of these assets and then deduct your debts against those assets. However, neither the federal formula nor the CSS formula looks at consumer debt, credit card debt, car loans, or personal loans. These are considered "lifestyle decisions," so if you owe $25,000 on your credit cards, that's too bad. The government is saying, in effect, "You chose to spend your money in this way. We're not going to give you aid for college just because you ran up your credit cards."

So what can you do to reduce your net assets without giving away your bank account and savings certificates? We noted that the federal formula no longer looks at home equity at all. So there's no incentive to lower that. In fact, you may wish to raise your equity, by paying off your mortgage with other assets that do count in the equation.

But be sure to remember this important fact. Schools don't have to follow any set guidelines and may very well do their own analysis of your assets. Some may still look at the current market value of your home, minus any outstanding debts against the home such as a first or second mortgage, as well as any outstanding balances on a home-equity line of credit.

DOLANS' SMART MONEY TIP: Find out which formula is used by the colleges you're interested in: the federal formula, the CSS formula, or some other formula. If they use a formula that still counts home equity, it may make sense to take out a home-equity loan and pay off all your consumer debt. In this way, you lower your home equity, enhance your chances of qualifying for aid—and probably lower the carrying costs on your debt while you're at it!

Another new wrinkle that was introduced to all the aid formulas in 1993 is that, for families with an adjusted gross income of under $50,000, all assets are excluded from consideration if you filed a 1040A or 1040EZ (or if you do not need to file a tax return at all). Which means that if you have considerable assets other than your home and you're considering filing a short form (and you're eligible for a short form), do so, even if it means sacrificing a few tax deductions. It could significantly raise the amount of financial aid you qualify for. In order to be able to qualify for this "simplified needs test" for dependent students, both the parents and the student must not file the long form, the 1040. If the student is an independent student, then only the student and (if he or she is married) the spouse of the student must not file the long tax form.

WHOSE NAME SHOULD THE ASSETS BE IN?

Does it make sense to transfer ownership of assets to your kids as part of asset management to maximize aid? It's true that you can reduce taxes that way. But the problem when you apply for aid is that 35 percent of those assets count when they're in the kid's name—but only up to 5.65 percent count when they're in the parents' name. So $10,000 will look like $3,500 when in the student's name, but only a maximum of $565 when in the parents' name.

What you might want to do is invest in growth stocks that don't generate much income and keep them in your (the parents') name. If you've gone through the aid process and find you're not eligible, gift the stocks that have gone up in value to the student. He can hold them for a while, then sell them; the capital gains and income will be in his name, meaning much lower taxes than if you sold the stocks yourself.

But wait to see what happens with the aid process before you start gifting those assets.

OTHER GIFTS CAN JEOPARDIZE AID

As you probably know, anybody can give as much as $10,000 per year to anybody, for anything, without triggering gift taxes (paid by the donor, in this case the parent). But if the gift is paid *directly* to an institution, then there is no limit on the money you can donate *for tuition only*. Dormitory fees, board, books, etc., are not eligible. But parents and/or grandparents should use this strategy only if you don't qualify for aid.

Gifting money for tuition will count against the student in the financial aid picture. For example, the school says, "You're expected to pay $10,000, and our school costs $25,000, so you get an aid package of $15,000." But if a grandparent gives $10,000 to the college, then it will say, "Great, now we're going to cut your aid $10,000, and you'll only get $5,000." So any kind of gift is a viable alternative only if you're sure the student is not eligible for aid.

DOLANS' SMART MONEY TIP: If the student qualifies for financial aid, hold off on the gift. Wait until after he graduates and then give him the money to pay off his student loans.

Another trap that lowers your aid is outside scholarships. Those are fine to look for, but if you are eligible for aid and you win one of those awards, they may not save you a penny, because again the school will reduce your aid by the size of the outside award.

DOLANS' SMART MONEY TIP: It pays to bargain. If the school doesn't have a fixed financial aid policy, you may be able to convince them to reduce your *loan* by half the amount of the outside scholarship and your *grant* by the other half. Your total package is the same, but the student will owe less in student loans when he or she gets out of school.

When you get an award from a community organization, a church, an ethnic foundation, whatever, you have to notify the school about it. But try to hold off notifying the school until after you get your initial financial aid package proposal. That way you can bargain. If you notify the school immediately, it's just going to take the award right off the top of the aid package. If you wait before you notify the school, then maybe you can say, "Well, take $500 off my grant and how about $500 off my student loans or the work-study program?"

WHAT ELSE WILL GET YOU MORE AID?

Say your son or daughter is in his or her junior year of high school. You've taken steps to minimize your income. You've lowered your net assets. You've held off on gifting money for tuition. Now what? It's time to start looking at colleges. To maximize aid, you want to look at the schools where your application will be considered most favorably. Many schools, especially the private ones, engage in a practice called "preferential packaging": the more desirable the student, the better the package.

DOLANS' SMART MONEY TIP: What makes a package good? Well, it's not just the total amount of money, although that certainly counts. You want to consider how much of the aid is in the form of grants and scholarships (which don't have to be repaid). The more, the better. You also want to look at how much the school will expect you to pay. This is the best way to compare aid packages.

What makes a student desirable? If you're from far away—in other words, you're from New York and you're looking to go to a private school in Iowa—you're going to be more attractive than a student from Iowa. In some cases, it can help to be a legacy, meaning a student who is a child of an alumnus or alumna of the school. (Of course, if you're famous, they may hit you up for a charitable contribution.)

Certainly, superior academics make a student more desirable. If his SAT scores and grade point average will put Junior in the top quartile or quintile of the freshman class at that college, that's an advantage. Sports talent can help, or other special talents, such as music, dance, or community service. Even if the school doesn't give athletic scholarships, athletic ability could get you a better aid package. Basically, the more the school wants you, the better the package.

STATE SCHOOL VS. PRIVATE

Conventional wisdom tells you that public state colleges are cheaper than private institutions. Well, that's right—as far as it goes. But that really only matters if the family is going to pay for the entire cost of the schooling. Once you start looking at financial aid, the picture changes. The amount of aid that eligible families receive is in part a function of the cost of the school. Once you meet what you're expected to contribute, the theory goes that the more expensive the school, the more aid you can get. So don't automatically rule out any school as being too expensive. In some cases, it can be cheaper to go to an expensive private college than to go to a state university.

In fact, the worst choice from a financial standpoint is often a state university in another state. You're tempted to push Junior toward a state school, assuming he will get the perspective of life in another part of the country without the expense of a private school. But it doesn't work out quite that neatly and cleanly. These institutions will spend the vast majority of their resources and aid helping in-state students, not you. You'll also probably have to pay an out-of-state tuition subsidy that can be as high as $10,000 in some states, such as Vermont and Michigan. In addition, you will most likely not qualify for state financial aid from your own state if you attend a school outside of your state.

You've probably seen those annual editions of popular magazines naming the "Best Colleges for the Bucks." The important thing to realize in terms of looking at those best buys is that they're only relevant if you've got to pay the whole sticker price. Because if you qualify for aid, the best buy may be Harvard, Yale, or Princeton.

Finally, look for two things when seeking a school with a good aid package: "the average percentage of need met" and "the average endowment per student." Both numbers indicate how much money you're likely to get, and how close the package will come to meeting your needs.

MEET THE DEADLINES!

While preparation for college starts in your child's junior year of high school, you cannot actually apply for aid until after January 1 of the student's senior year. And after that, it's a mad dash to the finish line. Figure it will take the processing service four to six weeks to process your application and then get the results to the schools you've listed on the application. Be sure to file the necessary forms by the deadlines listed in each school's admission materials; the deadlines will vary from school to school.

You want to apply for aid, get all your paperwork in, and get your taxes done as soon as possible, so that you can negotiate with the colleges' financial aid officers before you have to make a decision on where the student is going to go to school (which you usually have to make by May 1). Once the student has been accepted and has decided he's going to go to that school, you've lost some of your bargaining power. They know that they have you.

DOLANS' SMART MONEY TIP: Don't wait for your tax forms to be completed to fill out the financial aid applications. You can estimate your figures on the applications and then revise them later after your taxes have been completed.

WADING THROUGH THE PAPERWORK

As of January 1993, all students applying for aid have to fill out the Free Application for Federal Student Aid form (the FAFSA). Many private colleges and a few state schools may require you to complete the CSS's Financial Aid Form (FAF). (Samples are on pages 135 to 142.) On top of that, some schools may require their own aid form to be completed as well. You then send that form directly back to the college financial aid office, and all other forms to the appropriate processing company.

Usually both the FAFSA and the FAF forms are available in high

Free Application for Federal Student Aid

1993-94 School Year   CCCCC 1

U.S. Department of Education
Student Financial
Assistance Programs

FORM APPROVED
OMB NO. 1840-0110
APP. EXP. 6/30/94

WARNING: If you purposely give false or misleading information on this form, you may be fined $10,000, sent to prison, or both.

"You" and "your" on this form always mean the student who wants aid.

Section A: Yourself

1. Your name

   Last   First   M.I.

2. Your permanent mailing address
   (Mail will be sent to this address.
   See page 2 for State/Country
   abbreviation.)

   Number and Street (Include Apt. No.)

   City   State   ZIP Code

3. Your title *(optional)*

   ❑ Mr.   ❑ Miss, Ms., or Mrs.

4. Your State of legal residence
   State

   4a. When did you become a legal
   resident of the State you listed in
   Question 4? *(See the instructions
   on page 2.)*

   Month   Day   Year

5. Your social security number

6. Your date of birth

   Month   Day   Year

7. Are you a U.S. citizen?

   1 ❑ Yes, I am a U.S. citizen

   2 ❑ No, but I am an eligible noncitizen.
   (See the instructions on page 3.)

   |A| | | | | | | | | |

   3 ❑ No, neither of the above.
   (See the instructions on page 3.)

8. Will you have your first Bachelor's
   degree before July 1, 1993?

   ❑ Yes   ❑ No

9. As of **today**, are you married?
   (Check only one box.)

   1 ❑ I am not married. (I am single,
   widowed, or divorced.)

   2 ❑ I am married.

   3 ❑ I am separated from my spouse.

   9a. • If married or widowed, date married
   or widowed.
   • If currently divorced or separated,
   date separated.

   Month   Year

Section B: Student Status

		Yes	No
10. a.	Were you born **before** January 1, 1970?	❑	❑
b.	Are you a veteran of the U.S. Armed Forces?	❑	❑
c.	Are you a graduate or professional student?	❑	❑
d.	Are you married?	❑	❑
e.	Are you a ward of the court or are both your parents dead?	❑	❑
f.	Do you have legal dependents (*other than a spouse*) that fit the definition in the instructions on page 3?	❑	❑

• If you answered **"No"** to **every** part of question 10, go to Section C, and fill out the GREEN and the WHITE areas on the rest of the form.

• If you answered **"Yes"** to **any** part of question 10, go to Section C and fill out the **GRAY** and the WHITE areas on the rest of the form.

Section C: Household Information

PARENTS

11. What is your parents' current marital status?

    1 ❑ single   3 ❑ separated   5 ❑ widowed

    2 ❑ married   4 ❑ divorced

12. What is your parents' State of legal residence?
    State

    12a. When did your parent(s) become legal
    resident(s) of the State you listed in Question
    12? *(See the instructions on page 4.)*
    Month   Day   Year

13. Number of family members in 1993-94

    (Always include yourself [the student] and your parents. Include your parents'
    other children and other people only if they meet the definition in the instructions
    on page 4.)

14. Number of college students in 1993-94

    (Of the number in 13, write in the number of family members who will be in college
    at least half-time. Include yourself – the applicant. See the instructions on page 4.)

STUDENT (& SPOUSE)

15. Number of family members in 1993-94

    (Always include yourself and your spouse. Include
    your children and other people only if they meet the
    definition in the instructions on page 4.)

16. Number of college students in 1993-94

    (Of the number in 15, write in the number of family
    members who will be in college at least half-time.
    Include yourself. See the instructions on page 4.)

ED FORM 255

Section D: 1992 Income, Earnings, and Benefits

*(You **must** see the instructions for income and taxes that you should exclude from questions 19 through 23.)*

17. The following 1992 U.S. income tax figures are from...

Everyone must fill out the Student (& Spouse) column below.

PARENTS
(Check only one box.)

- ₁☐ a completed 1992 IRS Form 1040A or 1040EZ.   (Go to 18.)
- ₂☐ a completed 1992 IRS Form 1040.   (Go to 18.)
- ₃☐ an estimated 1992 IRS Form 1040A or 1040EZ.   (Go to 18.)
- ₄☐ an estimated 1992 IRS Form 1040.   (Go to 18.)
- ₅☐ A tax return will not be filed.   (Skip to 21.)

STUDENT (& SPOUSE)
(Check only one box.)

- ₁☐ a completed 1992 IRS Form 1040A or 1040EZ.   (Go to 18.)
- ₂☐ a completed 1992 IRS Form 1040.   (Go to 18.)
- ₃☐ an estimated 1992 IRS Form 1040A or 1040EZ.   (Go to 18.)
- ₄☐ an estimated 1992 IRS Form 1040.   (Go to 18.)
- ₅☐ A tax return will not be filed.   (Skip to 21.)

TAX FILERS ONLY

18. 1992 Total number of exemptions (Form 1040-line 6e, or 1040A-line 6e; 1040EZ filers, see instructions on pages 4 and 5)   ☐☐

19. 1992 Adjusted Gross Income (AGI)–Form 1040-line 31, 1040A-line 16, or 1040EZ-line 3, or see instructions on page 5. $_____.00

20. 1992 U.S. income tax paid (Form 1040-line 46, 1040A-line 25, or 1040EZ-line 7) $_____.00

21. 1992 Income earned from work   Father $_____.00

22. 1992 Income earned from work   Mother $_____.00

23. 1992 Untaxed income and benefits *(yearly totals only)*

23a. Social security benefits $_____.00

23b. Aid to Families with Dependent Children (AFDC or ADC) $_____.00

23c. Child support received for all children $_____.00

23d. Other untaxed income and benefits from Worksheet #2 on page 11. $_____.00

STUDENT (& SPOUSE) column — TAX FILERS ONLY

18. ☐☐

19. $_____.00

20. $_____.00

Student **21.** $_____.00

Spouse **22.** $_____.00

23a. $_____.00

23b. $_____.00

23c. $_____.00

23d. $_____.00

Section E: Federal Stafford Loan Information (Formerly Guaranteed Student Loan [GSL])

If you have never received a Stafford Loan (GSL) or a Federal Insured Student Loan (FISL), go to question 29. Skip questions 24 through 28.

24. What is the total unpaid principal balance on **all** your Stafford Loans (GSLs)? $_____.00
(If you answered "0," go to question 29. Skip questions 25 through 28.)

25. What is the unpaid principal balance on your **most recent** Stafford Loan (GSL)? $_____.00

26. What is the interest rate of your **most recent** Stafford Loan (GSL)?   ₁☐ 7%   ₂☐ 8%   ₃☐ 9%   ₄☐ 8%/10%   ₅☐ Variable Rate

27. What was the loan period of your **most recent** Stafford Loan (GSL)?   from ☐☐☐☐ through ☐☐☐☐
                                                                              Month Year   Month Year

28. What was your class level when you received your **most recent** Stafford Loan (GSL)?
(Check only one box.)

- ₁☐ Freshman
- ₂☐ Sophomore
- ₃☐ Junior
- ₄☐ Senior
- ₅☐ 5th year or more undergraduate
- ₆☐ 1st year graduate or professional (beyond a Bachelor's degree)
- ₇☐ Continuing graduate or professional

29. What is your permanent home telephone number?   ☐☐☐☐☐☐☐☐☐☐
                                                         Area Code

30. What is your driver's license number? *(Be sure to include the abbreviation of the State that issued it.)*   ☐☐☐☐☐☐☐☐☐☐☐☐☐☐☐☐☐☐☐☐☐
                                                                                                                  State

Section F: Your Veterans Education Benefits Per Month
(for the student only)

Expected Amount
July 1, 1993 through June 30, 1994

31. Your veterans education benefits
(See the instructions on page 6.)

31a. Amount per month $_____.00

31b. Number of months   └─┴─┘ months

Section G: College Release and Certification

32. What college(s) do you plan to attend in 1993-94?   *(Note: By answering this question, you are giving permission to send your application data to the college(s) you list below.)*

	College Name	Street Address	City	State
32a.				
32b.				
32c.				
32d.				
32e.				
32f.				

33. Do you give the U.S. Department of Education permission to send information from this form to the financial aid agencies in your State as well as to the State agencies of any college listed in question 32?

☐ Yes   ☐ No

34. ☐ Check this box if you give Selective Service permission to register you. *(See the instructions on page 7.)*

> **Note:** Contact the financial aid administrator at your school if:
> * your family has tuition expenses at an elementary or secondary school,
> * your family has unusual medical or dental expenses, not covered by insurance,
> * a member of your family is a dislocated worker, or
> * you have unusual circumstances not covered in this form that would affect your eligibility for student financial aid.

School Use Only

Dependency
Override: enter D or I   └─┘

Title IV Inst.
Number   └─┴─┴─┴─┴─┴─┘

FAA Signature: _____

Dept. of Ed Use Only
(Do not write in this box.)   └─┴─┴─┴─┴─┴─┴─┘

35. Read and sign

Certification: All of the information provided by me or any other person on this form and the Supplemental Information (Sections H and I), if completed, is true and complete to the best of my knowledge. I understand that this application is being filed jointly by all signatories. If asked by an authorized official, I agree to give proof of the information that I have given on this form and the Supplemental Information (Sections H and I), if completed. I realize that this proof may include a copy of my U.S., State, or local income tax return. I also realize that if I do not give proof when asked, the student may be denied aid.

I certify that I, the student, do not owe a refund on any Federal student grant, am not in default on any Federal student loan, and have not borrowed in excess of the Federal student loan limits, under the Federal student aid programs, at any institution.

Everyone giving information on this form must sign below. If you don't sign this form, it will be returned unprocessed.

1 Student

2 Student's spouse

3 Father (Stepfather)

4 Mother (Stepmother)

Date completed └─┴─■─┴─┘ Year   ☐ 1993
            Month Day   ☐ 1994

Preparer's Use Only   *(Students and parents: don't fill out this section.)*

36a. Preparer's Name   └─┴─┴─┴─┴─┴─┴─┴─┴─┴─┴─┴─┴─┴─┴─┴─┴─┘ └─┴─┴─┴─┴─┴─┴─┘ └─┘
                  Last   First   M.I.

36b. Firm's Name and Address (or yours if self-employed)
Firm Name └─┴─┘

Number and Street (Include Apt. No.) └─┴─┴─┴─┴─┴─┴─┴─┴─┴─┴─┴─┴─┴─┴─┴─┴─┴─┴─┘

City └─┴─┴─┴─┴─┴─┴─┴─┴─┴─┴─┴─┴─┘ State └─┴─┘ ZIP Code └─┴─┴─┴─┴─┘

36c. Employer Identification Number (EIN) └─┴─■─┴─┴─┴─┴─┴─┘

36d. Preparer's social security number └─┴─┴─■─┴─┴─┴─┴─┘

36e. Certification: All of the information on this form and the Supplemental Information (Sections H and I) if completed, is true and complete to the best of my knowledge.

Preparer's Signature _____   Date ____/____/____

─── **ATTENTION** ───

If you are filling out the GREEN and WHITE areas, go to page 7 and complete WORKSHEET A. This will tell you whether you must fill out Sections H and I. You may be able to skip Section H, if you meet certain tax filing and income conditions.

If you are filling out the GRAY and WHITE areas, go to page 7 and complete WORKSHEET B. This will tell you whether you must fill out Sections H and I. You may be able to skip Section H, if you meet certain tax filing and income conditions.

─── *Supplemental Information* ───

Section H: Asset Information

		PARENTS		STUDENT (& SPOUSE)	
37.	Write in the age of your older parent.	⊔⊔		37. XXXXXXXXXX	
		What is it worth today?	**What is owed on it?**	**What is it worth today?**	**What is owed on it?**
38.	Cash, savings, and checking accounts	$_____.00	XXXXXXXXXX	38. $_____.00	XXXXXXXXXX
39.	Other real estate and investments *(Don't include the home.)*	$_____.00	$_____.00	39. $_____.00	$_____.00
40.	Business	$_____.00	$_____.00	40. $_____.00	$_____.00
41.	Farm	$_____.00	$_____.00	41. $_____.00	$_____.00
42.	Is the family living on the farm?	❑ Yes ❑ No		42. ❑ Yes ❑ No	

(STOP) If you are applying for Federal aid, you must complete questions 45b, 45e, 46, and 47 below. You **may** need to fill out **ALL OF** Section I, below, if you are applying for State or college aid. Check with your financial aid administrator. If you are not required to fill out Section I, you have finished the application. Recheck your application. **MAKE SURE THAT YOU HAVE COMPLETED SECTION G. Mail the application to:** Federal Student Aid Programs, P.O. Box 6376, Princeton, NJ 08541.

Section I: State Information *(Fill out this section if you are applying for State aid. Your school may also require you to fill out this section. Also, your State or school may require additional information. If you are required to fill out this section, be sure to see the **deadline dates** under "Deadline for State Student Aid" on page 10. Check with your financial aid administrator.)*

43. a. What is the highest grade level your father completed? *(Check only one box.)*

   1 ❑ elementary school (K-8)   3 ❑ college or beyond

   2 ❑ high school (9-12)   4 ❑ unknown

b. What is the highest grade level your mother completed? *(Check only one box.)*

   1 ❑ elementary school (K-8)   3 ❑ college or beyond

   2 ❑ high school (9-12)   4 ❑ unknown

44. If you (the student) did or will receive your high school diploma by...

graduating from high school, give the date here:

⊔⊔ ⊔⊔
Month   Year

-OR-

earning a GED, give the date here:

⊔⊔ ⊔⊔
Month   Year

45a. If you are (or were) in college, do you plan to attend *that same college* in 1993-94?   ❑ Yes   ❑ No

45b. What will be your enrollment status during the 1993-94 school year?

School Term	Full Time	3/4 Time	1/2 Time	Less Than 1/2 Time	Not Enrolled
	(Check only one enrollment status for each term that applies.)				
Summer '93	1 ❑	2 ❑	3 ❑	4 ❑	5 ❑
Fall '93	1 ❑	2 ❑	3 ❑	4 ❑	5 ❑
Winter '94	1 ❑	2 ❑	3 ❑	4 ❑	5 ❑
Spring '94	1 ❑	2 ❑	3 ❑	4 ❑	5 ❑

45c. What will be your degree/certificate and course of study? *(See the instructions on page 9.)*   ⊔⊔⊔ - ⊔⊔⊔⊔   Degree/Cert.   Course of Study

45d. When do you expect to complete your degree/certificate?   ⊔⊔ ⊔⊔   Month   Year

45e. What will be your year in college during the 1993-94 school year? *(Check only one box.)*

   1 ❑ 1st   3 ❑ 3rd   5 ❑ 5th year or more undergraduate

   2 ❑ 2nd   4 ❑ 4th   6 ❑ graduate

46. What will be your housing status?

   1 ❑ Campus housing   2 ❑ Off-campus   3 ❑ With parents/relatives

47. For how many dependent children will you pay child care expenses in 1993-94?   ⊔⊔

FAF Financial Aid Form — 1993-94   ▢ ▢

This form is not required to apply for Title IV federal student aid. However, information from the FAF is used by some colleges and private organizations to award their own financial aid funds. CSS charges students a fee to collect and report this information. By filling out this form, you are agreeing to pay the fee, which is calculated in question 44.

Section A — Student's Identification Information — Be sure to complete this section. Answer the questions the same way you answered them in Section A of the Free Application for Federal Student Aid (FAFSA).

1. Your name

Last   First   M.I.

2. Your permanent mailing address
(Mail will be sent to this address.)

Number, street, and apartment number

City   State   Zip Code

3. Title (optional)

₁ ▢ Mr. ₂ ▢ Miss, Ms., or Mrs.

4. Your date of birth

Month   Day   Year

5. Your social security number

⎿⎽⎽⏌–⎿⎽⏌–⎿⎽⎽⎽⏌

Section B — Student's Other Information

6. If you are now in high school, give your high school 6-digit code number.

7. What year will you be in college in 1993-94? (Mark only one box.)

₁▢ 1st (never previously attended college)

₂▢ 1st (previously attended college)

₃▢ 2nd

₄▢ 3rd

₅▢ 4th

₆▢ 5th or more undergraduate

₇▢ first-year graduate/professional (beyond a bachelor's degree)

₈▢ second-year graduate/professional

₉▢ third-year graduate/professional

₀▢ fourth-year or more graduate/professional

8. a. If you have previously attended any college or other postsecondary school, write in the total number of colleges and schools you have attended. ▢

b. List below the colleges (up to five) that you have attended. Begin with the college you attended most recently. Use the CSS code numbers from the list in the FAF instruction booklet. If more space is needed, use Section M.

Name, city, and state of college	Period of attendance From (mo./yr.)	To (mo./yr.)	CSS Code Number

9. During the 1993-94 school year, you want institutional financial aid

from ⎿⎽⏌ ⎿⎽⏌   through ⎿⎽⏌ ⎿⎽⏌
   Month Year   Month Year

10. Mark your preference for institutional work and/or loan assistance.

₁▢ Part-time job only

₂▢ Loan only

₃▢ Will accept both, but prefer loan

₄▢ Will accept both, but prefer job

₅▢ No preference

11. If it is necessary to borrow money to pay for educational expenses, do you want to be considered for a Stafford Loan? (optional)

Yes ▢₁ No ▢₂

(If you mark "Yes," your information may be sent to the loan agency within your state.)

12. a. Your employer/occupation _____

b. Employer's address _____

c. Will you continue to work for this employer during the 1993-94 school year? Yes ▢₁ No ▢₂

13. If you have dependents other than a spouse, how many will be in each of the following age groups during 1993-94?

Ages 0-5 ⎿⏌   Ages 6-12 ⎿⏌   Ages 13+ ⎿⏌

14. 1992 child support paid by you $_____.00

Section C — Student's Expected Summer/School-Year Income

	Summer 1993 3 months	School Year 1993-94 9 months		Summer 1993 3 months	School Year 1993-94 9 months
15. Income earned from work by you	$____.00	$____.00	**17.** Other taxable income	$____.00	$____.00
16. Income earned from work by spouse	$____.00	$____.00	**18.** Nontaxable income and benefits	$____.00	$____.00

Print your name   Last ⌊|||||||||||||||⌋   First ⌊|||||||||⌋

Section D — Student's (& Spouse's) Assets

What is it worth today?   What is owed on it?

19. Cash and checking accounts $ _____ .00   **21. Other real estate** $ _____ .00 $ _____ .00

What is it worth today?   What is owed on it?

20. Home (Renters write in "0.") $ _____ .00 $ _____ .00

22. Investments & savings (See instructions.) $ _____ .00 $ _____ .00

Section E — Family Members' Listing

Give information for all family members but don't give information about yourself. List up to seven other family members here. If there are more than seven, list first those who will be in college at least half-time. List the others in Section M.

23.

	Full name of family member / You — the Student Applicant	Age	Relationship (Use code below*)	In the 1993-94 school year, will attend college for at least one term full-time half-time	Name of school or college this person will attend in 1993-94 school year	Year in school 1993-94	If attended college in 1992-93, give amount of: 1992-93 Scholarships/Grants	1992-93 Parents' Contribution
1	You — the Student Applicant							
2				₁☐ ₂☐				
3				₁☐ ₂☐				
4				₁☐ ₂☐				
5				₁☐ ₂☐				
6				₁☐ ₂☐				
7				₁☐ ₂☐				
8				₁☐ ₂☐				

Write in the correct code from below. ↑

* Relationship Codes:
1 = Student's parent   3 = Student's brother/stepbrother or sister/stepsister   5 = Student's son or daughter   7 = Other (Explain in Section M.)
2 = Student's stepparent   4 = Student's husband or wife   6 = Student's grandparent

If you were directed to provide parents' information when you completed the Free Application for Federal Student Aid, you should also give parents' information in the following sections. Some colleges may require your parents' information even if you were not directed to provide it on the Free Application for Federal Student Aid. See page 5 of the FAF instruction booklet if you are unsure about whether you should provide parents' information.

Section F — Parents' Information — See page 5 of the FAF instruction booklet.

24. Check one: ☐ Father   ☐ Stepfather   ☐ Legal Guardian   ☐ Other - Explain in Section M.

25. Check one: ☐ Mother   ☐ Stepmother   ☐ Legal Guardian   ☐ Other - Explain in Section M.

a. Name _____ Age ⌊|⌋   **a.** Name _____ Age ⌊|⌋

b. Occupation/Employer _____ No. years _____   **b.** Occupation/Employer _____ No. years _____

26. Parent(s) address (if different from address in question 2):   Street address: _____
City/State/Zip: _____

Section G — Divorced, Separated, or Remarried Parents

(To be answered by the parent who completes this form, if the student's natural or adoptive parents are divorced, separated, or remarried.)

27. a. Year of separation ⌊|⌋   Year of divorce ⌊|⌋

b. Other parent's name _____
Home address _____
_____
_____
Occupation/Employer _____
_____
_____

c. According to court order, when will support for the student end? ⌊|⌋ ⌊|⌋   Month   Year

d. Who last claimed the student as a tax exemption? _____
In which year? ⌊|⌋

e. Is there an agreement specifying a contribution for the student's education?   Yes ☐   No ☐
If yes, how much for the 1993-94 school year? $ _____ .00

Section H — Parents' 1992 Taxable Income & Expenses

28. Breakdown of 1992 Adjusted Gross Income (AGI)

Tax Filers Only

a. Wages, salaries, tips (IRS Form 1040 — line 7, 1040A — line 7, or 1040EZ — line 1)   **28a.** $ _____ .00

b. Interest income (IRS Form 1040 — line 8a, 1040A — line 8a, or 1040EZ — line 2)   **b.** $ _____ .00

c. Dividend income (IRS Form 1040 — line 9 or 1040A — line 9)   **c.** $ _____ .00

d. Net income (or loss) from business, farm, rents, royalties, partnerships, estates, trusts, etc. (IRS Form 1040 — lines 12, 18, and 19). If a loss, enter the amount in (parentheses).   **d.** $ _____ .00

e. Other taxable income such as alimony received, capital gains (or losses), pensions, annuities, etc. (IRS Form 1040 — lines 10, 11, 13-15, 16b, 17b, 20, 21b, and 22 or 1040A — lines 10b, 11b, 12, and 13b)   **e.** $ _____ .00

f. Adjustments to income (IRS Form 1040 — line 30 or 1040A — line 15c)   **f.** $ _____ .00

29. 1992 child support paid by parent(s) completing this form.   **29.** $ _____ .00

30. 1992 medical and dental expenses not covered by insurance.   **30.** $ _____ .00

31. 1992 total elementary, junior high school, and high school tuition paid for dependent children.   **31.** $ _____ .00

Section I — Parents' 1992 Untaxed Income & Benefits

32. Write in below your other untaxed 1992 income and benefits.

a. Deductible IRA and/or Keogh payments from Form 1040, total of lines 24a, 24b, and 27 or 1040A, line 15c $ _____ .00

b. Payments to tax-deferred pension and savings plans (paid directly or withheld from earnings) Include untaxed portions of 401(k) and 403(b) plans. $ _____ .00

c. Earned income credit from Form 1040, line 56 or 1040A, line 28c $ _____ .00

d. Housing, food, and other living allowances (excluding rent subsidies for low-income housing) paid to members of the military, clergy, and others (Include cash payments and cash value of benefits.) $ _____ .00

e. Tax-exempt interest income from Form 1040, line 8b or 1040A, line 8b $ _____ .00

f. Untaxed portions of pensions from Form 1040, line 16a minus 16b and line 17a minus 17b or 1040A, line 10a minus 10b and line 11a minus 11b (excluding "rollovers") $ _____ .00

g. Foreign income exclusion from Form 2555, line 39 $ _____ .00

h. Credit for federal tax on special fuels from Form 4136–Part III: Total Income Tax Credit $ _____ .00

i. Any other untaxed income and benefits (See instructions.) $ _____ .00

Section J — Parents' 1993 Expected Income

33. 1993 income earned from work by father $ _____ .00

34. 1993 income earned from work by mother $ _____ .00

35. 1993 other taxable income $ _____ .00

36. 1993 nontaxable income and benefits $ _____ .00

Section K — Parents' Assets

37. Cash and checking accounts $ _____ .00

38. If parents own home, give

   a. year purchased | 1 | 9 | | | b. purchase price $ _____ .00

39. Parents' monthly home mortgage or rental payment (If none, explain in Section M.) $ _____ .00

	What is it worth today?	What is owed on it?
40. Home (Renters write in "0.")	$ _____ .00	$ _____ .00
41. Other real estate	$ _____ .00	$ _____ .00
42. Investments & savings (See instructions.)	$ _____ .00	$ _____ .00

1

Section L — Student's Colleges & Programs

43. List the names and CSS code numbers of up to eight colleges and programs to which you want CSS to send information from this form and from the Free Application for Federal Student Aid. Enclose the right fee. See the FAF instructions and **44**.

44. Fee: Mark the box that tells how many colleges and programs are listed in **43**.

Name	City and State	CSS Code No.	Housing Code*

CSS Only

₁☐ **$9.75** ₃☐ **$25.25** ₅☐ **$40.75** ₇☐ **$56.25**
₂☐ **$17.50** ₄☐ **$33.00** ₆☐ **$48.50** ₈☐ **$64.00**

Make out your check or money order for the total amount above to the College Scholarship Service. Return this form, the fee, and the Free Application for Federal Student Aid in the mailing envelope that came with your FAFSA/FAF. **You must send the correct fee with your FAF. If you fail to do so, the FAF will be returned to you unprocessed.** However, CSS will process your FAFSA without a fee.

*Housing Codes for 1993-94 (Enter only one code for each college.)
1 = With parents   2 = Campus housing   3 = Off-campus housing   4 = With relatives

Section M — Explanations/Special Circumstances
Use this space to explain any unusual expenses such as high medical or dental expenses, educational and other debts, or special circumstances.

Don't send letters, tax forms, or other materials with your FAF as they will be destroyed.

Certification:

All the information on this form is true and complete to the best of my knowledge. If asked by an authorized official, I agree to give proof of the information that I have given on this form. I realize that this proof may include a copy of my U.S., state, or local income tax returns. I also realize that if I don't give proof when asked, the student may not get aid. I give permission to send information from my FAFSA and FAF to the colleges and programs in **43**.

Everyone giving information on this form must sign below.

1 _____
Student's signature

2 _____
Student's spouse's signature

3 _____
Father's (Stepfather's) signature

4 _____
Mother's (Stepmother's) signature

When you have completed this form, make a copy for your records.

Date this form was completed:

☐☐ ☐☐ 1☐ 1993
Month Day   2☐ 1994
                  Year

Write in the month and day.
Mark the year completed.

Page 4

☐ ☐

21701-02582 • CW122M

school guidance offices by December for the following academic year. Check each college's admission material carefully to see if it requires only the FAFSA form, or the FAFSA and the FAF. If you are applying to schools that require only the FAFSA form, you can use any version of the FAFSA and send it to the respective processor. If, however, at least one of the schools to which you are applying for financial aid requires the FAF form, then you should use the version of the FAFSA form that will be processed in Princeton, New Jersey, as well as the FAF form that goes to the same location. These two forms come together in a packet at the guidance office. There is a processing fee involved when filing the FAF form.

DOLANS' SMART MONEY TIP: Be sure you're using the current version of the financial aid forms. There's a new version of the forms for the 1994–1995 school year.

By the way, even if you don't qualify for financial aid, you can get an *unsubsidized* Stafford loan (see below), but you still have to fill out the FAFSA form. On top of that, there could be the school's own aid forms. And every school sets its own deadlines. So read each school's bulletin carefully, and be sure to supply everything they require.

Believe it or not, it even matters what color pen you use when you fill out your aid application. If it says a #2 pencil, use a #2 pencil. If it says black ink pen, use a black ink pen. If you don't, the processor could send it back to you to fill out properly, and you'll be even further behind.

You have to fill out an application for financial aid every year your child is in college. Of course, after the first year you're just doing the form for one school. And the most important application is the first one, since the college figures on giving you four years of aid, even though it is only offered one year at a time. But you do have to go through the paperwork four times (or more).

The best guide we've ever seen to help you maximize your aid eligibility and assist you with completing the aid forms is a book written by our friend Kal Chany—*The Princeton Review: The Student Access Guide to Paying for College,* co-authored with Geoff Martz ($14.00; 800-733-3000).

DOLANS' SMART MONEY TIP: Even if you're turned down for aid the first year, continue to apply each and every year your child is in college. A change in your job status or the addition of another child in college could make a big difference.

FINANCIAL SAFETY SCHOOLS

While you are applying for financial aid, your young student is applying to college and you may want to consider including a copy of your FAFSA aid application with the college admissions application, especially if you're running late in applying for schools. Eventually, the processor will send the completed forms to any schools you designate, but the sooner the school sees the form, the better. Also, if the income you're listing on the aid application is unusually high (remember, it's based on just one year, from January of the junior year to December of the senior year), write a letter explaining that to the financial aid officer. If it includes a one-time payment (which, as we discussed, you'll try to avoid), say so.

When you're applying to colleges, include at least one or two "financial safety" schools. Those are schools where the student will be accepted, or at least has a very good chance of being accepted, and you know you can pay the cost if you don't get any aid. For most parents, that will mean your home state university or local community college. That way, Junior's going to college somewhere!

Remember, even at these "safety" schools, if you're not eligible for any need-based aid, you can still take out an unsubsidized student loan (see below). Also remember that a college diploma carries the name of the school from which you graduate; your child could attend an inexpensive local community college for the first two years and then transfer to a more prestigious (and, of course, more expensive) college for the last two years. In fact, if the student lives at home for those first two years, you'll save even more money and have more to spend on the junior and senior years.

THE AID PACKAGE

Once the school has established your "need" (remember, that's the amount of money you can't afford to pay), each school that accepts your child for admission will send you its aid package proposal. This package may include a combination of grants and/or scholarship money (which is the best because you don't have to pay it back), government-subsidized loans, and a work/study opportunity to meet out-of-pocket expenses. If you are approved for government-subsidized loans, you do not have to pay them back until after graduation. You get the money for your two or four years of college, and the student starts repaying it when he or she leaves school (hopefully wearing a cap and gown).

DOLANS' SMART MONEY TIP: While grants are better than loans, there are also a few ways to turn loans into grants! Take advantage of some loan forgiveness programs. The government will "forgive" (cancel) some student loans if the student:

- Becomes a teacher and teaches in certain understaffed locations;
- Becomes a doctor, nurse, or other health professional and works in certain understaffed regions of the country;
- Goes into military service after graduation.

WORKING WHILE YOU'RE IN SCHOOL

Work/study will normally be part of a financial aid package, and that could be a good deal. A lot of parents are hesitant about letting their kids work while in college, but surveys have shown that students who work generally have higher grade-point averages than those who don't. Many are able to do their homework on the job, and relatively few schools penalize students if they don't fully meet their work/study agreement.

Work/study is a need-based program subsidized by the federal government and the school. But even if you don't demonstrate need to qualify for work/study jobs, most schools have employment services where any student who wants a job is able to get one.

STAFFORD AND PLUS LOANS

Banks love to make student loans because they're guaranteed by the government. With most regular loans, you go to the bank and if you qualify you get the loan. With Stafford loans (college loans for *students*, named for the former Republican senator from Vermont) and Parent

Loans to Undergraduate Students, or PLUS loans (college loans for *parents* of students), the school certifies how much you are eligible for, and the bank is just the financial intermediary for dispersing the funds.

So banks have no problem giving out student loans to virtually anyone, because they are really just the clearinghouse for government money. If the student doesn't prove "need," the interest on the Stafford loan will not be subsidized while the student is still in school. In other words, the student will have to pay interest while he or she is in college. (And interest is always due on PLUS loans, even while the student is in school.) Even so, these loans are still a good deal because Stafford loans and PLUS loans offer very competitive interest rates that are capped at 9 percent and 10 percent, respectively.

The maximum amount of the Stafford loan is $2,625 for the freshman year, $3,500 for the sophomore year, and $5,500 each for the junior and senior years (and fifth year, if necessary). The interest rate is calculated by taking the 13-week Treasury bill rate plus 3.1 percent, so at press time it was running at about 7 percent to 7.25 percent. Better still, it has that 9 percent cap.

There's a neat deal available with Stafford loans after graduation, too. Through Sallie Mae's* Great Rewards Program, if the student pays off the first 48 months of the loan in a timely fashion, the interest rate will be lowered by 2 percent for the remaining repayment period on the loan. To get a list of banks that participate in this Sallie Mae program, you should contact the financial aid office at the school your child will be attending as soon as you know what school that will be.

In the past, PLUS loan limits were $4,000 per student per year in college. The new rules say that, for a dependent student, parents can borrow the total cost of college attendance minus any other aid that the student receives, provided the parents pass a credit test. The new rules also state that you must begin repaying a PLUS loan within 60 days of receiving the funds. The interest rate on PLUS loans is the 52-week Treasury bill rate plus 3.1 percent, which worked out to about 7.5 percent at press time. And it has a 10 percent cap. The interest on the loan is no longer deductible, but the reason we like the PLUS loan is because of the cap. Frankly, since you can now borrow the total cost of tuition through

---

* Sallie Mae is the acronym for the Student Loan Marketing Association, a government agency that guarantees the bank repayment of the student loan, even if the student defaults.

Stafford and PLUS loans, there's really no need to borrow from anywhere else, although borrowing from the equity in your home would allow a tax deduction.

Your aid package may well include a PELL grant sponsored by the federal government. It could also include a Supplemental Educational Opportunity Grant (SEOG) and/or a grant from your state government. But, as Washington and state governments become more and more strapped for cash, we expect these grants to make up less and less of the aid package. Many colleges have their own grant funds available to assist students. In some cases, these grants can be as high as $10,000 or $15,000 a year.

There are a lot of other sources of private scholarships and grants. Any group you belong to—ethnic, religious, community, civic, business, whatever—is worth a phone call. And for a good one-stop guide, check out Laurie Blum's books *Free Money for College* and *Free Money for Graduate School* (Henry Holt; 800-488-5233).

DOLANS' SMART MONEY TIP: Apply for all aid, including the Stafford loans, first. Then apply for a PLUS loan, since the interest rate will be slightly higher. Remember, whatever you don't get from other sources, you can get from the PLUS loan. To get the most financial aid for college, you should begin planning before January 1 of the student's junior year in high school. But even if your kids have already started college and you're mortgaged up to the roof, it's not too late. You can still qualify for the PLUS loan and they can still get a Stafford loan, even if you don't demonstrate need.

WHAT THE SCHOOLS WON'T TELL YOU

While schools are going to say, "We have all this aid money available, and we'll help you," when it comes right down to it, this is still a business transaction. Even though they'll be forthcoming about what aid is available, don't expect schools to show you how best to represent your situation to qualify for the most financial aid. Schools won't tell you that it's possible to negotiate a package, to play one school's aid package against another and bargain for a better deal.

It's important for families to realize when they're dealing with the schools that they're trying to get you to pay *as much money as possible* while you're trying to pay the *least* amount. When pressed, the school will say, "Oh, yes, if you get a package from another school, send it to us. Maybe we overlooked something." But read between the lines. What they're really saying is, "If we want you, we won't lose you."

A BUYER'S MARKET

In fact, for all but the most highly selective schools, it's a buyer's market. There are not that many 18-year-olds out there; demographically they will be at a low point for the next few years. Schools have to fill their classrooms. They have businesses with fixed expenses that must be met, in large part, by tuition fees.

Even the most selective colleges are still interested in maintaining the quality of their applicant pool. So if a selective private college accepts you, and you have a choice of going there or to a competitor school in the same group, they don't want to lose you. They'll fight hard to get you.

And if you have special talent (the athletic coach wants you because he needs a tennis player or the wind ensemble needs an oboe player), they may come up with some creative aid packages that will meet their needs as well as yours.

DOLANS' SMART MONEY TIP: Don't say, "We'd like to get a better package. Is there anything you can do to improve it? But we love your school and even if you can't do anything, we're going to come to your school anyway." That's no incentive. Why would they give you a better package? Keep your cards close to your vest.

ESTATE PLANNING TIPS

Many estate-planning attorneys recommend putting money for children into a trust, such as a charitable remainder or Crummey Trust. *A charitable remainder trust* is a trust you set up when you want to avoid capital gains taxes on a large capital gain and donate property to charity (eventually). You can set up the trust, as most people do, to pay you a certain percentage of the assets in income each year, which you can use for whatever you want, including tuition and other college costs. Most charitable remainder trusts are set up so that the annual income received is less than the annual appreciation of the assets within the trust, so the assets continue to grow each year, and go to the charity at some predetermined future date, as specified by the creator of the trust.

A *Crummey Trust* is an irrevocable trust with "demand rights," which means that the beneficiaries must have the right to withdraw ("demand") their portion of the assets from the trust, within a certain predetermined window of time (usually 30 days), each time the creator puts property into the trust. The creator of the trust also specifies when and under what conditions the assets of the trust are distributed to the beneficiaries, apart from the demand right. With a Crummey Trust, for example, you can be very specific about how and when the beneficiary gets money out (much more so than with a gift under the Uniform Gifts to Minors Act). But here's the problem. Trusts are considered assets in the aid formula. And the problem gets even worse. Although you can't touch the money, *every year* the college will assess the student 35 percent of the value of the trust. So if you have a $10,000 trust, after 4 years the trust has been assessed 4 times 35 percent, or 140 percent on 100 percent worth of assets.

What about giving your kids real estate? In some cases, this is smarter than paying for dormitory life. You may want to consider buying a condo near campus for your child to live in. Rather than simply shelling out living expenses, you'll be able to take some nice real estate deductions, use your child as "property manager," and maybe even turn a tidy profit when you sell the property after graduation—*maybe!*

DEALS WE *DON'T* LIKE

We don't think very much of computer scholarship services. You know, the ads that read, "Send us $95 and we'll send you our computer list and you can go find a whole bunch of money." The Better Business Bureau recently found out that many of these services were scams and rip-offs.

As we mentioned before, we're not great fans of buying annuities to finance a college education because of the penalties and the costs associated with them.

Nor do we love prepayment plans for college, in most situations. Even if you have the funds to do it, what could you be earning on your money? Will you be able to make more on the money if you invest it than you'd save by not paying the annual tuition increases? Prepayment plans should be used only if you know it's the only way you'll manage to put some money together for Junior. In other words, use them only if you are financially undisciplined.

FINANCIAL AID CONSULTANTS

One deal we *do* like is a financial aid consultant. These consultants try to maximize a family's chances of qualifying for federal, state, and college aid. They look at money the school controls either from the government or from their own institutional funds. They can also relieve you of the nightmare of wading through and filling out all those lengthy forms.

How should you pick a financial aid consultant? Ask your friends for referrals. Look for parents whose kids are already in college and who got a financial aid package they were satisfied with. Also ask them if the consultant was receptive to follow-up questions and phone calls.

If you can't get a good referral, you'll have to sift through the candidates yourself. A few questions you might ask:

- Which year's income and assets do I list on my application? You already know the answer to this one: The base income year is from January of the student's junior high school year to December of the senior high school year. Don't hire a consultant who knows less than you do!
- How long have you been doing this, and what is your background and experience? You don't necessarily need a CPA, but you do want someone with experience in the personal finance and financial aid fields.
- What state grants are available in our state? A good financial aid consultant should be able to list them off the top of his or her head.
- How do you make your money? You want a fee-based consultant, not an insurance salesman! Steer away from anyone who is trying to sell commission-based products.
- What are the new rules for PLUS loans? You know that one, too: PLUS loans can now be taken to make up the entire difference between the rest of the aid package and the cost of the school. Of course, your consultant should also know that PLUS loans are given to parents, not students.

• Does it make sense to take out a home-equity loan? As we discussed, the rules have changed, so that some schools no longer count home equity as an asset. The correct answer to this question is, "It depends on which formula the school is using to determine your assets. The federal formula no longer looks at home equity." If that's not the answer you get, this consultant may not be aware of the new rules of the game.

The bottom line is that a financial aid consultant can be a great help and relief—and can find a lot of untapped aid—if you choose your consultant with care.

DOLANS' SMART MONEY TIP: Don't assume that your accountant or financial planner is an expert on financial aid. While the aid forms do ask questions about your income taxes and your finances, it's important to know that financial aid planning and tax planning often conflict with each other, and many times accountants or financial planners may give you suggestions that will help you on your income taxes only to hurt you when you apply for financial aid. So be sure if you're having a professional fill out the forms that he or she has particular expertise in the financial aid process.

We hope you now feel a little less anxious about being able to afford college for your children. Remember, there are billions of dollars out there to help you pay for school. Using the tips we've shared with you here, you should be able to get a piece of that pie and ensure that your family finances survive the process.

CHAPTER SIX

One More for the Road

The Best Way to Buy, Lease, and Finance Your Car . . . and Keep It Purring like a Kitten

Racers, start your engines. We're about to take a little ride to our friendly neighborhood car dealer. You know, the one who's always having a huge "sale" and giving new meaning to the phrase "sticker shock." But this time, it will be the fast-talking dealer who will be shocked—at just how much you know and how much you're going to save on your next car!

Don't you just love the smell of a new car, the fresh look of new paint and an untouched interior? Too bad it's such a trauma to buy one. Either you haggle so long you don't even remember what it is you're buying, or you do the "minute waltz" with a salesman who has you signing on the dotted line before you know what hit you. Either way, you feel taken advantage of.

Well, it doesn't have to be that way. In fact, armed with a little insider information and the tips we'll give you in this chapter, you should be able to drive a fantastic bargain without raising your voice or breaking into a sweat. And that goes for new cars, used cars, even selling your car. It goes for sports cars, sun roofs, extended warranties, auto financing. We're about to show you how to spend less and keep more in your pocket in every area of car buying.

THE THREE NUMBERS TO KNOW BEFORE YOU ENTER THE DEALERSHIP

Before you set foot on a new-car lot, there are three numbers you must know: how much the dealer paid for the car you want, how much to pay for the options you want, and how much the car will be worth in four years. *Consumer Reports* has a great service called the Consumer Reports Auto Price Service. For $11.00 per car or less (the price per car goes down if you ask for multiple quotes), you can get a printout of exactly how much the dealer paid for the car that is sitting on the showroom floor (this is known as the "invoice price"). The Consumer Reports service will give you the base invoice price for any car (it covers more than 1,000) and also the price for all factory-installed options. In this way, you can pick and choose the custom-tailored car of your dreams and know *exactly what the dealer paid*. For more information, call this service at 303-745-1700.

You also want to know the likely resale value of this car, *before* you sink your hard-earned dollars into it. You know what they say: "A car loses 20 percent of its value when you drive it off the lot." Yes, 20 percent! So let's see if it has any value left at all by the time you're done paying off the loan. We'll tackle auto financing in a minute.

The best place to find the resale value of a car is in the so-called "blue book." But did you know that dealers typically ignore the official blue book, raising or lowering prices to suit the circumstance? That's right, their book conveniently lowers the value of cars for the purposes of trade-ins, but somehow also mysteriously raises the value of used cars on the lot that they're trying to unload on unwitting buyers.

DOLANS' SMART MONEY TIP: Go to your local library or bank loan department and look in its "blue book" (officially *The National Automobile Dealers Association Guide* or NADA). In libraries, ask for it at the reference desk. Find out the current value of a four-year-old car of the same make, model, and options as the one you want to buy. Add 20 percent (four years' worth of inflation), and you have a good idea of what the blue book will say your brand-new car is worth four years from today. If you have a car to trade in, look that up in the library blue book, too. That way, you won't be cheated on your trade-in.

READY FOR THE FIRST VISIT

Now you're ready to visit your friendly neighborhood dealer, who is totally unprepared for a knowledgeable, confident buyer like you. Start by wandering around the lot. Check out the sticker prices on the cars you're interested in and see how they compare to what you know the dealer paid. What's the markup? 10 percent? 20 percent? 30 percent? Don't forget to add in those ridiculous and meaningless extras dealers love to charge for, like "dealer prep" and "undercoating." Look at the very bottom line of the sticker. That's what they want you to pay.

Invariably, as you're browsing through the lot, you'll be approached by an eager and smiling salesman. Never trust a smiling salesman. In fact, never trust any car salesman. It's not that they're terrible people; it's just that their highest priority (their only priority) is to get as much money from you as they possibly can. The more you pay, the more they make; it's that simple. Frankly, who can blame them for trying to make a better living? Just don't let you and your family be their next restaurant meal!

DOLANS' SMART MONEY TIP: Tell the salesman you don't need any help, you're just looking today. Usually, he'll let you look (at least for a while) before trying to move in for the kill.

SUCKER QUESTIONS FROM A CAR SALESMAN

At some point, a salesman will try to engage you in conversation to warm you up for the sale. You probably won't be able to avoid it. That's fine—remember, you know the real price of the car, and that's what you're going to offer. But first, the car salesman will try to trap you with one of these classic questions:

1. *"What would it take to get you to buy this car today?"* Correct answer: "I'm not ready to buy today. I'm still just looking." You'll probably have to repeat this answer several times, since it's most definitely not what the salesman wants to hear.

2. *"How much of a monthly payment can you afford?"* Never fall for the monthly payment trick. It's a car dealer's favorite. Focus on the total price of the car, not the monthly payment. Do not quote a monthly payment, because the salesman will come up with a way to meet that monthly number and still overcharge you by hundreds, perhaps thousands of dollars. ("You don't mind a six-year loan, do you, Mr. Jones?")

3. *"If I can match your price, will you buy this car today?"* This is just another version of Question #1, and the correct answer is "no." Once you enter into negotiations, you are certainly allowed to change your mind (believe us, the salesman will be only too happy to oblige if

you decide you do want to buy today), but your first answer to this question should be "no." And the reason is simple. You want to control the negotiation. Don't get into a conversation about buying a car today. It almost guarantees that the salesman will be running the show and will talk you into buying the car before you're really ready.

4. *"Will you buy this car if we give you $1,000 on your trade-in?"* No surprise here. That "extra" $1,000 the salesman gives you with one hand he'll take away with the other hand on the price you pay for the new car. Don't be fooled with these trade-in tricks. The bottom line is still the bottom line.

5. *"Would you like to be the one buyer I need to win a trip to the Bahamas?"* Not really. Enjoy your vacation, Mr. Salesman, but don't take it out of my wallet!

MORE SNEAKY SALESMAN TRICKS TO WATCH OUT FOR

Once you make it past these questions, the salesman knows he's dealing with a tougher customer than usual. No problem, he thinks, as he digs further into his bag of tricks. The next tactic he'll probably hit you with is the "test drive." Now, you certainly want to take a test drive before you buy any car. Just don't allow yourself to be swept out of the car and into the salesman's office after your first drive. Never buy a car on your first visit to the dealership, and *never* buy a car without visiting at least two dealerships.

Take a test drive, then thank the salesman and tell him you'll be back next weekend. Believe us, the car will still be there. And while we're on the subject of test drives, only test drive the actual car you want to buy—not the showroom demonstration car. You want to feel how the actual car you plan on owning handles.

Don't turn the AM/FM radio on full blast either. With Mick Jagger and the Rolling Stones roaring through the speakers you won't be able to hear the rattle in the back seat or make out the wheezing sound of air seeping through the sun roof. And don't take a test drive with the salesman if you can avoid it. He will talk your ear off, making it virtually impossible to focus on the car. If you are forced into taking him along for the ride, politely tell him to keep his mouth shut!

As you try to make your getaway, the salesman may well pull out another handy device from his bag of tricks: the famous someone-else-wants-"your"-car pressure tactic. The salesman will tell you that some-one else test drove the car just yesterday (maybe earlier today!) and will be back to snatch it out from under you. Don't buy it (neither the car nor the line). Remember, as our good friend and car negotiating expert Re-mar Sutton says, "There is always a nicer car waiting for you on another lot."

SMART BUYING ACTION PLAN

You're going to come to the dealership prepared. Make sure you have the key figures written down and in your pocket. You're going to check out the sticker prices and see just how high the markups are. You're going to try to fend off the advances of an eager salesman and make it clear you are *not* buying a car today. You are going to write down the sticker prices of the cars you're interested in, itemizing the options and extras. You may even take a test drive. But you are *not* going to get talked into the salesman's office.

Instead, you are going to go to another dealer and repeat the whole process. You'll start to notice that the salesman at the second dealership uses a lot of the same tactics the first salesman used. Funny, isn't it? But that's how they sell cars. It is not, however, the smart way to *buy* a car.

One week later, perhaps the following weekend, you're ready to talk price. Go back to the dealership you preferred (or both, if you're not sure) and tell the salesman you're ready to buy. Tell him exactly what car you want, what options you want, and then—the killer—the price you are willing to pay. Remember, that price is what the dealer paid, not a penny more. Once the salesman recovers from the shock, he'll tell you he couldn't possibly sell the car at that price—his family will starve, his boss will fire him, etc. Then he'll probably make a counteroffer. Fair enough. But you want to respond with a counteroffer of your own—and it should be no more than 2 percent above your original offer. In the end, never pay more than 5 percent over what the dealer paid. If the salesman says no, simply say, "Thank you anyway," and leave.

Feeling guilty about a 5 percent profit margin? Don't cry too much. Most car dealers don't own the cars on their lots, anyway. They get them from the manufacturer and then pay carrying costs, like interest, while the cars are on the lot. A $20,000 car will probably cost the dealer only $300 per month. His 5 percent net profit, or $1,000, is more than double his money.

"DON'T LEAVE YET!"

We said that if you can't agree on a price, simply leave. Well, far be it from a car salesman to let a ready buyer walk out his door and off his lot! This is the time to watch out for some negotiating sleights of hand that make you think you're getting a good deal when you're really getting taken to the cleaners.

1. *Your trade-in.* One of the favorite targets of car dealers is that old clunker you want to trade in. Many times a salesman will agree to the hard bargain you've driven on the new car, then wipe you out on your trade-in. Use the blue book so you know the real value of "Old Bessie."

> DOLANS' SMART MONEY TIP: If a salesman tells you your trade-in value depends on what you pay for your new car, walk away. Your trade-in value has nothing to do with your new car price. This is just a sneaky way of wringing more money out of your wallet.

2. *Being double-teamed.* The nice salesman will agree to your price, then tell you he just has to get his manager to approve it. He may even come back with a nice "note" from the manager saying they'd love to do business with you but can't possibly meet your price. *Don't believe it!* This is a common ploy—and chances are very good that the salesman went out and smoked a cigarette and came back with one of a dozen little fake notes he carries around in his pocket all day. Negotiate with one person, and one person only. Tell the salesman you want definite, quick answers, and you want your agreed-upon price *in writing*.

3. *Dealer financing.* You've made it through the gamut of negotiating a price, and you're feeling pretty good. You got a good deal, and you can't wait to drive away in that new car. There's one more hurdle to clear: the finance manager. Car dealerships don't care how they make their money, just as long as you pay it to them somehow. If they don't get you on the price or the options or the trade-in, watch out for the financing "deal."

> DOLANS' SMART MONEY TIP: Arrange for financing in advance with your bank or credit union. You'll almost certainly get a better deal, and you can sidestep the finance manager's office entirely. In fact, don't tell the salesman that you have outside financing already arranged until after you have agreed upon a

price for the car in writing. If he knows in advance that he won't be able to scalp you on financing, he'll try harder to squeeze you in other ways.

If you have a great deal of equity built up in your home and your mortgage payments are low, consider using a home-equity loan to pay for your car. The application process is a bit more time-consuming, but the great benefit is that your interest payments are tax deductible.

4. *Extended warranties.* Most manufacturers these days offer such good warranties with their cars that you're wasting your money if you buy an additional, extended warranty. If you really want the protection, don't pay more than $250 for it. And most times your best deal will be through your insurance company, not the dealer.

DOLANS' SMART MONEY TIP: If you really, really want an extended warranty from the dealer, buy it at the end of the month when the salesman is trying to meet his quota. He'll be much more motivated to give you a price break in order to make the sale.

5. *Rust-proofing, undercoating, glazing.* You simply don't need it. Most car manufacturers have done a good enough job on this already. Again, if you really want it, you'll get a much better deal from an independent company.

6. *Bonuses, premiums, sales, and prizes.* These are old-time favorites of car dealerships to get you in the door and writing a check. Don't believe in ''sales.'' They've just marked the prices up to mark them down again. And as for prizes and bonuses, you're buying a car, not a TV or a weekend in the mountains. Focus on getting the best deal you can for the car.

DOLANS' SMART MONEY TIP: The best book we've ever seen on negotiating for a car (it's fun to read, too) is Remar Sutton's *Don't Get Taken Every Time* (10th edition, Penguin Books). Read it before you shop.

IS LEASING A CAR BETTER THAN BUYING?

You've heard the ads: ''Pay just $298 a month, and drive off in a BMW, with no money down . . .'' Sounds enticing, doesn't it? But your common sense is probably asking, "What's the catch?" The catch is that this is not a purchase, it's a lease, and that makes all the difference.

While the lower monthly payments of a lease may seem attractive at first blush, we believe you are better off owning something at the end of two to four years, even if you pay more each month. The final amount you wind up with in your pocket is almost always greater when you buy than when you lease. Remember that car salesman's trick of asking you what you can afford in monthly payments? The same principle applies here. The dealer gets you focused on your monthly payments, and unfocused on the total amount you're going to pay and the terms of the agreement.

Here's some straight talk on how a lease really works: You agree to make monthly payments to cover the cost of the car, interest, and the dealer's profit, just as when you buy a car. But your monthly payments are less (usually) and you make no down payment (usually) because you are paying only for the part of the car's life you are using. For a two-year lease, you pay for two years of the car's life; for a four-year lease, you pay for four years' worth of car. At the end of the lease, the dealer owns the car, not you.

How does a dealer figure out how much a car is worth at the end of a four-year period? He uses what is known as "residual value." Basically, this refers to the market value of the car at the end of the lease period. The dealer figures out how much the car will be worth when the lease is over and charges you the difference between the residual value and the cost of the car when new. The higher the residual value placed on your car, the lower your monthly payments will be. Therefore, in most cases, you want the residual value quoted in your lease to be as high as possible.

Exactly what happens at the end of the lease depends on what kind of lease you sign, and you want to be sure it's the right kind! First, you want a closed-end lease, not an open-end lease. A closed-end lease allows you to walk away from the lease at the end of the period, regardless of whether or not the residual value of the car is indeed what the dealer had projected it would be. Remember, future residual value is just an estimate, and estimates vary greatly (not to mention the fact that they often turn out to be wrong). With a closed-end lease, if the dealer had estimated that the car would have a high residual value at the end of the lease period and he turns out to have been optimistic, that's his tough luck, not yours.

With an open-end lease, you are on the hook if the car turns out to be worth less than expected. You have to make up the difference to close out the lease, and this possible nasty surprise is why we stress having a closed-end lease.

The ease of walking away at the end of the lease depends upon your taking good care of the car. The lease will specifically spell out what is meant by "normal and acceptable wear and tear." For instance, small dents and scratches in the car doors are generally considered normal on a four-year-old car. Larger dents and scrapes are not. It also assumes you have not put 100,000 miles on the car in two years. All leases place a cap on the mileage you can rack up, and if you go over the limit you pay extra *per mile*. Generally you are allowed 15,000 miles per year.

DOLANS' SMART MONEY TIP: Since damage and mileage are the two likely places for you to get hit with extra charges at the end of a lease, make sure you understand exactly what is considered "normal and acceptable wear and tear" and that the mileage limit will accommodate your travel and commuting habits.

BUYING THE CAR AT THE END OF THE LEASE

We talked a moment ago about the benefit of having a high residual value figured into your lease. The higher the residual value, the less you pay over the term of the lease. Now comes the exception (you know what they say, "For every rule . . ."). If you plan to buy the car at the end of the lease—even if you think you *might* buy the car at the end of the lease— consider having a purchase option included in your lease. This option allows you the opportunity (but not the obligation) to buy the car at a predetermined price, usually the residual value. Unlike buying any used car, this car was used by you, so you know exactly what went wrong, how it was fixed, and how well it was maintained. The nice part about a purchase option in a closed-end lease is that you hold all the cards. If at the end of the lease your car is worth more than the residual value, you can buy it at this bargain price; if it's worth less, you can walk away.

DOLANS' SMART MONEY TIP: Car experts tell us that if the car is worth less than the residual value, you can most likely negotiate a better price if you really want to buy; after all, the dealer probably won't do much better trying to sell it to someone else anyway, if the value is indeed lower than you both expected.

NEGOTIATING A GOOD LEASE DEAL

The first rule of leasing, as we explained, is to choose a closed-end lease. Next, you want the lowest price possible. And that means approaching a lease just as you would a purchase. Don't focus on monthly payments, and don't forget to look at the total amount you're paying. Go through the same process you did for buying a car; namely, find out what the dealer paid, what the options cost him, and what the blue book value will be at the end of the proposed lease period. Negotiate the best (lowest) purchase price you can for the car you want, then tell the salesman you might consider leasing *at this purchase price.* In other words, never let the salesman know up front that you are going to lease the car. Negotiate a sale. Drop the bomb about leasing after you've agreed on a good price, following our guidelines for buying a car.

Your monthly lease payment should be no more than what the dealer paid for the car minus the car's residual value, plus 10 percent more (annually) to cover financing and dealer profit, divided by the number of months in the lease.

Once you've agreed upon a price (divided by the number of months in the lease, to come up with your monthly payment), then you want to watch out for a few "potholes":

- Make sure you read and understand the lease's limit on wear and tear and mileage. If you think you'll be driving more than the lease allows, negotiate that into the contract before you sign.
- Be aware that there will probably be a modest fee at the end of the lease to cover cleaning and preparing the car for resale, usually $150 to $200. Make sure you understand what this fee is, and don't be afraid to negotiate it down.
- Don't go for a longer lease period than you really want in order to get the monthly payments down. Not only will you wind up paying more money in the end, but if you want to get out early, you'll get scalped (more on early termination in a minute).
- Don't buy insurance or a maintenance contract through the dealer. You will be required to carry car insurance, but if you go through an insurance company you'll almost certainly get a better deal. As for maintenance contracts or extended warranties, we don't believe you need one. But if you insist, at least don't overpay. Buy

through an independent provider (check with your insurance company on this, too).

• Shop at two or three different dealers and an independent leasing company to find the best price and terms.

"PLEASE RELEASE ME, LET ME GO . . ."

When you lease a car, you probably are doing so because you don't plan on keeping the car forever. Maybe you like to have a new car every three years. Or maybe you think your needs and/or buying power will be a whole lot different in four or five years. The point is, since you're choosing an option that is designed for fickle drivers, don't shoot yourself in the foot by signing up for a long-term lease. We recommend three- or four-year leases, but no longer than that.

It can be very expensive to get out of a lease early. You see, your lease payments are equal over the length of the lease. You pay, say, $295 per month, every month for four years. But that's not the way the car depreciates. Depreciation is steep at the beginning of a car's life and then levels off in years three and four. So for most of the lease you're playing catch-up. The car is worth less than what's left to pay on your lease. And if you want to "terminate" early, you have to make up the difference!

For example, if you've paid $295 per month for one year, you've paid $3,540. And if 10 percent of that is interest and dealer profit, you've actually paid off only $3,186. But after a year, the car may have depreciated by $5,000. Your bill: $1,814. But wait! You may also be required to pay the finance charges you would have paid for the life of the lease, and there could also be a cash penalty. Add it all up and you could easily find yourself faced with a charge of $2,000 to $10,000, depending on the purchase price of the car and on how much time you have left on your lease. That's why we say to keep your lease period to four years or less, and don't plan on getting out early.

BUYING A BARGAIN, NOT A LEMON

If you think buying a new car is dangerous, imagine going the used car route! But, then again, when you consider that a car loses 25 percent to 35 percent of its value in its first year of use, a used car could be a great way to get the car you really want at a price you can afford. As long as you don't get stuck with a lemon.

You have several different options when shopping for a used car. You can buy from a dealer who sells both new and used cars, you can buy from an independent used car lot, you can buy from a private individual, a rental car agency, even at auction.

Buying from a dealer is probably the safest route, but unfortunately it's also usually the most expensive. Unless you feel comfortable taking risks, we recommend buying through a dealer. You can get a warranty and go back for service, and you have more government protection.

All dealers are required to post a buyer's guide in the window of all used cars they sell. The guide will spell out the condition of the car and what's known about any problems or potential problems, as well as any warranty included with the car. Some cars are sold ''as is,'' in which case you should expect a much better price, and possibly bigger problems. Several states, however, no longer even allow dealers to sell used cars ''as is.''

DOLANS' SAFETY WARNING: Watch out for the words "laundered," "salvaged," or "rebuilt" in a buyer's guide. These refer to cars that were seriously damaged or totaled in an accident and then pieced back together with parts—usually parts scavenged from other used cars or even from junkyards.

Your next choice of a place to buy a used car might be a rental agency. Again, you're likely to get a later-model car (closer to new) in relatively good condition. Also, a major rental agency is not likely to go out of business overnight, which means you have someplace to go back to if something goes wrong. You're also likely to get low mileage. However, as with dealers, there is high overhead that translates into a higher price for you. If this option sounds appealing, call one of the big rental companies like Avis or Hertz and ask them where their closest used car lot is.

STEER CAREFULLY WITH THESE SELLERS

Speaking of used car lots, independent used car companies are the most plentiful of your shopping options, but you must be careful. You're apt to find dealer ''rejects''—cars that even the dealers refuse to sell because their condition was so bad—picked up at auction and sold to you at a "bargain." Remember, a low price is no deal if the car breaks down the day after you buy it. Also, used car lots are known to disappear quickly, so only buy from a lot that's been doing business in the same location for several years.

Your best price will probably come from a private seller who has no overhead to cover, and no inventory to pay for. At the same time, you have absolutely no guarantee of protection if something goes wrong. This is a true "as is" sale, so be sure you know exactly what you're getting (we'll tell you how in a moment).

Finally, for the truly adventurous, you can buy used cars at auction. You'll almost certainly get a great price, but you are buying the car on the spot with little or no time for an inspection. It's very easy to get a lemon. Also, most auctions require cash up front; no financing or trade-ins here.

SPOTTING A LEMON

Before you buy from anyone, you want to make sure the car doesn't hold any nasty surprises under the hood—or anywhere else! Here are a few tips from the experts on how to check out a car:

Compare the tire wear with the odometer. If the tires are bald but the odometer says 12,000 miles, you may be looking at an odometer that's been turned back! Also check the tires for uneven wear, which could be the sign of bad alignment or poor suspension.

Look over the car thoroughly for rust—in the wheel wells, under the carpeting on the inside floor of the car, the edges of the doors, in the trunk. Check the fluids for rust, too. Take the radiator cap off (when the engine is cold) and make sure there's no rust in the coolant.

You can also spot leaks by checking under the car for stains or puddles, by checking for excess residue of lubricants on the engine, transmission, hoses, or radiator, and by looking for greenish-white stains on the radiator cap. Also, take a sniff of the car's interior—a musty smell can signal a water leak.

Check all doors, windows, and trunks/hatchbacks to make sure they close easily and snugly. Poor fits (not to mention paint that doesn't match) are telltale signs of accidents that have been repaired.

Push on each corner of the car and see how quickly it bounces back to an even keel. Stand back and see if the car *looks* balanced. Take a look at the driver's seat for broken springs or sagging. All these can mean heavy use, bad suspension, and an uncomfortable ride.

Shake the tires and listen for the clunking sound of loose or worn wheel bearings or suspension joints. Check all electrical features, including fancy extras like power locks, power windows, sun roofs, etc. Don't forget to check the basics, too, like lights, blinkers, locks, radio, clock, horn, emergency brake, etc.

THE TEST DRIVE

Next, you want to drive this car you're thinking of buying. You're not just looking to see if you like it. Just as important, you're testing the safety and general operating health of the car. You want a car that starts easily and smoothly (no whining, chugging, or loud rumbling, thank you); you want a car that steers well and true; you want a car that stops and corners accurately and safely; you want a car that shifts smoothly and quietly.

Make several stops and starts, all kinds of turns to the right and left, try parking the car, backing up, slowing down and speeding up, coming to a sudden stop and cruising on the open road. Have a friend go with you, so he or she can stand back and watch the car drive down the street. If the front and back tires do not follow in a straight line, this could be the sign of a car whose frame was bent in an accident.

Finally, do your own comfort test. Can you reach the controls comfortably while steering? Can you see clearly out the windows and mirrors? Is there enough head room? Enough leg room? Remember, once you write the check, it's yours. So make sure it's what you want.

And, of course, *never* buy a car without taking it to an independent garage or mechanic for an objective inspection and appraisal. Ask for a written report, including an estimate on how much repairs of any defects would cost.

GETTING A GOOD PRICE

You'll get a better price from an independent seller, and possibly from a used car lot, than from a car dealer or rental agency. But let us share with you a few more tips on getting the best price you can.

1. Comparison shop. As with almost anything, a little work can have a big payoff. So visit at least two or, even better, three or four different sellers to find the best price on the car you like. With used cars, however, it's almost impossible to avoid the problem of comparing apples with oranges.

2. Another rule of thumb: Sporty cars and racers tend to hold their value better than sedans, which means higher prices on used sporties than used family vehicles. If you don't mind four doors and even station wagons, that's where you're likely to find the bargains.

3. *Mileage* and *condition* are the two biggest factors affecting price. So shop for the best combination, depending on your own needs. If you'll be driving around town with clients and business associates but not taking any long trips, go for high mileage in mint condition. If you plan on taking to the road but have no one to impress but yourself, go for low mileage and a few scuffs and scratches.

4. By all means haggle! Make an offer you feel comfortable with, then let the seller counter your offer. Keep raising your offer in small increments—1 to 2 percent at a time.

DOLANS' SMART MONEY TIP: Consult the experts for proper price ranges. Try *Consumer Reports Used Car Buying Guide* ($8.95 plus $2.00 postage and handling; 800-272-0722); Edmund Publications' *Guide to Used Car Prices* (800-394-4545); Pace Publications' *Used Car Price Guide* (800-272-0246); or the National Association of Automobile Dealers' *Guide to Used Car Prices at Dealerships* (800-248-6232).

GETTING A LOAN FOR A USED CAR

One of the reasons it's harder to buy a used car is that it's harder to get a loan. But don't be discouraged. If you have good credit, you should be able to get a two- or three-year loan from your bank, your credit union, or the dealership if you're buying from the dealer. (The credit union or bank will almost certainly give you a better deal.)

DOLANS' SMART MONEY TIP: Ask your bank about a car loan *before* you go shopping. This will put you in the driver's seat when you start your negotiations. And no matter how good a financing deal you find, keep your eye on the ball (i.e., the car). Don't buy a used car you don't really want just because you "can't pass up" the low-interest financing or some other "bargain" feature.

FIXING YOUR CAR (NEW OR USED)

No matter what type of car you buy, where you buy it, or how much you pay, at some point you're going to have to fix something on it. Here again, you can get a fair deal or get ripped off—depending on how much you know and how carefully you proceed. So let's take a few minutes to talk about getting good service, finding a mechanic you can trust, and spending as little as possible while still keeping your car in tip-top shape.

Most people who buy a car from a dealer wind up using that dealer for service and repairs. Not a bad idea. The people at the dealership know the car, they know you, and the garage is probably in a location convenient to your home and/or office. Frankly, as we said earlier, this should be one of your considerations when buying a car in the first place. Before deciding to buy from a dealership, arrive there on a Monday morning between 7 and 8 A.M. and talk to the people in line at the service department. Ask them how they rate the service they get, if they feel well treated, if their problems are solved the first time around, and how cooperative the service people are at trying again if the problem isn't fixed the first time. Talk to the service manager and ask how they handle appointments and emergencies. Listen to the answers *and* the tone (are these folks going to be easy to deal with or not?).

It makes a lot of sense to go back to the dealer for any repairs covered by warranty. But when the money is coming out of your own pocket, you may want to use an independent mechanic, who is usually cheaper. How do you find one you can trust?

1. *Go with a specialist.* If you have a Honda, find a mechanic who specializes in Japanese cars, or even Hondas in particular. If you have a BMW, go with a BMW mechanic. If you have a Ford pickup, go with an American-truck mechanic.

2. *Ask friends for referrals.* Ask everyone you know with a car like yours who they use for a mechanic. If they're satisfied, their mechanic is worth a look. Ask about the quality of work, the prices, the wait (two hours or two weeks?), and what kind of guarantee is offered.

3. *Avoid shops that pay mechanics on commission.* If the mechanic

makes more money the more repairs he performs, this could work against you in two ways: You could be talked into repairs you don't need, and the mechanic could rush through jobs in order to fit more work in.

4. *Beware of shops with a big advertising budget.* The money for all those TV, radio, and newspaper ads has to come from somewhere—and it's probably your wallet!

5. *Look for shops that have been in business a long time.* Like any other business, longevity suggests good business sense, satisfied customers, and at least a good chance that they'll be around next week if you have to go back.

6. *Find a mechanic before you need him.* When you have an emergency, you may not have the time or attention to shop around carefully. So do your shopping now, and try out the mechanic on something relatively minor. A "test drive" for your mechanic is just as wise as a test drive for your car.

AVOIDING A CAR REPAIR RIP-OFF

Once you've chosen a mechanic or service department, you still want to protect yourself against unnecessary or poorly done repairs. Here's how to keep your serviceman on the straight and narrow:

1. Put everything in writing. That means your needs, the mechanic's diagnosis, and the estimate of cost.

2. Ask questions if you don't understand. Most folks are reluctant to ask questions of doctors, including car doctors. Consequently they get talked into fancy-sounding (and high-priced) treatments without the slightest idea why these "repairs" are being done. If you don't understand what or why, ask questions until you do!

3. If you don't feel satisfied with the answers you're getting, get a second opinion, especially on problems you can't see.

4. Make sure your mechanic asks your approval for any and all extra repairs above and beyond his written estimate. You don't want to get a call like this: "Mr. Peters, your car is ready, and the bill comes to $1,349," especially when the estimate was for $625!

5. Stay in touch. If you're asking the mechanic to get your OK on extra expenses, you've got to give him the opportunity to ask you! So make sure he can call you, or arrange to check in with him at a certain time.

6. Ask to see all replaced parts along with the box the new part came in. You want to be sure not only that your old air filter was taken out, but also that a new one of good quality was put in.

DOLANS' SMART MONEY TIP: You don't need high-priced dealer parts to stay under warranty. As long as you use name-brand parts and get regular checkups, your auto company cannot refuse to honor the warranty.

7. Pay the going rate. Reasonable charges for common fixes: wheel alignment, $100–$150; brake replacement, $400–$500; new muffler, installed, $125–$250; water pump replacement, $200–$350; headlight replacement, $50–$100; basic tune-up, including spark plugs: $100–$200. Expect to pay more in a big city than in a small town.

TWO THINGS NEVER TO SAY TO YOUR MECHANIC

No matter how foreign you feel in a car repair shop, here are two things you should never say:

"I don't know a thing about cars." That's like giving your mechanic an open invitation to trump up repairs and maintenance that aren't really necessary.

"I don't care how much it costs, just fix it." That's like giving your mechanic a blank check. It's almost irresistible to inflate the cost just a little—or a lot!

CAR INSURANCE

Finally, let's talk about protecting this car you've worked so hard to buy right and keep running like a charm. Everyone must buy car insurance. The key is to pay for what you need without overpaying and/or overinsuring. First of all, don't insure the car for more than it's worth. If the car can't be sold for more than $1,000, don't worry about collision insurance. Just make sure you are covered to pay for the other guy's damage and injury, in case of a multiple-car accident. If damage to your car is under $1,000, pay for it yourself; if it's over $1,000, it's time for another car. Which leads us to the subject of a deductible. You can save a lot of money on your car insurance premiums by raising the deductible to $500, even $1,000. After all, insurance is protection against disasters, not for regular expenses.

Even if you're using your car primarily for business, purchase and register it in your name. Personal insurance policies cost less than business policies. And take advantage of multiple-policy discounts by insuring all cars, as well as home and other property, with the same insurer. Make sure, too, that you get discount credits for things like a burglar alarm, an air bag, automatic seat belts, and a good driving record.

Cars are meant to provide safe transportation for you and your family—and a little fun en route! Follow the rules of the road we've laid out for you here, and you should be able to drive a hard bargain and keep your engine purring.

CHAPTER SEVEN

The Company You Keep

How to Find the Right Job, Your Rights as an Employee, and Your Self-Employment Alternatives

We've spent a lot of time so far talking about managing money for you and your family—shepherding it carefully, spending it wisely, investing it shrewdly. But where does all this money come from? Unless your rich aunt dies and leaves you her many millions, the money comes from years of hard work. In this chapter, we're going to give you advice and guidance on getting, keeping, and making the most of your job. We'll start with some insider's tips on cover letters, résumés, and interviews, we'll follow up with employee benefits packages and your rights as an employee. We'll close with a discussion of one of the fastest-growing segments of the work force—the self-employed.

STANDING OUT FROM THE CROWD

We hate to start on a negative, but let's face it: There are an awful lot of people looking for a job these days. After the no-holds-barred corporate expansion and leveraged buy-out craze of the 1980s, the 1990s seem to be shaping up as the decade of small business and corporate downsizing. And that means you have to work even harder than before to get noticed when you're looking for a job.

The first question is, where should you look? Good news! There are a lot of places and sources of information, many of them free. You can find out which jobs will be in the greatest demand over the next 10 to 20 years, including starting salaries and salary ranges, from your State Labor Information Center. Or call the Bureau of Labor Statistics at 202-272-5278, and ask for its Office of Economic Growth and Employment Projections. You can also get a copy of *Workforce 2000,* a study by the federal Department of Labor that looks at the best job fields for the next century. Call the Government Printing Office, at 202-783-3238.

WHERE THE JOBS ARE

On page 173 is a list of the metropolitan areas that made the biggest employment gains in a year when, overall, U.S. companies lost 360,000 positions.

New companies are often in need of employees or independent contractors, and you can get a list of new businesses in your state by contacting your state government and asking for the Office of Corporations or the Office of the Secretary of State.

If you know the field or fields you're looking for work in, your State Licensing Office has a computerized list of all professionals that are required to carry a license to work in your state. It will give you that list for a small fee. In fact, you can often get the list on ready-made mailing labels, so you could do a mass mailing of your résumé and cover letter to prospective professionals in your area.

Together with the federal government, your state government also has a computerized list of specific job openings, called ALEX (Automated Labor Exchange), located at your local job service center. ALEX lists job openings in the private sector, as well as federal job openings. For any opening listed on the network, you can get a complete profile of the position, including the name and general location of the employer, the contact person, phone number, job title, salary, job requirements, hours, and job description. Call your local reference library to find the ALEX nearest you.

If you're looking for a high-tech job, your state government probably publishes a directory of high-tech companies in your state. Contact your state office of economic development. You can find national high-tech jobs by contacting the National Aeronautics and Space Administration's (NASA's) small business office (202-453-2088) and asking for a

U.S. Metropolitan Areas Rated
By Number of New Jobs Created*

Listed below are the 20 metro areas across the country that boasted the biggest increase in new jobs in 1992. As you can see, the increases were not impressive, ranging from 26,000 new jobs in Minneapolis to 3,100 new jobs in Charlotte, North Carolina.

Rank	Metro Area	Total Employment 3Q/1992 (000's)	No. of New Jobs (000's)	% Change '91–'92
1	Minneapolis	1,395.7	25.9	1.89
2	Indianapolis	692.4	14.2	2.09
3	Salt Lake City	522.3	13.9	2.73
4	Denver	863.3	11.9	1.40
5	Las Vegas	396.7	9.7	2.51
6	Atlanta	1,472.1	9.5	0.65
7	Portland, Ore.	650.6	8.6	1.34
8	San Antonio	533.6	8.5	1.62
9	Gary, Ind.	256.8	8.1	3.26
10	Tampa, Fla.	851.7	7.1	0.84
11	Austin, Texas	391.9	6.3	1.63
12	Milwaukee	753.1	6.0	0.80
13	Tucson, Ariz.	260.8	5.9	2.31
14	Louisville, Ky.	492.8	5.6	1.15
15	El Paso, Texas	214.1	5.2	2.49
16	Fort Lauderdale, Fla.	500.9	4.5	0.91
17	Fort Worth, Texas	592.7	4.2	0.71
18	Colorado Springs, Colo.	160.9	4.1	2.61
19	Mobile, Ala.	189.2	4.1	2.22
20	Charlotte, N.C.	612.5	3.1	0.51

copy of its free directory of large contractors who do work for the agency.

Interested in teaching abroad? Consider working for one of the Department of Defense's (DOD's) elementary or high schools overseas, which are attended by "army brats" stationed abroad. These schools are always looking for new teachers—it's a great way to get a teaching job, and to see a different part of the world! The DOD even pays for your

Places with the Most Technical, Sales, and Administrative Jobs*
This table shows the 20 areas in the country with the most jobs in the technical, sales, and administrative fields. Each area is either a Metropolitan Statistical Area (MSA) or a Primary Metropolitan Statistical Area (PMSA), and
over 35% of all jobs in these areas are considered technical, sales, or administrative. The three right-hand columns in this table show the total employed
population (that's the number of people with jobs in any field), the number
employed in these three occupations, and the percentage of the total workforce represented by these three occupations in each area.

Rank	County (MSA or PMSA)	Total Employed Population	Number Employed in These 3 Occup.	% of Total in These 3 Occup.
1	Fayette, Ga. (Atlanta)	62,415	31,844	40.0
2	Gwinnette, Ga. (Atlanta)	352,910	203,387	39.6
3	St. Bernard Parish, La. (New Orleans)	66,631	27,859	39.5
4	Sarpy, Neb. (Omaha)	102,583	45,877	39.0
5	Polk, Iowa (Des Moines)	327,140	176,499	38.9
6	Arapahoe, Colo. (Denver)	391,511	210,935	38.7
7	Henrico, Va. (Richmond)	217,881	120,294	38.6
8	Cobb, Ga. (Atlanta)	447,745	253,096	38.6
9	Johnson, Kan. (Kansas City)	355,054	196,066	38.5
10	Jefferson Parish, La. (New Orleans)	448,306	207,479	38.4
11	Sangamon, Ill. (Springfield)	178,386	91,949	38.3
12	Albany, N.Y. (Albany)	292,594	149,954	38.0
13	Dakota, Minn. (Minneapolis)	275,227	153,515	38.0
14	Prince Georges, Md. (Washington)	729,268	412,742	37.8
15	Denton, Texas (Dallas)	273,525	153,373	37.7

(*continued*)

Rank	County (MSA or PMSA)	Total Employed Population	Number Employed in These 3 Occup.	% of Total in These 3 Occup.
16	Clayton, Ga. (Atlanta)	182,052	96,580	37.7
17	Clay, Fla. (Jacksonville)	105,986	48,601	37.7
18	Richmond, N.Y. (New York)	378,977	177,265	37.6
19	Collin, Texas (Dallas)	264,036	145,946	37.6
20	Santa Cruz, Ariz.	29,676	11,286	37.5

transportation to and from the school, plus free room and board! Contact the Department of Defense Dependent Schools, Teacher Recruitment Section, 2461 Eisenhower Avenue, Alexandria, VA 22331; 703-325-0885.

Remember we mentioned "downsizing"? That means the best job opportunities are no longer with the big giants of corporate America. New jobs are more likely to be found in small and medium-sized companies, at least for the next five years. Of course, you can look at the help-wanted ads in your local newspaper, but that's what everyone else will be doing. Why not try the *National Business Employment Weekly,* which has dozens of positions advertised each week, plus articles on interviewing, outplacement, up-and-coming fields, and more. Call 800-JOB-HUNT to subscribe.

Here are a few of our other favorite places to look for jobs. Most are far too often overlooked, but that's what makes them even more valuable to you, the savvy job hunter! Consider: job fairs, college placement offices, alumni organizations, professional associations, and business and trade publications.

If you decide to use an employment agency, make sure the employer (not you) is paying the fee. That's standard operating procedure—remember, you're looking to get paid, not pay someone else! While you're at it, protect yourself and your family by checking out any counseling or placement services beforehand. Contact your State Consumer Protection office and the Better Business Bureau and ask about these services. Have they had any complaints registered against them? How long have they been in business? Or call the Federal Trade Commission (FTC) and ask the same questions. The FTC also has information on how to select a legitimate employment service and how to complain if you feel you've been abused. Call the FTC Bureau of Consumer Protection, at 202-326-3650.

WHICH CAREERS ARE HOT?

You probably won't be surprised to hear that by the year 2000, the job market will look considerably different from today's. If you're a long-range planner, here are some up-and-coming specialties that should be in high demand in the future: chief information officer, computer network administrator, desktop publishing designer, electronic publishing specialist, environmental accountant, environmental engineer, estate planning attorney, family physician, intellectual property lawyer, investment counselor, member services director, merchandise manager, nurse midwife, outplacement consultant, personal services provider (shopping, housekeeping, child care), restaurant site selector, special education teacher, technical administrative assistant, training manager, and wireless specialist.

WHEN TO LOOK

Of course, like anything else, you're better off considering your next job before desperation sets in. You probably don't have time to actually look for a new job while you're scrambling to keep the one you have. But here are a few tips for everyone with a job, just in case that pink slip ever arrives on your desk.

1. Keep your résumé and references updated. That doesn't mean you have to retype them every 60 days. Just keep a folder to which you can add performance appraisals, complimentary notes from your boss, new skills learned, lists of your achievements and accomplishments, samples of your work, and your history of raises and bonuses.

2. Keep a contact/networking list. Ugh, networking! But the fact is that most jobs (and the higher up they are, the truer it is) are landed through personal contacts and references. So stash business cards, join profes-

sional clubs (and go to the meetings once in a while!), be visible in civic organizations, find out what the other parents at your kids' school do for a living, the other families at your church, the other folks at the health club or community pool. People love to talk about themselves—get friendly and start listening! You might find a great lead on a new job; at worst, you might find some new and interesting friends.

3. Have a plan. Write down exactly what you will do if you get fired or laid off. Make a list of questions you'd ask your boss, including what kind of severance you'll receive, whether or not you'll get help from an outplacement service, if you can keep your office for a while, if the company will help pay for trips or phone calls in your job search, and what both parties will give as your reason for leaving the company.

The point is that if you start preparing today for your next job, you'll be a whole lot more likely to land a good one fast when you need it. And, by the way, contrary to popular opinion, the holiday season is not a bad time to be job hunting. Many people think employers don't hire then, but they do!

AN IRRESISTIBLE COVER LETTER AND RÉSUMÉ

OK, let's say you're out of work already, looking for a job. What you want is an interview, and it usually takes a great cover letter and résumé to get one. One of the most impressive things you can do in a cover letter is show you know something about the company you want to work for. It shows that you're hardworking and that you do your homework. Basically you want your letter to show that you are absolutely the perfect candidate—just what they're looking for and maybe even a little bit better. So talk about yourself as a problem solver, an achievement-oriented person (it's not the hours put in, but the end result), and a team player. If you can, show bottom-line impact such as how you saved your former company money, how you boosted profits, how you increased sales, etc. If nothing else, show you are aware of and devoted to the bottom line. Don't discuss money or titles; at this point, you're just trying to get your foot in the door.

The best format we've ever seen for a cover letter is what Martin Yate, author of *Knock 'Em Dead,* calls an "Executive Briefing." Very simply put, it matches the job requirements with your abilities and experience. The letter starts with a paragraph that goes something like this: "Dear

Mr. Jones, I read with great interest your ad in Sunday's paper for a computer technician. While my attached résumé outlines my work experience and accomplishments in greater detail, here is a snapshot of how my skills meet your needs.'' Then, in a column on the left, you list ''Your Requirements,'' taken from the classified ad or (better yet) the phone conversation you've had with the company. On the right half of the page, you list ''My Qualifications,'' those skills and experiences that match up with the job description. You look organized, to the point, and well informed. This approach is almost sure to get your résumé to the top of the pile.

SPEAKING OF RÉSUMÉS

Your résumé itself should be brief, clearly written, and easy to understand. Avoid industry or company jargon and abbreviations. Remember, you want to put your best foot forward, and that means that the reader of your résumé must understand what he or she is reading! Don't assume that someone in the field will know what you're talking about. Be clear, specific, and to the point. Write your résumé so that someone *not* in the field will be able to understand it, too, because the first person to screen résumés is often unfamiliar with the jargon.

Your résumé should be no more than two pages; if it's longer than that, you'll run the risk of looking disorganized or, at the very least, long-winded. Most interviewers are already pressed for time, so make their job as easy as possible. If possible, tailor your résumé to the specific job you're applying for, without naming it. Make it look as if you are the ideal candidate (which you are, naturally). You're just what they're looking for. And don't go for one of those professional résumé services. The résumés they turn out look canned and fake, not the real you. If you're worried about your spelling or punctuation, have a bookworm friend read your résumé over.

And don't lie, or even exaggerate, on your résumé. Not only is it wrong, but it's too easy to get caught. Nowadays employers are checking résumés.

There are two ways to organize your résumé. Use the one that best shows off your unique qualities. If you've had a steady career track, with progressive growth and responsibility, use a chronological résumé, listing your jobs from the most recent to least recent. Leave off your college waitressing or delivery boy job, unless they're relevant. If you've had long periods of unemployment or you've gone off track a few times into unrelated ventures, use a functional résumé, grouping your jobs by function, not date. Whichever format you use, try to state your past jobs with fairly general titles, so they have broad appeal. Again, avoid giving salary history, and avoid stating a narrow job objective, unless it's tailored expressly to the position you're applying for. The résumé and cover letter should both be typed.

TELEPHONE COVER LETTERS

Sometimes you have the opportunity to have a "pre-interview" over the phone. Perhaps you're calling because a friend referred you to someone who was hiring, or perhaps you've been dying to work for a company and just decided to call up and see if there are any openings! It is often a great way to get your foot in the door. But you have to overcome a few obstacles. When you call, you are forcing the hirer to talk to you on your schedule, not his or hers, so you must be particularly sensitive and persuasive.

Here's how to make a good first impression and end the call by setting up a person-to-person interview. Try to do your best to talk to someone who might actually be interviewing and hiring (not a secretary or personnel officer). If you don't know the person's name, call the switchboard and get the name, then call back and ask for that person. If you get a computerized answering system, dial any extension and plead technological ignorance. "I'm sorry, I guess I got the wrong extension. Would you mind transferring me to the sales manager (or whatever)?"

When you get through to the right person, be brief and to the point. Tell him or her who you are and why you are calling. If you're calling about a specific opening, say so. If you're calling because a particular person referred you, say so. If you're just fishing, say you think you have some skills that might be particularly attractive to the company and would appreciate the opportunity to come in and talk for 15 minutes or so.

Follow up by describing just one or two key skills, backed up by your specific experience and accomplishments. Don't go through your entire résumé over the phone. One or two key points are enough. Let the other person talk, but be sure to ask questions about what the specific job requirements are, what kind of person he wants, what is most important to him in a candidate. Your goal: a meeting in person.

Write a script, or at least have crib notes, before you call. Don't read from a piece of paper, but have your notes handy so you won't forget what you want to say. If you're responding to an ad, have that in front of you, too.

AVOIDING THE BRUSH-OFF

When you call potential employers, whether you're responding to an ad or "cold calling," they can't afford to waste time. So they may try hard to disqualify you over the phone. Your job is to convince them you could very well be the person they are looking for, and that you are worth talking to face to face.

One great way to disqualify yourself and get the brush-off is to establish that you are outside their price range. So don't bring up salary. If they ask how much you're looking for, ask what the salary range is. If pressed, give a wide range, but make sure it's one you're comfortable with. Don't undersell yourself. In most cases, employers figure they get what they pay for.

If they ask, "How much experience do you have?" again respond with a question of your own. Ask what kind of experience they are looking for—overall work experience, or experience in a specific field or role. And ask what kind of experience is most important.

Sound evasive? Not really. We're not saying never answer a question. Just be clear on what the question is, and get as much information about the position and the company as you can before you answer. If the potential employer suggests you send a résumé, don't argue. Say, "Fine, I'd be happy to. And so I can be sure my qualifications meet your needs, what specific skills are you looking for?"

If you're calling cold, you're very likely to hear the line "We don't have any openings right now" or something similar. Your best tack is to get the person talking about what kind of people work there, what qualities the company is looking for in an employee, and what type of position is most likely to open up. One way to find a place where you might fit is to ask this person where he or she feels most understaffed. This question is nearly irresistible for anyone in management. Few managers feel they truly have all the help they need, and you may get them talking about that one critical additional employee they wish they had. It could be you!

You're getting the brush-off when you hear this line: "We only hire from within.'' Your answer: ''That's one of the things I admire about your company, the opportunity for advancement and growth. But when you do hire from the outside, what convinces you to do so?'' Notice you've assumed that, when the candidate is right, they *will* hire from outside, as almost every company does at some point or other.

What if the person at the other end of the line simply says, ''I don't have time to see/talk to you now''? Again, don't argue. Say, ''I understand. In fact, I'd like to talk to you about how I might help you save more time during the day. When is the best time of day to call again?'' And if the person tries to pass you off to personnel, say you know that he is the real decision maker, and might it not save everyone some time to talk directly? If the potential employer insists, don't argue. Call personnel, and tell them Mr. So-and-so sent you. At least that will earn you more attention than a ''cold call'' to personnel.

TIPS FOR A SUCCESSFUL INTERVIEW

If you send a convincing letter and your résumé shows you have the basic skills and experience (or if you convince the potential employer over the phone that you are a viable candidate), you'll probably get an interview. Now what? Sweaty palms and a queasy stomach? Not at all! One of the best ways to avoid being nervous is to be prepared. Review your résumé and cover letter before you go into the interview, review any notes you have on the company and the position, and know in advance how to answer some tough questions. When you know what you're going to say, you'll look forward to the interview as a way to convince the employer you are his dream come true.

Before you say anything, your body language will talk for you. So pay attention to the signals you're sending out. Stand up straight (this is *not* your mother talking), walk slowly, shake hands firmly, and smile. Try raising your eyebrows rather than flashing a toothy grin; you'll look alert and interested without seeming nervous or insincere. Have two or three copies of your résumé with you, plus a copy of your cover letter, the ad you are responding to, a pad, a pen, and a list of questions *you* want to ask about the company and the job.

Don't sit down until invited to, and then don't slouch or slump—and, for goodness sake, don't put your feet up anywhere! Don't cross your arms in front of you, don't fidget with a pen or paper clip, don't nod incessantly, don't tap your pen or check your watch. Never smoke. Never argue.

What *can* you do? You want to make eye contact without staring, so try thinking of the interviewer's two eyes and mouth as a triangle. Look at each point of the triangle for three or four sentences, then refocus. It's OK to look away, particularly as you're thinking about an answer. Just don't *avoid* eye contact (you'll look nervous or, worse yet, untrustworthy). It's also OK to ask the interviewer to repeat the question, if you need more time to think or if you didn't understand the question. It's also OK to take a minute to think about your answer. It may even be an advantage. Hesitating while you think the question through will make you look serious and thoughtful. If it's a hard question, try starting your answer with "Good question!"

SHOW YOUR STUFF

No matter what questions your interviewer asks, remember that your goal is to show you have the experience, the skills, and the personal traits that make you perfect for this job. You want to leave the interview having shown that you are:

A *problem-solver*. Look for chances to talk about specific problems that you helped solve, including how you spotted the problem and the steps you took to solve it.

A *team player*. You want to avoid complaining about people you worked with or for in the past. Show, instead, how you work well with others, perhaps using stories of group projects or simply talking about staffs you managed and how you helped them become productive and motivated.

Bottom-line oriented. You want to show that you understand the business from an owner's or manager's point of view and that you are committed to the company's success, not just your own. Whenever possible, quote specific dollar results or projects you worked on that affected the bottom line.

Achievement oriented. No one wants to hear about how many hours you worked, they want to know what you actually accomplished. Quality, not quantity is what counts. Putting in more hours than the next guy could simply mean it takes you longer to get things done. So make it clear that you are hardworking *and* productive. Use examples of projects completed, deadlines met, work finished. Bring samples, if appropriate.

GREAT ANSWERS TO TOUGH INTERVIEW QUESTIONS

Let's get to the questions. We'll start with three of the most common questions asked in interviews, and discuss the best way to answer each one. Then we'll talk about some good answers when the interviewer throws you a curve.

Common Question #1: "Why do you want to work here?" Talk about the company first, you second. Here's where your research pays off. The more you know about the company, the better your answer will be.

Common Question #2: "What's a typical day like for you at your current job?" Your answer should show that you are organized, efficient, productive, flexible, and focused, and that you work well with others. How can you possibly show all that? Think out this question in advance. Write down a description of a particularly productive day you had recently. Then you'll have a specific day in mind when you're answering this question for real.

Common Question #3: "Why are you leaving your old job?" Be positive. No personnel problems, no complaints about your old boss. Your answer should be some version of "I love my old job, but this one is even better, because . . . " Fill in the blanks before you walk into the interview. If you were fired, you need to address this question more carefully. Being laid off or fired due to a company downsizing or general industry reduction is common, so say so and move on. But if you were fired for a reason, you'll have to tread more carefully. Find out what your previous employer will say if contacted. Will he say you were fired or that you resigned? By asking you will be prepared. Then package your answer in the best possible light. If you deserved it, say so and explain why. "I let personal problems affect my work." "I lost my motivation." Even though former employers are called only about 10 percent of the time, tell the truth and then explain how you learned from the experience.

Now let's turn up the heat. After the interviewer asks you about your experience and skills, be on guard for these tough questions:

Tough Question #1: "What is the least relevant job you've ever had?" Answer: "No job is irrelevant. I've learned something from every single one!" After making this point, you can use the opportunity to talk about an interesting summer job or volunteer job from your past.

Tough Question #2: "What would you like to be doing in five years?" Answer: "I'd like to be working here, one or two steps up from the position I'm interviewing for." Figure out what position that might be, but be careful if it belongs to the person interviewing you! If it does, work into your answer a line like, "I'd hope to enable you to advance, too."

Tough Question #3: "How do you work under pressure?" Answer: "I work fine under pressure, but I try to keep things under control so I avoid crises." Your answer should also include some acknowledgment that no one can avoid last-minute crises 100 percent of the time, and that your approach when this happens is to stay cool and try to help those around you stay focused. Give examples of your effectiveness under pressure, like a tight deadline or unforeseeable complication (the time the computers went down the night before the big presentation; the day your partner got stuck in a blizzard with all the sales reports; the time your annual meeting was held and the annual reports never showed up).

Tough Question #4: "How do you take directions?" Answer: "I take them very well, and I think it's because I try to make sure I understand the directions clearly and fully at the outset. I'm not afraid to ask questions, and I'm not ashamed to take notes so I remember all the details." The interviewer can see you have a pad and pencil in your lap.

Tough Question #5: "What do you think of your last boss?" Answer: "I respect and admire him/her." There's really nothing to be gained with any other answer.

Tough Question #6: "Tell me about yourself." Answer: "What would you like to hear about?" With such an open-ended question, you need clarification before you answer. Does the interviewer want to hear about your hobbies, your personal traits, your work style, your skills, your experience, your training? Don't be afraid to ask politely for a more specific question.

Tough Question #7: "What kinds of things do you worry about?" Answer: "Getting the job done well, on time, and with the good feelings of everyone involved." No true confessions here! Stick to sensible, job-related concerns that show you are practical and flexible, not a dreamer, and not one to get stuck when things don't go exactly as planned.

Tough Question #8: "What's the most difficult situation you've ever faced?" To answer that question, talk about a truly difficult situation and how you solved it. Focus on solutions, not the problem, and avoid complaining about co-workers.

Tough Question #9: "What kind of working atmosphere do you like?" Answer: "Informal, cooperative, an atmosphere that's conducive to getting the job done, exactly the kind you seem to have here." And keep your answer short; the more specific you get, the more it's likely to sound different from where you're interviewing. (Another variation on this question is: "Do you like to work with your door open or closed?" The answer to this one is: "I like interacting with people, so I usually leave my door open. But when I need total concentration and focus, I do shut my door.")

Tough Question #10: "How have you benefited from disappointment?" Note: The question asked about disappointment, not failure! To answer it, pull out a story from your past about disappointment, then show how you learned from it and didn't let it get you down.

Almost all other tough questions you will get are variations on the 10 listed above. Just keep in mind that your own objective is to show that you are *a problem solver, a team player, bottom-line oriented,* and *achievement oriented.* Look over these questions and construct answers that show these traits. You'll be irresistible!

GETTING PAID FOR ALL THIS HARD WORK

Be careful when the interviewer turns to salary. Unless a specific dollar amount has already been established in the ad and it is assumed you wouldn't be applying for the job if it wasn't satisfactory, the salary may be negotiable. But try to avoid talking salary until you are face to face with the potential employer. If pressed, give a range that starts 10 percent above your current salary. But don't lie about your current salary, if asked. You don't have to quote dollars and cents, but don't inflate it by more than rounding to the nearest $5,000—it's just too easy to get caught in a lie.

At some point, however, the time will come to talk dollars, and you want to be prepared. First, find out what the going rate is for that position. Check the classified ads in the paper to get an idea of comparable salaries, and then call a few trade organizations or employment agencies for more specifics. Two more good sources of info: The Bureau of Labor Statistics (BLS) has compiled Area Wage Surveys, which tell you what the average salary is for someone in your profession or business with your level of experience; call 202-523-1208. BLS also publishes an annual study of white-collar salaries called *The Professional, Administrative, Technical and Clerical Survey*; call the same number for information.

Ask your potential employer for more than you expect, in order to leave yourself some negotiating room. If you have a range in mind, go for the high end (why not the top?) of that range. Don't be afraid to explain why you think you deserve the high side, and be a cool cookie. Stay calm; don't get nervous or impatient. The best negotiators wait for the other party to make the first move. These experts say that most people negotiate against themselves when they get nervous and end up giving things away just to keep the conversation going. Don't be afraid of silence.

If the final offer is less than you'd hoped for, don't turn it down immediately. Ask for time to consider it. You might also agree to a starting salary that's not quite as high as you'd hoped if it comes with a written agreement that you'll get a salary review (better yet, a raise) in six months.

A BENEFITS PACKAGE YOU CAN LIVE WITH

It used to be fairly simple: More money was more money. But now a good salary is just one part of your total compensation package. Before you accept a position, you want to be sure that you get not only a nice-looking paycheck but also a competitive package of benefits. These include major medical insurance, short-term disability insurance, life insurance, and some sort of tax-deferred retirement savings plan.

With health-care costs skyrocketing, companies have become very innovative in cutting these costs or sharing them with employees. You will probably be asked to:

- Contribute money toward your health-care premiums, or
- Join a health maintenance organization, or
- Participate in a "cafeteria-style" plan in which you choose the health-care coverage you want from a menu of options (and, usually, set aside pretax money to pay for part of these options), or
- Shoulder a big deductible and pay for 20 percent of your nonhospital care yourself, or
- Pay for wellcare (checkups and vaccinations) yourself, or
- Some combination of the above.

If you're comparing packages from several different prospective employers, sit down with a pad and list your anticipated health-care costs for the coming year. Use last year's expenses as a guide, unless you anticipate significantly different expenses—like having a baby, for instance. Then figure out how much you'd pay with each of the packages you've been offered. This is the best way to compare packages and see which really is best for you.

"DESIGNER" BENEFITS PACKAGE

Increasingly, you are being given more and more choice about what benefits you want to have and how to construct a package of benefits that best protects your and your family's health and financial security. For example, you may be offered the choice between an HMO (Health Maintenance Organization) and a traditional major medical insurance policy. Which should you choose? First, let's be clear on the difference. An HMO is a plan that focuses on preventive care and wellness checkups; major medical kicks in when you get sick or are injured. With an HMO, you usually pay minimal charges or no money for checkups and preventive care. The downside is less personal choice. You go to the doctors that belong to the plan; you usually cannot go to just any physician you choose. Thus an HMO is best for young, healthy families with no current severe illnesses or disability.

Major medical insurance usually does not cover the costs of staying healthy. It pays when something goes wrong. The advantage, however, is that you can go to any doctor you choose. Major medical coverage is usually the best choice for middle-aged or older families or couples, especially if you are wedded to a particular specialist for a medical condition.

ASKING YOU TO FOOT THE BILL

As more and more companies search for ways to cut health-care costs, they are asking their employees to help pay for health insurance. We like the pretax plans the best. These are plans that allow you to set aside a part of your salary into a health-care account before taxes are deducted. Then, when you encounter a health-care cost (including checkups, prescription drugs, dental care, sometimes even contact lenses), you draw from your account.

The great advantage for you is that you're paying for your health-care costs with pretax dollars. Thus, if you're in the 28 percent tax bracket you're really only spending 72 cents on each dollar you pay (Uncle Sam would have gotten the other 28 cents anyway). What's the catch? If you don't spend the money you've set aside in your pretax account by the end of the year, you lose it.

The solution is to be conservative in the money you set aside. For example, take a look at the amount of money you spend each year on regular health-care expenses, including your deductible, which is not covered by your health insurance. If you are certain you will spend this much money, set it aside in a pretax plan. If you're not sure, deduct 10 percent, and contribute this amount to the plan. You'll run little risk of spending less, especially when you consider the 28 percent Uncle Sam would be getting anyway.

Another way for companies to spend less on you and your family is to take you off their insurance plan altogether if you are covered by your spouse's plan. Two-income families often have double coverage, and companies have gotten wise to this as an area of fat to trim. So many companies will offer cash incentives to get employees to opt out of the company health insurance plan and go with their spouse's plan, which is paid for, of course, by some other employer.

DOLANS' SAFETY WARNING: Don't agree to give up your company-sponsored health-care plan unless you have a written guarantee that you can get back into the plan if your spouse's work situation changes. We also advise that you agree to do this only if the cash incentive will cover at least one year of your deductible—preferably two—and only if your spouse's job is reasonably secure.

RETIREMENT SAVINGS PLANS AT WORK

The other important component of your benefits package is the plan the company has set up to help pay for your retirement. If there is no "qualified" plan (qualified means the government has given the plan its tax-deferred seal of approval), your conclusion is easy: This is not a great package of benefits. Beyond that, the decisions get harder.

Pension plans, funded by the employer and set up to pay retired employees a certain percentage of their salaries after they retire, are largely becoming obsolete. These plans are known as "defined benefit" plans, since the benefits they pay out to retired employees are predetermined.

But today more and more companies are opting for retirement savings plans funded partly or completely by the employees. Most companies are using ''defined contribution'' plans, in which the amount of money you contribute is predetermined by you (and may or may not be matched by your company). Usually you are offered a menu of investment choices, such as a growth fund, a bond fund, a money market fund, and a guaranteed-interest contract (like a CD). The capital appreciation of the growth choice and the interest of the fixed income choices grow tax deferred, but the amount you receive when you retire is not guaranteed. Defined contribution plans include the most currently popular form of retirement savings plan: the 401(k) or the 403(b) for nonprofit organizations.

We talk a lot about how to save for retirement in Chapter Nine, but for now let's focus on these plans as they apply to your career choice. Which type of plan is better for you? In most cases, the more money the company contributes, the better. After all, why not have your retirement funded by your employer? All other things being equal, we definitely prefer a 401(k) that includes employer contributions over one that does not. But you must also look at the past performance of the plan and the number of investment options it offers. Make sure performance has been consistent and solid (8 percent or more in average annual gains is reasonable, with *no* years of double-digit losses) and that you have at least three investment choices (blue chip stocks, high-grade bonds, and savings/money market).

In a defined benefit pension plan, the employer contributes 100 percent, which seems to make this the best benefit of all at first glance. Unfortunately, pension plans have run into increasing financial difficulty, and more than one large corporation has gone bankrupt and left employees with an underfunded plan. What happens is that distressed companies, desperate for cash, fall victim to the almost irresistible temptation to syphon off assets from a pension plan to pay current bills. For more about pensions see Chapter Nine, page 219.

DOLANS' SAFETY WARNING: Customarily, a company's health-care and retirement packages are presented to you *after* you accept employment. But if they are important considerations in making a job choice, ask for the information. If the company is interested in hiring you, you'll get it.

KEEPING BENEFITS WHEN YOU LEAVE

It's appropriate here for us to talk about keeping your health-care benefits and protecting your retirement savings when you leave a job, whether it's to retire, work somewhere else, or start another job hunt.

First, let's talk health-care insurance. Federal law requires that your former employer let you keep your health-care insurance coverage generally for up to 18 months after you leave (up to 36 months for your dependents) if you work in a company with 20 or more employees, according to the Consolidated Omnibus Reconciliation Act of 1986 (COBRA). It's not free, not by a long shot. You have to pay the full premiums plus 2 percent yourself, but generally we recommend using this option. It's getting increasingly difficult to find a cheaper policy with similar benefits by shopping around yourself. Be sure you have coverage. Don't cancel your COBRA benefits until you sign up for something else. For more information about your rights under COBRA write or call the U.S. Department of Labor, Pension and Welfare Benefits Administration, Room N-5658, 200 Constitution Avenue, N.W., Washington, DC 20210; 202-219-8776.

Your company will also probably let you keep your life insurance for 30 days after you leave, during which time you can convert your company-paid policy to an individual one—or find a better deal on your own. Disability insurance stops the day you leave, so be sure you get coverage before you walk out the door, if possible. See our chapter on insurance (Chapter Eight) for details.

If you worked for a company with fewer than 20 employees, state insurance laws may require that your insurer allow you to convert from a group to an individual health-care plan with no questions asked. These plans typically charge a lot for less-than-comprehensive coverage but may be worth considering if you or your dependents have a condition that prevents you from buying your own policy.

If you need to shop for insurance, send $3.00 for a copy of *Buyer's Guide to Insurance,* from the National Consumer Insurance Organization, 121 North Payne Street, Alexandria, VA 22314; 703-549-8050. You can also call the National Insurance Consumer Helpline, at 800-942-4242, for general information.

If you think you may be uninsurable, here are three good options: 1) Call your local Blue Cross/Blue Shield to see if it has an open-enrollment period during which it accepts all applicants. 2) Try to find a health maintenance organization (HMO) with an open-enrollment period. Contact the National Consumers League, 815 15th Street N.W., Suite 928, Washington, DC 20005; 202-639-8140, for the league's booklet ($4.00) on choosing an HMO. 3) Call your state department of insurance to see if your state has a high-risk pool.

As for your retirement savings plan, some companies require that you leave the money with them until your actual retirement or the age of 55, in which case there's not much you can do. Some allow you to keep the money with them, others require that you withdraw it. But generally we recommend you take it with you. You'll feel better about having an account you can control.

But a new law went into effect in January 1993 that could be very costly for you if you withdraw your money in the wrong way. Now, whenever you take a payout from a company retirement plan, the IRS requires your employer to withhold 20 percent. Whether it's a lump-sum payment at retirement or simply a check you plan to deposit into a new retirement savings plan, like an IRA or your new employer's 401(k), you'll only get 80 percent if you simply withdraw your money. Meanwhile, unless you are 59½ or older, you have to roll over the entire 100 percent (including the 20 percent you never got) into another "qualified" plan within 60 days; otherwise you get slapped with income taxes, plus a 10 percent penalty tax. Yes, it's unfair, but this is the new law.

How do you get 100 percent of your retirement money from an old plan to a new one without all this trouble and cost? Simple. Just have the money in your old plan transferred directly to the new plan. If you don't touch the money yourself, you don't fall victim to withholding, income taxes, or penalties. All this requires is a little advance planning. If you know you're leaving, set up an IRA account at a bank or broker before you leave the company. Then ask your current plan administrator to transfer your money directly into this new account.

DOLANS' SAFETY TIP: Don't have the money transferred into an existing IRA. This could cause a bigger tax bite down the road (as we describe in Chapter Nine). Set up a new account; it's called a conduit IRA.

YOUR RIGHTS AS AN EMPLOYEE

As an employee, you have the responsibility to work hard, do your job well and on time, follow the rules, and maybe even help your fellow workers. But you also have some rights. Let's run through what those rights are, and then what to do if you feel they've been violated.

First, you have the right to a fair wage. The Fair Labor Standards Act (FLSA) has defined "fair wage" as at least the current minimum wage, equal pay for equal work, plus time and a half for overtime and/or comp time for hourly wage workers. (Comp time is time off with pay to make up for unpaid overtime worked. In effect, your employer gives you extra vacation time, rather than paying you directly for your extra work.) Specifically:

Minimum wage. The minimum wage is currently $4.25 per hour. This can consist of salary plus commissions. But if your commissions for any given pay period don't bring you up to the minimum wage, your employer must pay you the difference. Minimum wage applies to the hours you work; there is no guarantee that you'll get paid vacation or sick time, which the law does not require (perhaps your employer will offer this, however).

Equal pay for equal work. This part of the law, enforced by the Equal Employment Opportunity Commission (EEOC), states that you must be paid just as much as anyone else doing the same job at the same level, regardless of your age, sex, race, color, religion, or marital status.

Time and a half for overtime. FLSA states that if you are paid an hourly wage, your employer must pay you at least 50 percent more than your regular wage for any hours you work in excess of 40 hours in a given week. That doesn't mean you must be paid extra for longer than an eight-hour day; overtime kicks in only when you've worked more than 40 hours in a week. Also, if some of your wage comes from commissions or tips, so that your official wage is below minimum wage, your employer must pay you your regular wage plus 50 percent of minimum wage for overtime.

Comp time. If you're an hourly wage worker, your employer is permitted to give you comp time rather than straight overtime, meaning you get paid time off to compensate for extra time worked (over 40 hours in a week). Like overtime, comp time must be given at 1.5 times your regular wage, so if you work 3 extra hours in a week, you are due 4.5 hours of comp time.

Restrictions on child labor. The FLSA also severely limits the amount and type of work a child can do. Children under age 14 are not permitted to work (except for having paper routes and serving as crossing guards). And children age 14 to 15 can work only 18 hours per week, no more than 3 hours on a school day, no more than 8 hours on a nonschool day (weekend or holiday), and no more than 40 hours in a nonschool week. The only exceptions are for certain hazardous businesses, such as manufacturing or mining, in which no one under 16 can work, and farming, for which less strict rules apply and kids under 14 can work with their parents' consent.

If you feel that your employer is failing to obey any of these laws, contact your local office of the Wage and Hour Division of the U.S. Department of Labor (look in the federal government section of your phone book). If you don't get satisfaction, consider taking the employer to Small Claims Court (contact your county courthouse for information on how to proceed).

In addition to a fair wage, the government has a very powerful law preventing employers from discriminating against employees on the basis of gender, age, race, religion, color, and sexual preference when making decisions regarding hiring, firing, promotions, raises, working conditions, etc. It's called Title VII of the Civil Rights Act of 1964. Call your city hall for the number and address of the nearest office of the EEOC or the Fair Employment Practices Agency.

Title VII also protects you against sexual harassment. True harassment occurs when submitting to sexually related conduct or conditions is a condition of continued employment or is a condition for pay raises and/or promotions, or when sexually oriented conduct or conditions create a hostile or abusive working environment. Again, contact the EEOC.

QUESTIONS THE INTERVIEWER CAN'T ASK

There are certain questions an interviewer is not allowed to ask an interviewee. These are important to review, whether you're being interviewed or conducting an interview.

Interviewers cannot ask you about your age, race, religious belief, sexual preference, childbearing plans, credit history, or drug/alcohol use. The law says these areas are off-limits. Other hiring abuses to watch out for: false advertising and brochures, false promises of support, false promises of earning potential. Your best defense is to talk to others who work for the same employer and for the employer's competition, and to the person you are being interviewed to replace. It can't hurt to ask!

DOLANS' SMART MONEY TIP: If you are asked to sign an employment application, get a copy. It could come in handy if you feel later on that you were misled about the job. And if you feel you have been subjected to any illegal hiring practices, contact the National Labor Relations Board, at 202-254-8064, or the Equal Employment Opportunity Commission, at 800-669-3362.

"DON'T LET THE DOOR HIT YOU ON THE WAY OUT"

A great businessman once said, "Every good worker has been fired at least once." As terrible as it is to be fired, you do have rights and some protection. There are things you cannot be fired for, and rules for proper dismissal.

First of all, you cannot be fired for taking military leave, nor on the basis of gender, age, religion, race, creed, color, or because you've filed an FLSA complaint. Second, the firing cannot involve breach of an implied contract or breach of good faith and fair dealing. For instance, an employer cannot fire you to prevent you from collecting commissions due you, nor can he fire you in order to hire someone cheaper. Employers are also prohibited from defamation and blacklisting, where they seek to ruin your good name and reputation.

In addition, you must be paid for work completed, plus any sick or vacation time accrued, within a month of firing. Different states have different rules on this. Some require payment within a week; some give employers a full month. The only states that have no applicable laws are Alabama, Florida, Georgia, Mississippi, Ohio, and Tennessee.

If you feel you've been fired illegally, proving it can be an uphill battle, not to mention an expensive process. But if you have the stamina and the determination, here's how you should proceed: If you feel you were fired because of racial, sexual, or other illegal discrimination, contact the EEOC. If you feel you were fired because you had filed an FLSA complaint, contact the Labor Department. And if you feel your firing constituted a breach of contract or good faith, hire a lawyer.

DOLANS' SMART MONEY TIP: If you are fired, immediately request a copy of your employment file and a letter outlining the reasons for your being fired. These documents may come in handy if you wind up in court. They may even help keep you out of court! Do not sign a waiver of your right to sue. This can often be disguised as some sort of exit interview form, but don't sign. After all, what can they do to you if you refuse? They've already fired you. Remember, they must pay you what you're due, and you can contact your state labor department, at the state capital, for help in collecting unpaid wages.

For a complete rundown of your rights and remedies as an employee, we recommend *Your Rights in the Workplace*, by Dan Lacey (Nolo Press, Berkeley, CA, $15.95).

ENTREPRENEURS IN THE 1990S

After all this talk about employer abuse, maybe the corporate rat race doesn't sound so appealing. As a matter of fact, more and more callers to our radio show are asking employment questions with a twist: They're asking about being their own boss! It takes a special kind of person to be successful as an entrepreneur and, frankly, most people don't have what it takes. But maybe you do! Give yourself the following test. And be honest—you'll only hurt yourself and your family by taking a wrong turn on your career path.

If you can answer "yes" to all the following questions, you may be successful at being your own boss:

1. Do you get more done when you work alone than when you work with a group?
2. Are you willing to answer your own phone and open your own mail?
3. Do you make lists of things to do at work regularly—and then regularly get them done?
4. Do you have an idea for a business that you understand, that can be profitable, that you can afford to start with your current resources, and that you have some experience with?
5. Do you have enough money set aside to support your family for at least six months while your business is getting up to speed?
6. Do you have a place to work, and will your family be cooperative and supportive as you struggle along? (The kitchen table is not conducive for work!)
7. Are you able to keep going when the going gets tough (we mean really tough)?

If you find yourself answering "yes" enthusiastically to all these questions, starting your own business (or buying one that already exists) could be the right career move for you and your family. Just remember that 80 percent of self-employed workers go out of business within five years of launching their own business. You'll have to beat the odds to be successful.

START SMALL AND HAVE TWO PAYCHECKS

It's easy to be excited on the first day of your new career working for yourself. It's a lot harder being upbeat after 10 weeks of no income, computer breakdowns, big telephone bills, and jelly-stained invoices courtesy of your two-year-old. That's why one of our favorite suggestions for starting a business is to start part-time. Try your idea on the weekends, if you can, or in the evenings, or both, while you still have a paycheck. This way you get to work out the bugs and see what some of the problems and challenges will be, before you burn your bridges behind you.

TAX BREAKS FROM YOUR HOME-BASED BUSINESS

Taxes for the self-employed are a double-edged sword, as any entrepreneur will tell you. Yes, you may get to write off your home office, your business phone, your business credit card interest, your business travel, up to $10,000 per year spent on equipment, etc. But you'll now be responsible for quarterly estimated tax payments, your own Social Security taxes, and state, county, and local business (or "mill") taxes, just to name a few. And while you're busy working, the IRS may decide you're not a business at all, but a "hobby," not entitled to many business deductions!

The question of whether you have a business or merely a hobby comes under careful scrutiny when you try to take losses. As long as you have a profit, you can take a deduction for the expenses incurred by the activity. When the expenses are more than the income, you can take the loss only if you can prove you are engaged in an activity to make a profit. Typically, that means showing some net income in three of the last five years. Hobby losses are deductible only against hobby income; any excess loss is considered a nondeductible personal loss.

DOLANS' SMART MONEY TIP: Use your home office exclusively for business. Your desk should not sometimes be the dining room table. The IRS will disallow a home office deduction unless the space is exclusively for business. That doesn't mean your entire home must be an office, just the portion you use for work. Also, list your home address as your principal place of business, with its own desk, filing cabinet, and separate phone line. All of which will make your deductions stand up under IRS scrutiny.

Keep a daily log of the time spent in your home office. Log in, give a brief description of the work done, and log out when you're finished. Then have that log notarized once a month. That turns it into a sworn statement, and the IRS can't come back and accuse you of sitting down the night before filing and concocting an office log.

DOLANS' SMART MONEY TIP: For added protection, file form 8275 (a Disclosure Statement) with your tax return. On this form you can explain why you need your home office and how it is used.

Remember, you cannot deduct more than you make. So your home office expense deductions cannot be larger than your business income. And that's net income, after other business expenses have been deducted. You can, however, carry forward losses into the following years.

UNTANGLING THE WEB OF NETWORK MARKETING

If you're thinking about working from home, you may have been approached about selling a product, like cosmetics or cleaning supplies, through "network marketing." How do you tell the difference between a legitimate business opportunity and a downright scam?

A legitimate multilevel (network) marketing company has a line of consumer products (like Amway cleaning supplies) that you, as an independent "distributor," purchase at wholesale prices and then sell at retail, usually in a potential customer's home. As a distributor, you set your own hours and earn money on your sales ability. If the customer buys the product or service, you're in business. These companies also encourage you to build and oversee your own sales force. It's your job to motivate, train, and supply products to your sales reps. In return, you get a percentage of each rep's sales, as well as the profits from your own sales.

On the other hand, a network marketing scam dangles the promise of a quick buck by "selling" you the right to recruit other people to sell some product or service. You try to recoup your investment by recruiting more and more people from an ever-dwindling pool rather than by selling a product or service. Sometimes you never even learn what the product or service is because you're recruiting bodies, not selling products—products that usually aren't even saleable!

DOLANS' NETWORK MARKETING "SCAM BUSTER" CHECKLIST

You can quickly identify a legit company by asking these four questions:

- Are the company's start-up costs reasonable for the products being sold? Most legitimate companies have small (under $250) or no start-up costs.
- Will the company buy back inventory if you decide the job's not for you? Legit companies should be willing to buy the inventory back for at least 80 percent of your cost.
- Is there a market for the product? Legit companies depend on your sales in order to make money, so they have to give you a product that will sell.
- Does the company offer an orientation to help you get started, and free sales training classes so you can build your sales and marketing skills?

If a company passes this test, it's probably a legitimate multilevel marketing company. Now you're ready to make sure the company is profitable. Ask the company to send you its sales literature, annual report, and the names of four or five new "distributors" you can contact. Then see if the company makes the grade on these counts:

- Does the sales literature and marketing plan show that the company has a well-defined plan and knows where it's headed?
- Do the company, its officers, and its products get a clean bill of health from the Better Business Bureau in your state and the company's home state, and from the district attorney or state attorney general's office?

- Is there a written buy-back policy and an itemization of start-up costs?
- Have new distributors had a good experience with the company and its products?

DOLANS' SMART MONEY TIP: If you don't want to wait for a legitimate company to track you down, contact the Direct Selling Association (1776 K Street, N.W., Washington, DC 20006), which is the national trade association for legitimate firms. They'll help you find companies that carry products you want to sell.

THREE WAYS TO GET WASHINGTON'S HELP WITH YOUR SMALL BUSINESS

Two free reports from the Small Business Administration that you should find useful are *How to Start a Home-Based Business* and *How to Raise Money for a Home-Based Business,* both available from the Office of Business Development and Marketing, 409 Third Street, S.W., Washington, DC 20024; 202-205-6665.

The government may also be a great customer. Your local Small Business Administration office will help you find a Small Business Development Center or Procurement Assistance Office near you, which can give you a complete listing of every government agency and program that buys your product or service.

To get on the government's list of suppliers, call the local Procurement Assistance Office and ask to be listed on its computer data base, with your name, address, number, and the product or service you offer. This is a great way to really put your tax dollars to work for you!

You should also know that the government sells all sorts of equipment, furniture, and supplies at bargain basement prices, if you know where to shop. Call the General Services Administration's headquarters, at 703-557-7785, to find out about government auctions in your area.

FINDING MONEY FOR YOUR HOME-BASED BUSINESS

If you think it's hard raising money to start your own business, you're wrong—*it's harder!* But we have a technique we like that will get you the cash you need without sinking your business under the carrying costs of a loan. Trade a percentage of your business income (say, 25 percent) for start-up money from a friend or family member. You both share in the profits—and the risks. Plus you don't have to pay until you start actually making some money. If your lender doesn't like putting all his or her money at risk, go halvsies. You agree to pay back half in cash, no matter what, and the other half with equity in the business.

DOLANS' SMART MONEY TIP: Whatever you do, don't take out a home-equity loan to fund a new business. If the business fails, you not only lose your job, but the bank will foreclose on your house as well.

If your business is one that benefits the public good, another source of very good information on "free" start-up capital is *Free Money for Small Businesses and Entrepreneurs*, by Laurie Blum (Wiley and Sons, $14.95). There are grants available from foundations for a business that hires the handicapped or the homeless or in some other fashion gives something to the community while being a for-profit business.

The economic climate of the 1990s promises to be a turbulent one. Knowing some of the inside tricks to getting the job you want at the salary you desire, knowing what your employer can and cannot do once you've signed on, and knowing how to start and finance your own business can help ensure that your workday is spent productively, enjoyably, and fruitfully for you and your family.

CHAPTER EIGHT

Protecting Your Family—No Matter What!

How to Buy the Right Kind of Insurance for the Right Price

We work, make investments, and plan ahead to achieve special goals and milestones for one reason and one reason alone: to make life for ourselves and our families the best we possibly can. Some families fare better than others. But the one thing that can profoundly affect every family's future is the catastrophe of disability or death. That's why it is imperative that we talk about both life and disability insurance in this book of family financial planning.

Through the years, in talking with our TV viewers and radio listeners, we have come to realize that more people are scammed by insurance salespeople than by almost any other type of financial services salesperson. We lose money in many investments because the salesperson appeals to the greed that (to one extent or another) lurks in all of us. But we lose money in insurance "investments" in a far more dangerous way. We are made to feel inadequate, and the unscrupulous salesperson plays on our fears. "If you really loved your family you'd buy this insurance." Psychologically it is a much more dangerous sales pitch than being advised to buy gas and oil futures or rare coins. And, most amazingly, people who have been taken by bad insurance investments don't scream about it the way they do when the stock they were sold goes down in price. Yet far more families lose more money by buying insurance that is inappropriate to their real needs or that is an outright rip-off.

Insurance is the one thing you cannot buy when you need it. You must buy it *before* you need it—and then hope that you don't need it for a very long time, if ever. Yet, while people hope they never have to use it, life insurance is a huge business. It's a $1.6 trillion industry, into which people pay $79 billion in premiums every single year. Yikes! Where is all this money going? And how can you make sure you get the protection your family needs without getting scalped?

WHO NEEDS INSURANCE ANYWAY?

Do you need it at all? *Don't buy insurance as an investment,* and don't buy it to make the kids rich when you are no longer around. In our opinion, the reason to buy life insurance is to provide for your dependents when you're gone—period. For that reason, we believe you should carry it only as long as you have outstanding debts, dependent children, or a spouse who doesn't work.

A young, single person doesn't need life insurance, unless you have extraordinary debts that you would want paid if you died. Insurance sales people like to scare you into buying a policy by claiming it will prove you are "insurable" in case you have a real need for insurance later on. But no one is even going to check your health if it's a policy of $100,000 or less, so don't bother. If you're in good health and have yearly checkups, then you don't even need to mess around with the nominal policy.

Should you insure both spouses? Definitely. Even if the wife is the stay-at-home spouse or the husband is a house husband, you still want to insure for at least enough money to pay for child care and housekeeping, neither of which come cheaply.

HOW MUCH INSURANCE DO YOU NEED?

How much life insurance is appropriate? Ideally, you need 10 times your annual salary to be completely, 100 percent insured. But most people blanch at that formula. If there is only one member of the family missing, then you probably can do with less. But we'd say *no less than* five to six times that person's salary. The replacement salary for a housewife is something like $50,000 to $60,000 a year for all the services they perform. Don't skimp on a stay-at-home spouse.

WHAT KIND OF INSURANCE SHOULD YOU BUY?

Young couples should buy term life insurance, period. Term insurance is pure death protection without any cash (investment) buildup. Young is defined as under 50. Why term? Because it is the cheapest and, consequently, the best bang for your insurance buck.

Here's what to look for in a term policy:

- You want it to be guaranteed renewable annually (meaning you don't need a checkup every year to renew your policy).
- You want *level premiums* (meaning you lock in a fixed premium), preferably for 5 or 10 years. This will cost more in the early years, but knowing exactly what the premium will be year in and year out will give you financial peace of mind.
- You want to be able to convert to a whole life policy at the end of the term. Whole life combines the death protection of term insurance with an investment portfolio.
- You want a safe insurance company.

Guaranteed renewable means the insurance company guarantees it will allow you to renew the policy each year for the term of the policy at the same premiums without a physical. At the end of the contract, if you continue to need life insurance, then you'll probably buy a new policy at a higher premium because you are older.

During the term of the policy, the company can't cancel your policy, but you can. In fact, the company wishes you would, because then it would never have to pay off on the policy. If you cancel and you're still alive, then the company has won its side of the gamble.

Level premiums mean your annual premiums don't go up but are the same dollar amount for the entire term of the policy. It's going to cost you more in the early years to have a level premium, but we believe you should know exactly how much you're going to pay from the outset. Otherwise the company can guarantee to renew your policy annually, but the premiums could be so outrageous that you can't afford them. The longer the term of the policy, the more expensive it's going to be, but you're guaranteed that annual premium cost with no surprises.

When your term policy expires, both parties walk away without further obligation. The insurance company does not have to pay you anything nor continue to insure you, and you do not owe anything to the insurance company. The whole idea is that you will reach a point in your life (you hope) when you no longer need life insurance, so why pay for it? Ideally, your term insurance will run out at the same time that you no longer need it, but life isn't always so accommodating.

What happens when the term is up and you still need insurance protection for your family? You buy another term policy, if you're still young enough and able to afford it. If you can't afford term (which gets quite expensive as you get older), you're back to square one—and you have to qualify for whole life insurance. That's why we like term policies that promise you the opportunity to convert to a whole life policy without a medical exam, so you can avoid being rejected for whole life at the very time you can no longer afford term.

As for safety, the insurance company will probably quote you their A. M. Best rating. A. M. Best is one of several companies that rate the financial stability of insurers and the most widely quoted by the industry. Frankly, however, A. M. Best is just not tough enough. We believe you've got to spend $15.00 and check out the insurer with Weiss Research (800-289-9222). The reason we recommend Weiss Research is that they are the toughest. The Weiss ratings indicate the company's ability to meet policyholder commitments under current economic con¬ ditions and also project its ability to pay in a declining economy and in a liquidity crunch. Call 800-289-9222. It's worth the money. And just so you understand the ratings, Weiss's top rating is A+, A. M. Best's is A++, Duff & Phelps's is AAA, Standard & Poor's is AAA, and Moody's is Aaa.

GETTING THE BEST PRICE

Once you satisfy these four criteria, choose the term policy with the lowest premiums you can find. One great way to comparison shop is with our friend Milton Brown's Insurance Information, Inc. For a $50 fee, it will comparison shop five policies within your needs. If the lowest quote doesn't save you the $50, you won't be charged the fee. Call 800-472-5800 and get quotes. Another good way to find the lowest premiums is through Select Quote, which charges no fee for quotes on the cost of the term insurance policy. It acts as an insurance broker for 18 different insurance companies and collects a commission if you buy one of the quoted policies; call 800-343-1985.

OVER 50? BUY PLAIN VANILLA WHOLE LIFE

Once you reach age 50, term policies become prohibitively expensive. At that point, if you still need insurance, we like a plain vanilla whole life policy. No bells, no whistles, because like anything else in life, the fewer the options, the cheaper it is. And once you lock it in, your premiums never change. Granted, if you shop for whole life insurance in your fifties, it will be more expensive than it would have been in your thirties, but your premium will not change once you buy the whole life policy. Term insurance at this stage becomes very expensive and will continue to cost more if you find you need to renew it each year.

Here's how whole life works: Insurance companies take in X number of dollars in premiums. They turn around and fund the actuarial side for the death benefit. With the remainder, they invest in, among other things, long-term bonds. They give you a set rate of return on the investment part. The difference between what they credit you and what they get by investing in long-term bonds is their profit.

Of course, as with any other insurance product, you must make sure the insurer is safe before shopping for the lowest premium. And you should understand that the insurance agent gets a commission every year; it's an ongoing thing. It's called a "trailing commission." The big hit is in the first year, when 50 percent to 90 percent of your premium is skimmed right off the top and paid to the broker. But it takes 10 years before you get rid of the real weight of that broker commission, so the lower the commission, the better.

We love low-commission insurance that you buy direct from the insurance company (no agents involved). Three such companies we like are USAA (800-531-8000), Lincoln Benefit (800-525-9287), and Ameritas (800-552-3553), all highly rated by Weiss. Obviously anytime you can cut the commission out, you're putting more of your money to work for you. It's like no-load mutual funds. For more info, get a copy of Glenn Daily's *The Individual Investor's Guide to Low-Load Insurance Products* (call 800-488-4149) or contact the Life Insurance Advisors Association at 800-521-4578. We also like United States Annuities' quarterly report *The Annuity and Life Insurance Shopper,* which includes interest rate charges and safety ratings for 250 different insurance companies (800-872-6684; single issue, $20.00; one-year subscription, $45.00).

You can buy low-load whole life. Check with Ameritas and USAA. Ameritas charges a 10 percent fee in the first year and 2 percent every year thereafter. USAA charges a one-time start-up fee of $50, plus $30 and 3 percent each year. Another great thing about low-load policies is that the less you pay in commissions, the more money goes toward your cash value. So if you decide to cancel your policy and take the cash, there's more cash to take.

WHAT IS "CASH VALUE"?

You'll hear a lot about "cash value" when you shop for whole life insurance. Cash value is the amount of money you've paid into the policy plus the investment return—and it's the amount you can take out of your policy while you're alive. If you terminate the policy, its cash value on the day that you stop will be paid to you. But you'll have to pay income taxes on it, because it's been in a tax-deferred account up until the time you "cashed out." An insurance company would love to pay you the cash value, because it's a small fraction of the death benefit, and once you terminate the policy the company no longer has to worry about paying you a death benefit.

You can also borrow your cash value from the insurance company. But note: You're borrowing your own money and paying the insurance company interest, like 6 to 8 percent. And it's not deductible. You pay interest every year, and if you don't repay the loan, the company lowers the death benefit by the amount borrowed. Since Congress changed the tax deductibility of interest paid on personal and consumer loans back in 1986, borrowing on your cash value has become much less attractive. We would suggest you try to avoid borrowing unless it's an emergency.

LIFE INSURANCE TRAPS

Here are some of the pitfalls to watch out for when buying life insurance:

1. *Unrealistic projections and the "disappearing premium" fallacy.* One popular insurance salesperson's trick is to overinflate the projected rate of return within your account, promising it will mean lower premiums or a higher return on the investment side of the policy.

DOLANS' SMART MONEY TIP: Ask your agent what is *guaranteed* by the policy and what is contingent upon investment results. Ask if there is a *cap* on your premiums. You want to know the *worst case scenario,* not just the insurance company's wishful thinking.

Similarly, some policies are sold with a "vanishing premium" promise. Sounds great! The problem is that the premiums don't necessarily vanish when the insurance salesperson says they will. The theory behind this promise is that the investments the insurance company puts your money into will generate enough in dividends to pay the premium. But when the investments don't return the "projected" 16 percent (or whatever percentage rate the policy was "projected" to earn), the insurer comes back to you and says: "Gee, you're going to have to pay for one more year, three more years, five more years." The company doesn't *guarantee* that the premiums are going to stop. It only says that "based on this projection, you will be able to stop making premium payments in X years." Not so. The average person who is sold life insurance as an investment drops it by year 7 anyway, because he is tired of making the premium payments and not seeing much growth.

DOLANS' SMART MONEY TIP: Before you buy a policy based on the insurance agent's rosy projections, do a reality check on his or her numbers. Call Peter Katt, at Beacon Company, Inc. (800-824-1274) and for $108.00 he will evaluate the insurance company's projections for you.

2. *Insurance on your kids.* Unless your kid is Macaulay Culkin—that is to say, unless your kid is bringing in big bucks, upon which your family depends—it is a total waste of money.

3. *Insurance on seniors.* Many people think that the older they get the more insurance they need. We think it's quite the contrary. The older you get, the less life insurance you may need. Very often your kids are out of school, the mortgage is paid off, and you have amassed a reasonable amount of assets. Don't be suckered into: "Well, you can leave your kids so much money." Let your kids worry about themselves. In Chapter Eleven, we'll talk about a much better way to leave money to your heirs.

4. *Insurance to pay for college.* You should not buy insurance as an investment to pay for your children's college education. Invest the money you would have spent on insurance premiums and you'll be much better off. When tuition is due, you will have the money to pay it, or you can

seek financial aid alternatives (see Chapter Five). You should not borrow from insurance policies to fund a college education. But do buy insurance on your life to help pay for that college education in case you're not around when your kids are ready to start college.

Additionally, there are a few really disreputable insurance salespeople who will try to talk you into buying annuities (another type of insurance product) to fund your children's college education. An annuity is a contract between you and an insurance company that provides for a guaranteed life income or a lump sum at maturity. It grows, tax deferred, through the years and then becomes taxable as you opt to start taking payouts. Uncle Sam allows the money you pay into an annuity to compound tax deferred, as it would in an Individual Retirement Account. Uncle Sam also treats it like an IRA for tax purposes; money removed from an annuity before you reach 59½ years of age not only becomes fully taxable, but it also becomes subject to a 10 percent penalty for early withdrawal.

So the unscrupulous insurance salesperson who talks you into an annuity to fund your child's college education is walking you into a potential tax trap and costly investment mistake. Unless you started your family later in life, the odds of your being 59½ when Johnny starts college are slim. So kiss 10 percent of the money in your account good-bye!

What's even worse, some salespeople will try to talk you into putting the annuity in Johnny's name! Unless Johnny's a *real* late bloomer who opts to start college at the age of 60, you'll definitely watch 10 percent of your money go bye-bye!

Annuities should be used for retirement planning, *not* college planning. This is a very important distinction to understand. Insurance should not be "invested in" for the purpose of borrowing the cash value 18 years from now as a way to pay the registrar's bills. Instead, term insurance should be purchased now, in case you're not around to watch (and pay for) your kids' first steps behind those ivied walls.

QUESTIONS TO ASK AN INSURANCE AGENT

Before you sign on the dotted line, here are seven questions you want to ask your insurance agent. They will help protect you from bad deals, poor coverage, and an unreliable agent.

1. What is the safety rating of this company—not just from A. M.

Best, but from Standard & Poor's, Moody's, Duff & Phelps, and Weiss.

2. What is the death benefit, and is it enough for me? Remember, you want five or six times your annual salary, at the very least; the optimum amount is ten times. Make sure your agent understands this.

3. What will my premiums be every year, guaranteed? If they go up, how much will they go up?

4. Under what circumstances can my policy be canceled?

5. If term insurance, what happens at the end of the term? Can I renew without a medical exam? Can I convert to a whole life policy without an exam?

6. In the case of "whole life" or other "permanent" types of policies, what will my cash value be at various points in time (after five years, ten years, etc.)? What is that value based on? Is it guaranteed? Then check the projections with the Beacon Company (see page 207).

7. How will I keep track of my policy and how much it's worth? You should get a statement every year, showing your cash value, death benefits, and any withdrawals (borrowing) you've made.

WHAT YOUR AGENT WON'T TELL YOU

While we're at it, let's pull the curtain up on what an agent may not tell you in his or her neat little sales presentation. You know the saying, "What you don't know won't hurt you?" Not when we're talking about protecting your family! Chances are very high your agent won't tell you:

- That a company is unsafe. The agent will quote you the A. M. Best rating, which in our opinion is way too soft on insurance companies. Our concern with all these ratings services is that the insurance companies pay to be rated. If you're paying $25,000 year in and year out, will the rating always be objective? Am I going to give the full story to the world? Or am I going to try to give you the benefit of the doubt?
- That the investment projections are unrealistic. You may get a quote for lower premiums (even no premiums), but if they depend on the company making 15 percent in its investment portfolio, forget it.
- That you can get a better deal elsewhere. Don't hold your breath for this one.

- That you should buy "term" if you are under 50 years of age. Most agents get a much bigger commission on whole life—but that may not be the best deal for you.

MOVING TO ANOTHER COMPANY

If you find yourself with an unsafe company, move—if you can still qualify for insurance. You can use what is called a 1035 tax-free exchange to move your policy from one company to another. This exchange can be handled by your new insurer, and you don't need to get involved with embarrassing phone calls or messy red tape. Of course, you have to be approved by the new company. There may very well be an up-front commission, unless you use the low-load insurance companies we mentioned on page 205. If your medical history has changed for whatever reason, you may not be able to qualify for the same low premiums. But you won't owe any current taxes and you will be protected by a company that won't predecease you.

How do you make the switch? Approach the new company and say you want to switch. The company will do the paperwork for you.

LIFE INSURANCE BENEFITS WHILE YOU'RE LIVING

One life insurance feature that's getting a lot of attention right now is the accelerated death benefit (ADB). Designed for people who are gravely ill, ADBs allow them to tap into their insurance while still living.

It's a great idea, but the problem is the cost. Most policies add a 5 percent to 15 percent annual charge, on top of your regular premiums, for this feature. Also some policies are ridiculously restrictive, paying benefits only under rare circumstances. Study the policy's language closely. Make sure you understand what conditions must be met to get these benefits. Shop for a plan that doesn't charge more money every year but instead charges you only when—and if—you use the benefits.

For more information on ADB policies, contact the National Insurance Consumer Organization's Helpline, at 800-942-4242.

LIFE INSURANCE FOR RETIREMENT

Another product you've probably heard a lot about lately is annuities that are sold as "investments" for your retirement. If you have already used all the other tax-deferred retirement options available to you (like IRAs, Keoghs, 401(k)s, etc.), and you can afford to put the money away for 7 to 10 years and not touch it, annuities may make sense for you. They make a great deal of sense for many people in their late forties or fifties. But we feel they are a mistake for most senior citizens. When you're into retirement, giving up liquidity for a long-term type of investment is usually a bad trade-off unless you have money to burn. In your thirties annuities don't make much sense either, because it's so long before you can get your money out without that penalty, and so much can happen in 30 years.

With annuities, you have two choices: fixed or variable. Fixed annuities are like CDs, in which you lock in a predetermined, guaranteed rate of interest for a specific time period. Variable annuities are like mutual funds, in which you invest your money in different mutual funds and take your chances. Generally speaking, we say let the insurance company take the risk. Which means that we prefer "fixed" plans for many investors.

Stay away from 90 percent of the commissioned variable annuities. The commission structure, on top of the mutual fund fees, makes them extremely costly. The odds of the company doing as well as you'd like are pretty bad because it has to overcome all those commissions and expense ratios.

We do like some of the no-load mutual fund annuities, like Vanguard's. There is no commission, and you're working with companies that have good traceable track records, mutual fund companies that know what they're doing with investments. But remember, a variable annuity involves risk. If you are not one to take risk anyway, then why buy a variable annuity? If you have never bought an equity mutual fund before, or if at this point in time you're shy of stocks and bonds, then for heaven's sake don't pay that high commission and all those expenses to get a variable annuity!

As with an IRA or 401(k), you want to wait until you are past 59½ years of age to start taking your money out of an annuity. At that point, you can "annuitize" (make regular withdrawals) or you can take a lump sum. In most cases, it's better to annuitize, because you will owe taxes only on the amount withdrawn rather than on the whole thing, as with a lump sum. Besides, if the insurance company has done a good job to date, why not leave the rest of the money in the annuity to continue growing, tax deferred.

Since an annuity is a contract with an insurance company, you want to make sure it's a safe company. For more information, consult *The Annuity and Life Insurance Shopper* (see page 205).

HAVE YOU FORGOTTEN DISABILITY INSURANCE?

You probably have. One of the most overlooked areas of insurance is disability insurance. Most people need it, yet few have it. Ever hear the saying "You can't afford to get sick, you can only afford to die"? That's for a person who doesn't have adequate disability insurance. But workers between the ages of 35 and 65 are six times more likely to be disabled than they are to die!

Your employer's health insurance may cover disability, but it's almost certainly *short-term* disability. The real family disaster comes when you can't go back to work for years, or ever. As wage earners, we all have some disability coverage through Social Security. However, like everything else that comes out of Social Security, it is not nearly enough. You can find out what Social Security will pay you if you become disabled and then figure out how much more you need. Just call Social Security, at 800-772-1213, and ask for a Personal Earnings and Benefits Estimate Statement. Fill it out, return it, and in about three weeks you'll get it back showing, along with your estimated retirement earnings, how much Social Security disability you can expect to receive.

Remember, when buying disability insurance, you're aiming to replace your income and support yourself and your family. You want to get the best price with the safest company. Shop for long-term coverage that provides *at least 60 percent* of your pretax income.

WATCH OUT FOR THESE LOOPHOLES

Here's what to look for—and look out for—in disability insurance. You want a plan that is *guaranteed renewable*—meaning the company can cancel the policy only if you fail to pay. You want a policy that includes a *cost of living/inflation index* to help your benefits keep pace with rising costs. You want a policy that will pay *benefits if you cannot return to your previous job or line of work*. Watch out for plans that will pay only if you can't work at *any* job. That's virtually a waste of money. You might opt for (it's cheaper) a *residual benefit* option, which pays a partial amount if you can't earn as much as you did before you became disabled.

You want your policy:

1. To pay you if you cannot do the work that you were doing when you incurred the disability.
2. To pay you *if you go back to work and it happens again.*
3. To pay you *for as long as you are disabled,* generally until you reach age 65.
4. To waive the premium (meaning you don't have to pay) once you start collecting benefits.

To keep the costs down (because disability insurance can be very expensive), agree to an "elimination period" of 30 to 90 days or longer. That means your benefits don't start immediately upon your becoming disabled, but after a certain period of time. This acts as a "deductible." But you'd better have some assets behind you that you can tap while you are waiting for your disability policy to pay. Check the benefits package at your company and your personal savings.

If your employer has provided disability insurance to you, the benefits are taxable. If you have paid for the insurance yourself, they are not. For more info, call the Health Insurance Association of America, at 202-223-7780, and ask for *The Consumer's Guide to Disability Insurance.*

Remember, life insurance is not an investment, it's protection for your family. That being the case, your primary concerns are that you get a good deal, sufficient coverage, and an insurer you can count on to take care of your loved ones after you're gone.

CHAPTER NINE

Feathering Your Nest (Egg) for a Comfortable Retirement

How to Figure Out How Much You'll Need and How to Plan to Make Sure You Get It

As with so many things involving your money, the best way to make sure you and your family enjoy a comfortable and secure retirement is to take charge of your financial future. You can't count on Social Security and a company pension to provide the income you need and desire. The sad fact is that you may not have all the alternatives available in the way of retirement income that your parents have had. And the only way to ensure that your retirement is indeed a golden award for a lifetime of work is to plan carefully, starting today!

We talk to a lot of people who feel as if they've started their retirement planning too late and can't possibly catch up. We also talk to many folks who think retirement is so far in their future, it's just not worth worrying about now. Wrong on both counts! It's never too early—or too late—to plan for retirement. No matter what your age or financial situation, you can (and should) be building your retirement nest egg.

The first question you must ask yourself is, "How much will I need to retire?" To develop a sound and successful retirement savings plan, you must have a goal. You have to establish how much you're going to need to retire in style before you think about how to get there from here.

FIGURING OUT HOW MUCH YOU'LL NEED

Most experts agree that you need 75 percent or 80 percent of your pre-retirement income to maintain the same standard of living you had before retiring. Why do you need less than 100 percent? Your expenses and taxes will probably go down in retirement. You'll have less dry cleaning, you won't commute to work, your tax bracket most likely will be lower, you'll be paying less insurance, the kids will have finished college, often the mortgage will be paid.

At the same time, however, inflation will almost certainly reduce the value of a dollar between now and when you retire, meaning that a $50,000 income 10 or 15 years from now will not buy as much as a $50,000 income today. Take a look at the erosive power of inflation. The chart on page 216 will help you determine what income you will need, depending on the number of years until your retirement and the inflation rate during those years.

Here's how to use the chart. Assume you are planning to retire in 5 years and the annual rate of inflation during those years is 6 percent. Your annual income today is $50,000. What will you need 5 years from now to match that amount at a 6 percent annual inflation rate? Take $50,000 and multiply it by the appropriate inflation multiplier from the chart: $50,000 x 1.34 = $67,000. Now multiply this amount by 75 percent (remember, your expenses will be a bit lower in retirement) and you get $50,250.

Now that you have an idea of how much annual income you'll need in retirement, you must multiply that amount by the number of years you expect to be retired. Men are now living to an average age of 72, and women are living to age 77. And the further you are from retirement, the more likely it is that you'll exceed these averages. We like to use 20 years as a rule of thumb in planning. And, of course, if you plan to retire before 65, you'll need even more.

Using the annual income in the above example times 20 years, you get $1,005,000. This is the retirement nest egg you'll need! As shocking as that number may be, we have two pieces of good news. First, your money will continue to grow in retirement. So a nest egg at retirement of approximately $500,000, if it grows at 10 percent per year, will give you enough income, without even factoring in what Social Security and a pension might also pay you. Second, the money you save now will grow faster than you can possibly imagine when you put the power of com-

Inflation Multiplier Chart

Years in future	Average Inflation Rate						
	2%	4%	6%	8%	10%	12%	14%
1	1.02	1.04	1.06	1.08	1.10	1.12	1.14
2	1.04	1.08	1.12	1.17	1.21	1.25	1.30
3	1.06	1.12	1.19	1.26	1.33	1.40	1.48
4	1.08	1.17	1.26	1.36	1.46	1.57	1.69
5	1.10	1.22	1.34	1.47	1.61	1.76	1.93
6	1.12	1.27	1.42	1.59	1.77	1.97	2.19
7	1.14	1.32	1.50	1.71	1.95	2.21	2.50
8	1.16	1.37	1.59	1.85	2.14	2.48	2.85
9	1.18	1.42	1.69	2.00	2.36	2.77	3.25
10	1.20	1.48	1.79	2.16	2.59	3.11	3.71
11	1.22	1.54	1.90	2.33	2.85	3.48	4.23
12	1.24	1.60	2.01	2.52	3.14	3.90	4.82
13	1.27	1.67	2.13	2.72	3.45	4.36	5.49
14	1.30	1.73	2.26	2.94	3.80	4.89	6.26
15	1.33	1.80	2.40	3.17	4.18	5.47	7.14
16	1.36	1.87	2.54	3.43	4.59	6.13	8.14
17	1.39	1.95	2.69	3.70	5.05	6.87	9.28
18	1.42	2.03	2.85	4.00	5.56	7.69	10.58
19	1.45	2.11	3.03	4.31	6.11	8.61	12.06
20	1.48	2.19	3.21	4.66	6.73	9.65	13.74
21	1.51	2.28	3.40	5.03	7.40	10.80	15.67
22	1.54	2.37	3.60	5.44	8.14	12.10	17.86
23	1.57	2.46	3.82	5.87	8.95	13.55	20.36
24	1.60	2.56	4.05	6.34	9.85	15.18	23.21
25	1.63	2.67	4.29	6.85	10.83	17.00	26.46
26	1.66	2.77	4.55	7.40	11.92	19.04	30.17
27	1.69	2.88	4.82	7.99	13.11	21.32	34.39
28	1.72	3.00	5.11	8.63	14.42	23.88	39.20
29	1.75	3.12	5.42	9.32	15.86	26.75	44.69
30	1.79	3.24	5.74	10.06	17.45	29.96	50.95

(from *Smart Money Family Financial Planner*, Berkley Publishing)

pound interest on your side (see Chapter Five, page 120). Don't forget, risk-averse investors will have to use less than 10 percent per year as a calculation. The safer you keep your money, the lower the return.

PUTTING THE POWER OF COMPOUND INTEREST TO WORK FOR YOU

We're talking here about taking advantage of tax-deferred growth in a retirement plan like your IRA, or a pension plan, 403(b), or 401(k) plan at work. Taxes on the profits made from investments in these plans are deferred. The great part is not only deferring taxes (we all love to do that!), but also the fact that you make profits *on your profits*.

This difference between investing taxable and tax deferred really adds up over time. Say you're earning just 8 percent on your money. If you placed $2,000 in a taxable account, you'd have $27,568 at the end of 10 years, but you'd have $31,042 in a tax deferred account. In 15 years, the difference would be $48,343 taxable vs. $58,283 tax deferred—and by 30 years, the difference would be $160,326 vs. $243,532!

Let's take a look at just how quickly your money can grow. As we said, the earlier you start, the better. For example, if you placed $2,000 a year in your IRA for just five years, from age 14 through age 18, and then never put in another dime, you could retire at age 65 with a cool $1.184 million (assuming an average 10 percent return). Start at age 26, and contribute $2,000 a year until you retire, and you'll have a tidy $973,704. Even if you start at age 40, you'll still have $216,364 at age 65.

DON'T COUNT ON SOCIAL SECURITY TO PROVIDE A SECURE RETIREMENT

Statistics show that approximately 40 percent of the incomes of most retirees will come from company-sponsored pension plans and Social Security. Frankly, we're concerned that the percentage may be even lower if the Social Security program continues on its present course. The U.S. government has borrowed money from the Social Security Trust Fund, and that money may or may not be paid back. Furthermore, there just aren't enough people working now to support the generations yet to retire. By the year 2010, there will be more Americans over age 65 than ever in history, and the trend isn't stopping anytime soon.

The problem is that when Social Security was enacted in 1937, the average person had a life expectancy of 55 and the retirement age was set at 65, 10 years higher than life expectancy. Very few people ever collected. But now life expectancy is 10 years higher than retirement age and getting higher every year! In just your first three years of receiving Social Security benefits, you're probably going to take out everything you put in, plus interest. That's all it takes. The average person has withdrawn everything he or she has contributed in the first three years.

We can't predict whether or not Social Security will be around when you retire, although entire books have been written on both sides of the argument. Our point is simply that the more you can count on yourself and the less you have to rely on Social Security, the more secure your family's financial future will be. Social Security was never meant to be enough in and of itself for anyone's happy retirement.

WHAT WILL YOU GET FROM SOCIAL SECURITY?

If you're retiring within the next 20 years, you'll probably be able to count on collecting the Social Security money promised you. How much is that? It's easy to find out. Contact the Social Security Administration, at 800-772-1213, and ask for a Personal Earnings and Benefits Estimate Statement (PEBES). It takes about five minutes to fill out and return. In about three weeks you will receive an estimate of your benefits based on your anticipated retirement age, your past payments, and your projected payments until the time of your retirement.

> DOLANS' SMART MONEY TIP: We recommend you fill out the PEBES form every couple of years and mail it in, just to be sure you've been accurately credited for your Social Security payments. You have a little over three years (39 months) to correct a mistake if you find one. It pays to check up on your money!

> DOLANS' SAFETY WARNING: You'll reduce your Social Security benefits if you continue to work while receiving benefits. In 1993, if you are between the ages of 62 and 65 and earn more than $7,680, your benefits will be reduced by $1 for each $2 over the thresh-

old; if you're 65 to 70, your benefits will be lower ($1 for each $3 over the income threshold) if you earn more than $10,560. For the time being, if you're over 70, you can earn an unlimited amount without jeopardizing your Social Security benefits. But watch out for a revenue-hungry Congress. It could tax up to 85 percent of your Social Security benefits if your total income exceeds certain limits. We expect the IRS to go after even more retirees' income in the future. Call the IRS, at 800-829-FORM, and ask for publication #915, *Social Security Benefits and Equivalent Railroad Retirement Benefits.*

HOW MUCH WILL YOUR PENSION PAY?

How do you calculate a pension payout? If you are on a defined benefit plan, your company can tell you exactly how much you're going to get at retirement. If you're participating in a defined contribution plan (where you contribute a set amount each month), such as a 401(k), you should be able to get some idea of your future nest egg by asking the plan administrator for an estimate, based on the plan's track record and your level of contributions.

Once you've found out how much you can expect from Social Security and your pension, and compare that to the nest egg you know you need, you'll really be ready to roll up your sleeves and build a financial fortress.

SMART MONEY STRATEGIES FOR BUILDING YOUR NEST EGG

If Social Security and your pension won't keep you in champagne and caviar, what should you do? Start your own retirement nest egg! Everyone (yes, that means you!) should have an IRA (Individual Retirement Account); a company-sponsored profit-sharing plan or a tax-deferred plan—like a 401(k) or 403(b)—if you qualify; or, if you're self-employed, an SEP or Keogh. If your employer doesn't offer a plan, you can set up an IRA and salt away up to $2,000 per year, tax deferred. That means you don't pay current income taxes on that $2,000 and you don't pay taxes on the profits within the IRA until you start withdrawing your money. If you earn less than $25,000 annually ($40,000 for couples filing jointly), you can also deduct your IRA contribution, regardless of what plan your employer offers.

A company plan, like a 401(k), generally lets you save more than $2,000 pretax dollars per year. For 1993, the maximum contribution to a 401(k) is $8,994. If you're self-employed, you may be able to shelter as much as $30,000 per year in an SEP or Keogh.

After you've taken advantage of these opportunities and you want to put away even more for your retirement (God bless you!), consider an annuity. You can invest virtually an unlimited amount in an annuity and your account grows tax deferred until you start withdrawals, just as with an IRA. You can choose a fixed or guaranteed annuity (like a CD), where you lock in a rate of return, or a variable annuity (like a family of mutual funds), where you decide how to invest the money. In a variable annuity, your return is not guaranteed (but could end up to be more money than the fixed). Take a look at Chapter Eight for more on annuities.

How much will you need to achieve your goal of financial security? Again, you have to do a little math. There are two variables in this calculation: how much you'll be able to save and how fast it will grow. Only you can decide how much you can afford to set aside each year. Then just take your estimated annual growth rate and divide by our handy-dandy Rule of 72 (see page 83). For example, if you think your retirement portfolio will earn 8 percent per year, divide 8 into 72 and you will find that your retirement savings will double in value every 9 years.

We suggest planning on a growth rate of between 8 and 10 percent per year, depending on your willingness and ability to take risks. But please don't say, "Well, I should be able to do 20 percent a year." It's just not realistic. Especially if you've been a conservative investor all your life. Treasury bills have paid an average 7.75 percent per year for the past 20 years. Even five-year CDs have paid only about 8 percent per year. So don't base your family's financial future on outlandish projections that are totally out of step with your investing profile, and that turn out to be nothing more than wishful thinking.

THE MOST IMPORTANT MISTAKE OF RETIREMENT PLANNING

This brings us to what may be the single most important mistake of all in retirement planning, the one mistake you must avoid to build a secure nest egg: being too conservative with your retirement money.

We all tend to invest in guaranteed securities, like CDs, fixed annuities, bonds. But these investments simply will not grow fast enough to provide a comfortable retirement. When offered a choice in a 401(k) plan, 60 percent of us put our retirement money into guaranteed contracts or fixed interest rates, like a bank CD, guaranteed by the insurance company. You're never going to have enough money for retirement if you do that. In fact, most folks invest totally backward. We put our safest investments in our retirement accounts and our most aggressive investments in our taxable accounts. Not only does this mean your retirement account is not growing fast enough, but it also usually winds up costing you a lot more in taxes.

How so? Because aggressive investments, things like small capitalization stocks and growth mutual funds, tend to be bought and sold more frequently. The more you buy and sell, the more chances the IRS has to tax you.

DOLANS' SMART MONEY TIP: The smart place to trade actively (and wisely), if you can afford the risk, is in your retirement account, where no current taxes are due as a result of trading. Buy solid growth stocks and stock funds in your retirement plan. As the economic or stock market picture changes, you can shift into the best stock sectors without hesitation.

You should diversify in three or four solid growth funds with good long-term track records. Historically stocks return an average of 10 percent per year. Or, if you have sufficient assets, buy at least five or six individual stocks. Pick companies that range over broad-based industry sectors. Look for companies that have had both earnings and dividend growth and consistent payments of dividends. This usually indicates a well-run, profitable company; while you're waiting for the capital appreciation, you should be getting the reward of dividends. The kinds of companies you want to look at are good growth companies, including the utility sector.

DOLANS' SMART MONEY TIP: As you get closer to retirement, you'll want to shift some of your money into more conservative investments (such as bonds). Although it's difficult to generalize because each person's needs and objectives necessitate fine tuning, the best way we've found to figure out how much money to put into bonds is simply to use your age! If you are 25, put 25

percent in bonds and 75 percent in stocks. If you are 45, put 45
percent in bonds and 55 percent in stocks. If you are 65, put 65
percent in bonds and 35 percent in stocks. You see, even in
retirement you need growth (more on this a bit later).

IRA INVESTING FOR SCAREDY-CATS

If you are so totally risk-averse you can't bear the thought of putting your
nest egg in stocks, then put the initial amount —$2,000 if it's an IRA, up
to $8,994 if it's a 401(k) plan—into bonds or CDs, and when the interest
is paid, put those dollars into stocks or stock mutual funds. Over the long
term, we think you'll like what happens to the money invested in stocks,
and you'll find it a little easier to get over your fear.

DON'T LET UNCLE SAM GRAB YOUR RETIREMENT SAVINGS!

As you save for your retirement, there are a few logistical hurdles you
may face along the way. Know the rules and the smart money techniques
for keeping your money safe, and you should be able to leap over these
hurdles with ease.

First of all, whenever you switch from one plan to another—say from
an IRA with a bank to an IRA with a mutual fund, or from a 401(k) at
one company to a 401(k) at another company—you must comply with the
"60-day rollover rule." This states that money taken out of a tax-deferred
retirement account must be deposited (in full) into another tax-deferred
retirement account within 60 days to avoid penalties and taxes by the IRS.
If you do not roll over the money within 60 days, the IRS will charge you
income taxes on the amount you didn't roll over. If you're under the age
of 59½, not only will the IRS tax you, it will also hit you with a 10
percent tax. Unfortunately, only 13 percent of people who have received
a distribution roll it over into a new plan. Eighty-seven percent never do.
They keep it and they get nailed.

DOLANS' SMART MONEY TIP: If you really need to get at the money in
your 401(k) retirement plan (for college tuition bills for your kids,
for example), borrow from your company plan, if your employer

allows you to do this. There are no applications, credit approvals, or fees, and you pay yourself the interest. You also avoid the taxes and penalties you'd get hit with if you withdrew the money instead. The IRS generally requires that you pay back the loan within five years.

Another hurdle: If you've been saving for retirement in a company plan, what happens to your money when you leave that job? If it's a profit-sharing plan, you may not be eligible to receive all the money in your account until you are fully "vested." Under current law, you must be entitled to all the money after no more than seven years with the company; in some firms, five years is all it takes. And, of course, if you've been putting away a portion of your own income, such as in a 401(k) or 403(b), all the money and profits you've made in these plans are yours, subject to the rollover rules we just mentioned.

We believe that when you leave a job, generally you should take your retirement money with you. Most plans will allow you to do this. Find out by looking at the summary plan description (ask the plan administrator for a copy). Provided you are allowed to take the money out of the plan, you should always arrange for a "custodian-to-custodian transfer." *This is very important.* You don't want the company to send you a check personally, no matter where you plan to put it. Because, if it does, the IRS will get 20 percent of it before you see a dime.

Under a law that went into effect January 1, 1993, employers must withhold 20 percent of a qualified distribution to an employee if the employee takes direct receipt of the funds. They must withhold this 20 percent even if you do roll your money over into an IRA or new 401(k). You could save yourself taxes and a possible penalty by adding back the 20 percent from other savings at the time of the rollover, but not everyone can afford to do that. Plus, why would you want to leave 20 percent of your distribution sitting at the IRS earning nothing until you file your taxes and wait for the refund? Don't touch the distribution. Set up your new IRA or 401(k) and tell the company where to send the money directly to the new custodian.

Worse yet, remember the 60-day rollover rule? You have only 60 days to roll over the *full* amount (including the 20 percent deducted by the IRS) into another tax-deferred plan to avoid taxes and penalties. Tough, huh? So the bottom line is: You want to do a custodian-to-custodian transfer, where all the money goes from the old plan to the new plan and you never touch it yourself. The new plan can be an IRA or the 401(k) at your new job, as long as it is a *qualified* retirement plan.

Since most employers do not allow you as a new employee to partic-ipate in a plan until you've been on the job for a year, and many others have no retirement plan at all (and that's assuming you have a new job!), you will very likely have to put your rollover money into an IRA with a bank, broker, or mutual fund. Our first choice is a no-load mutual fund company, which gives you a wide range of investment options, easy switching (remember, there are no tax consequences for switching, so don't hold back!), the safety of diversification, low fees, and professional money management.

But no matter whom you choose as your new custodian, make sure you keep this rollover money in a *separate* IRA account—a "conduit" IRA. Even if you already have an IRA, keep this new money separate. If you don't, when you have an opportunity in the future to move into a 401(k) plan, you will not be able to specifically identify this rollover money and your new employer will not accept it.

"What are you talking about, Dolans? I know how much I've rolled over. I can find it when it's time to take it out!" Not so fast. The IRS won't let you mix 401(k) money with IRA money and then separate it out again. Once it's mixed, it's all IRA money. The reason: While an IRA cannot be withdrawn in a lump sum and then "income averaged" (we'll talk about that in a moment), 401(k) money can be income averaged, subject to restrictions. The two must be kept separate. Even if there is no 401(k) at your new job, you should still leave the money in a separate, conduit IRA. Statistics say you'll hold 11 jobs in your life, and you're very likely going to hit another 401(k) plan eventually.

HOW SAFE IS YOUR PENSION?

Once you've saved up all this money for retirement, you sure as heck want it to be there when you finally retire! A real retirement nightmare befell employees of Pan Am (and dozens of other bankrupt companies) who saw their lifetime of savings disappear when the company went under. What about government guarantees? The Pension Benefits Guar-antee Corporation (PBGC) does insure some pension money (just as the FDIC insures some bank accounts), but this safety net is full of holes. Theoretically, if the company can't meet its obligations, the PBGC will provide benefits (subject to limitations). But as more and more companies go down, this coverage will be harder and harder to maintain. Even now, $40 billion of benefits in corporate pension plans is underfunded by their sponsors, which means the PBGC would have to come up with this money if those companies were to go out of business. In fact, PBGC is running into financial problems of its own. PBGC, which insures the pensions of some 40 million Americans, is currently running a $2.5 billion deficit. By 1998, that deficit could be as high as $18 billion. For more information,

- Contact the Pension Benefits Guarantee Corporation, 2020 K Street, N.W., Washington, DC 20006. Ask for a copy of *Your Guaranteed Pension;* it's free.
- For $1.00 you can also get a copy of *Your Pension: Things You Should Know about Your Pension Plan* (Document #068-000-0000-2-5), from the Superintendent of Documents, U.S. Government Printing Office, Washington, DC 20402-9325.
- The U.S. Department of Labor's Pension and Welfare Benefits Administration offers a free booklet called *What You Should Know about Pension Law*. Write to Room N-5511, 200 Constitution Avenue, N.W., Washington, DC 20210.
- The International Foundation of Employee Benefit Plans, at 414-786-6700, offers a booklet called *Your Pension and Your Spouse— The Joint and Survivor Dilemma,* for $10.95.

And if you suspect foul play, financial trouble, or mismanagement with your pension plan, contact the Pension Rights Center, a nonprofit organization dedicated to helping workers and retirees protect their pensions. Write to them at 918 16th Street, N.W., Suite 704, Washington, DC 20006.

It pays to keep tabs on your pension fund, and to try to make sure the folks running it are doing a good, honest job. Federal law requires pension funds to treat all participants fairly and equally, to keep costs reasonable, and to invest responsibly and carefully.

Is your company's pension following the rules, or breaking them and jeopardizing your retirement security? Check it out. Every year (if your plan covers 100 people or more) or every three years (if it covers fewer than 100 people), you will receive a summary annual report. This document will give you a snapshot view of the plan, tell you how much money the plan made (or lost) in the past year, and shows whether or not money borrowed from the fund has been paid back on time.

DOLANS' SMART MONEY TIP: To find out what's really going on with your pension, request a copy of Form 5500 (5500 C/R for plans with fewer than 100 participants). This detailed, six-page financial statement will show you exactly where the plan's money (your money!) is invested. It will also tell you whether or not there is enough money to pay the benefits promised by the plan. To get a copy of Form 5500 (or 5500 C/R), request it in writing from your plan administrator.

The Pension Rights Center has a great little handbook to help you give your pension a checkup. *Protecting Your Pension Money* is available by sending $8.00 to Pension Publications, Suite 704, 918 16th Street, N.W., Washington, DC 20006. If you are unable to get this documentation or you suspect foul play in your company's plan, contact your state's Department of Labor.

COUNTDOWN TO RETIREMENT

As you approach retirement, you'll be faced with several key decisions, and making the right choices is crucial to your family's future. But don't worry. We'll help you get through this confusing period with confidence and ease.

First of all, you'll have to decide when to retire. Technically, that refers to when you start receiving income from your retirement plans and Social Security. You can retire (i.e., stop working) whenever you want to (as long as you can afford it) and your plan will begin paying benefits. But once you start receiving income from Social Security, your pension, your annuity, your IRA, or any other tax-deferred retirement plan, you trigger a series of chain reactions that can't be reversed.

Have we got your attention?

The first milestone (and decision point) is age 59½. Before that age, you cannot withdraw money from a retirement plan without incurring a penalty from the IRS (there is an exception to this rule, known as annuitization, that we'll talk about in a moment). The next age milestone is 62. At this point, you may start receiving Social Security benefits. *But we believe most people should wait until they reach age 65.* If you start getting Social Security benefits at age 62, you permanently forfeit 20 percent of your Social Security retirement benefits. If the life expectancy numbers continue to rise, your loss could be substantial. Age 65 signals traditional retirement age. Now you qualify for full Social Security benefits as well as Medicare (the government health insurance plan).

DOLANS' SMART MONEY TIP: You won't get your Social Security benefits automatically. You have to file an application form. Call 800-772-1213 for a copy of Form SSA-7004. We also suggest you have your Social Security checks automatically deposited directly into your bank account. That way you won't have to worry about checks getting lost in the mail.

As for your personal retirement plans, including pensions, IRAs, Keoghs, etc., we recommend you let your money continue to grow tax deferred for as long as possible. Don't start taking money out until you need it. The only limitation is that you *must* start withdrawing money from retirement plans by April of the year after you turn 70½.

DOLANS' SMART MONEY TIP: Withdraw the money from your taxable accounts first! Maximize the tax shelter for as long as possible!

Now that you've solved the question of when to start taking money out of your retirement plans, let's talk about how to take the money out. When you retire from a company, your 401(k), 403(b), or profit-sharing plan money may be distributed to you in a lump sum. Remember we talked earlier about lump-sum rollovers and conduit IRAs? The same advice applies here. If you decide to roll the money over into an IRA, don't touch the money yourself or the IRS will withhold 20 percent. Ask your employer to roll the money over into a conduit IRA that you've already set up with your bank or mutual fund company.

But before you decide to take your lump sum and roll it over into an IRA account, remember one very important point: A 401(k) may be "income averaged" (subject to certain restrictions) for tax purposes and an IRA may not.

Maybe you do want the entire lump sum at once. Perhaps you have a lump sum coming to you that's only a small portion of your nest egg. Or maybe you want to use the money to buy the home of your retirement dreams. If you do take a single lump sum payment, here's how 5- or

10-year income averaging works to help you reduce income taxes. If you were born in 1936 or before, you can elect 10-year income averaging, which allows you to pay the tax calculated as if you received the money in equal payments over a 10-year period. Five-year income averaging lets you make the same type of calculation/payment as if the lump sum was paid out over a five-year period. In other words, if you choose five-year averaging on a $100,000 lump sum, $20,000 would be added to your income during each of five years instead of the full $100,000 in one fell swoop. You still pay all taxes due in the year you receive the lump sum, but your rate will theoretically be lower, since you've spread the income over five or ten years.

So before you decide to roll over a lump sum, sit down and talk with your accountant. If you don't have an accountant, this would be a good time to ask friends and co-workers for a referral. Let a professional calculate which decision will cost less in taxes, because once you roll that money over into an IRA, the income averaging option is lost forever.

> **DOLANS' SAFETY WARNING:** Watch out for taking too much out of your retirement plans (we should be so lucky, right?). Seriously, the IRS will sting you with a 15 percent excise tax on any distributions you get from retirement plans in excess of $150,000. That applies to income from all plans combined!

CONTINUING TO GROW IN RETIREMENT

Even in retirement you're going to have to generate growth in your portfolio, because inflation is going to continue eating away at your purchasing power even after you retire. The clock doesn't stop. So no matter where you have your retirement nest egg parked, make sure you continue to invest it wisely. Our "age = bonds" rule still applies. At age 65, keep 65 percent in bonds and/or CDs and 35 percent in stocks or stock mutual funds. At age 75, you want 75 percent in bonds; at age 80, you want 80 percent in bonds.

EARLY RETIREMENT WITHOUT PENALTIES

Need to get at your IRA before you turn 59½? There is a way. The IRS allows you to withdraw money without penalty before you hit 59½ if you "annuitize" your withdrawals. That means you divide the total value of your IRA by the number of years you expect to live (we all want to live forever, but the IRS has a life expectancy table you must use in this case). Thus you'll be taking your money out steadily during your lifetime without penalty. Of course, the younger you start, the smaller your annual withdrawals will be.

DOLANS' SMART MONEY TIP: To beef up those withdrawals, the IRS will allow you to factor the future growh of your IRA into the equation. Instead of dividing your current account value by your life expectancy, you can divide the current amount plus reasonable earnings (say, 6 to 8 percent per year). The result: a bigger check each month. Even better, you have to stick with these annual withdrawal levels for only five years and until you reach age 59½. After five years or more, as long as you are 59½, you can withdraw as much as you want!

MANDATORY WITHDRAWALS AT AGE 70½

Many of our viewers and listeners are confused as to how much they *must* withdraw each year from their IRAs beginning April of the year following the year they turn 70½. Well, it is confusing. For more information, order IRS Publication 590, *Individual Retirement Arrangements,* by calling 800-829-FORM. But here's a chart showing *minimum* IRA distributions.

For example, if you are 70 and your spouse is 67, your joint life expectancy is 22 years. Hence, 1/22 of all IRA account totals must be withdrawn that year. The figure is recalculated each year, and you can, of course, also withdraw any amount above that minimum.

PENSION BENEFITS FOR ONE SPOUSE OR TWO?

One strategy for increasing retirement income we've heard a lot about lately is called "pension max life." It sounds fancy, but basically it involves taking maximum benefits from your pension and using some of that money to buy life insurance for your spouse as beneficiary. In order to receive maximum benefits, you agree that they will be paid only for as

IRA Minimum Distributions

If you are ↓	and your beneficiary is									
	65	66	67	68	69	70	71	72	73	74
	your joint life expectancy is									
70	23.1	22.5	22.0	21.5	21.1	20.6	20.2	19.8	19.4	19.1
71	22.8	22.2	21.7	21.2	20.7	20.2	19.8	19.4	19.0	18.6
72	22.5	21.9	21.3	20.8	20.3	19.8	19.4	18.9	18.5	18.2
73	22.2	21.6	21.0	20.5	20.0	19.4	19.0	18.5	18.1	17.7
74	22.0	21.4	20.8	20.2	19.6	19.1	18.6	18.2	17.7	17.3
75	21.8	21.1	20.5	19.9	19.3	18.8	18.3	17.8	17.3	16.9
76	21.6	20.9	20.3	19.7	19.1	18.5	18.0	17.5	17.0	16.5
77	21.4	20.7	20.1	19.4	18.8	18.3	17.7	17.2	16.7	16.2
78	21.2	20.5	19.9	19.2	18.6	18.0	17.5	16.9	16.4	15.9
79	21.1	20.4	19.7	19.0	18.4	17.8	17.2	16.7	16.1	15.6
80	21.0	20.2	19.5	18.9	18.2	17.6	17.0	16.4	15.9	15.4

long as you are alive. Once you're gone, the benefits stop and your spouse receives nothing more. The idea is that you receive a larger check each month while you're living and your spouse receives the insurance death benefit when you die.

Sounds clever, but we think it's a pretty poor idea, for several reasons. First of all, buying life insurance when you're over 60 is extremely expensive. The premiums will probably cost you just as much as the extra pension income you're receiving. You get more from your pension, and then turn right around and pay it to the insurance company. Another pitfall: It may take a lot longer to pay off the premiums than the insurance agent would like to admit. These plans are often sold with the promise that the premiums will pay themselves (out of the interest generated by the money in your plan) after the first seven years. Guess what? Seven years come and go, and you're still paying because the insurance company's estimates were, shall we say, optimistic. Another problem with this strategy is that you'll owe taxes on the extra pension money you receive, and you'll have to pay your premiums with after-tax dollars.

Do you need life insurance when you retire? Generally speaking, you don't. It goes back to the question of dependents. If nobody is dependent on you other than your spouse, and you own everything free and clear by the time you've reached retirement, then why spend any money on life insurance? It just doesn't make sense for most retirees. We say take the lower pension benefit and guarantee that your spouse is going to continue getting it when you're gone.

LIFE INSURANCE, NO. LONG-TERM-CARE INSURANCE, MAYBE

Although life insurance is not a necessary expense in retirement for most families, the fear of the costs brought on by a catastrophic illness and a nursing home stay frighten both retirees and their children. The insurance industry realized that nursing home costs can quickly bankrupt a family, so they set out to insure against this with long-term-care policies. In fact, on average, when one spouse is admitted to a nursing home, the couple's entire life savings are wiped out in about 13 weeks. Since statistically you have a one in four chance of spending time in a nursing home at age 65, and a one in two chance by the age of 85, a proper retirement plan must at least consider long-term-care insurance.

Although the earliest insurance policies issued for long-term care weren't worth the paper they were printed on, the new policies are getting better. Read the fine print on these policies before you sign on the dotted line. A good policy must have:

- An inflation rider. A guarantee of $100 a day may sound good today, but might only pay for aspirin in 10 years.
- Immediate payout to you without the need to be hospitalized first. Most nursing home patients come directly from home, not a hospital.
- Coverage for Alzheimer's disease without a diagnosis of the disease. Only a biopsy or autopsy can confirm a diagnosis of Alzheimer's.
- The willingness to pay for skilled, intermediate, and custodial care

in any type of facility. If they limit the payout to skilled-nursing care you may not be covered.

States are becoming tougher on families trying to shift assets to children in order to qualify for Medicaid to handle nursing home costs. For this reason we feel long-term-care insurance may make sense for more families. But there are pitfalls in the policies. So call your state division of insurance to find out whether your state has provided laws or regulations for your protection. Also ask for the names of companies that have been approved to sell long-term-care policies within your state.

Before buying a long-term-care policy, educate yourself. Two very thorough articles have been written by *Consumer Reports* magazine to help you. To order reprints of the May 1988, October 1989, and June 1991 articles ($4.00 per issue) write to: Consumer Reports, Back Issue Department, P.O. Box 53016, Boulder, CO 80322-3016.

TAPPING THE EQUITY IN YOUR HOME

Another strategy for boosting your retirement income is called a "reverse equity mortgage," which allows you to tap into the equity in your home without having to sell it and move out. Here's how it works. You and the bank switch traditional roles. The bank sends you monthly payments and gradually owns more and more of your house. You get current income while still living in your house.

But bear in mind one important fact of any loan: interest. Even a reverse mortgage has interest due. So when you or your heirs sell your house, the bank gets back not only the money it paid you, but also accrued interest. Furthermore, the size of your monthly check from the bank depends on your age, as well as the value of your house. That's because this loan works like an annuity. You keep getting checks for as long as you live, even if the amount of money you ultimately receive exceeds the value of your home (we're talking here about open-end reverse mortgages).

DOLANS' SAFETY WARNING: Don't, under any circumstances, take a reverse mortgage that could force you to sell your home after a fixed period, say 10 years. This defeats the whole purpose of the reverse mortgage!

Basically, the longer you live, the better this deal is for you. If you do "outlive your equity," the bank owns the house upon your death, but your heirs do not owe more. So what's the catch? First, you have to be very careful with the lender. If you deal with an outfit other than an FHA-insured reverse mortgage lender, they could easily low-ball the appraisal on the house so they don't have to pay you as much in your lifetime. Second, the fees on these reverse mortgages are extremely high. Closing costs and associated fees on a $100,000 home can easily top $4,500, plus $30 per month in service fees, plus insurance. And, of course, you're racking up interest charges on your reverse mortgage every year.

Take a look at these numbers. With a typical reverse mortgage, a $100,000 home would pay a 75-year-old home owner about $360 a month. After 10 years, you'd have received about $43,500, but with the interest on the loan you would owe more than $85,000! And after 17 years, the bank would "own" your home completely, even though you'd only received less than $74,000. Meanwhile, that $100,000 home would probably be worth close to $200,000 after those 17 years, assuming just conservative appreciation of 4 percent per year. It's true that if you outlive the equity in your home, the bank keeps paying you, but unfortunately very few people outlive the equity.

DOLANS' SMART MONEY TIP: Most times, you'll be better off selling your house. Chances are very good you'll wind up getting more money this way. And if you're house rich and cash poor, the house is still going to continue to be a drain on the income you are able to generate. Wouldn't you be better off taking the $100,000 sales proceeds, buying a $50,000 condominium, and investing the $50,000 at 5 percent for another $2,500 a year—and still have your principal intact? We know most seniors would rather stay put, but it may make more sense to sell and move. The numbers don't lie.

For more information: Our #1 choice of books available on the subject of reverse equity mortgages is *Retirement Income on the House,* by Ken Scholen. It costs $29.95 and is available by calling the National Center for Home Equity Conversion at 800-247-6553. Or call your local AARP (American Association of Retired Persons) office, if you are a member, and order a free copy of *Home Made Money.*

If you're not an AARP member, you should be. For information about AARP membership and national activities and services, write to AARP Headquarters at 601 E Street, N.W., Washington, DC 20049, or call 202-434-AARP. For information about AARP programs, chapters, and other activities in your state or community, contact the area or state office below that serves your state.

Area 1 Office (Connecticut, Massachusetts, Maine, New Hampshire, Rhode Island, Vermont)
116 Huntington Avenue
Boston, MA 02116
(617) 424-0400

Area 2 Office (Delaware, New Jersey, New York, Pennsylvania)
919 Third Avenue, 9th Floor
New York, NY 10022
(212) 758-1411

Pennsylvania State Office
225 Market Street, Suite 502
Harrisburg, PA 17101
(717) 238-2277

Area 3 Office (District of Columbia, Kentucky, Maryland, North Carolina, Virginia, West Virginia)
1600 Duke Street, 2nd Floor
Alexandria, VA 22314
(703) 739-9220

Area 4 Office (Alabama, Florida, Georgia, Mississippi, Puerto Rico, South Carolina, Tennessee, Virgin Islands)
999 Peachtree Street
Suite 1650
Atlanta, GA 30309
(404) 888-0077

Florida State Office
9600 Koger Boulevard
St. Petersburg, FL
(813) 576-1155

Area 5 Office (Illinois, Indiana, Michigan, Ohio, Wisconsin)
2720 Des Plaines
Des Plaines, IL 60018
(708) 298-2852

Area 6 Office (Iowa, Kansas, Minnesota, Missouri, North Dakota, Nebraska, South Dakota)
1901 West 47th Place
Westwood, KS 66205
(913) 831-6000

Area 7 Office (Arkansas, Louisiana, New Mexico, Oklahoma, Texas)
8144 Walnut Hill Lane
Suite 700 LB-39
Dallas, TX 75321
(214) 361-3060

Area 8 Office (Colorado,
  Montana, Utah, Wyoming)
6975 Union Park Center, # 320
Midvale, UT 84047
(801) 328-0691

Area 9 Office (Arizona,
  California, Hawaii, Nevada)
4201 Long Beach Boulevard,

#422
Long Beach, CA 90807
(310) 427-9611

Area 10 Office (Alaska, Idaho,
  Oregon, Washington)
9750 Third Avenue, N.E., #400
Seattle, WA 98115
(206) 526-7918

A SECOND CAREER IN RETIREMENT

Working in retirement can actually be a lot of fun, and many retirees do it for the stimulation and mental challenge, not (just) for the money. But no matter what motivates you to pursue a career in retirement, here are a few words to the wise.

1. Do what you know. Leverage your experience, skills, and professional contacts by working in a field you're familiar with. However, that doesn't mean you should do the same job you were doing before you retired. What's the point of retiring? But take advantage of your strong suit, whether it's gourmet cooking, decoy carving, chemistry, or carpentry.

2. Tap into the resources available to you. Two organizations that are ready and willing to help your "retirement" career: the Service Corp of Retired Executives (SCORE), at 800-368-5855 and your local AARP office.

3. Be your own boss. After years of punching the clock, give yourself a break. One of the best things about retirement is that you are the master of your own time. And you can still be the boss, even if you go back to work. Open a small shop or service business, work from your home, be a consultant, or buy an existing business in an industry you're familiar with. A good source of information on part-time income is *555 Ways to Earn Extra Money: The Ultimate Idea Book for Supplementing Your Income,* by Jay Conrad Levinson (Henry Holt & Co., $12.95).

Just remember, income earned in retirement will reduce your Social Security benefits until you reach age 70. Taxes on your paycheck and your Social Security benefits will eat up even more of your income in retirement.

ENJOYING THE FRUITS OF YOUR LABOR

As each year goes by, we have to take more and more responsibility for our own secure retirement. We hope we've shown you that this added responsibility need not be a burden. Instead it can be a wonderful opportunity to take advantage of the chance to save, tax free, and to handle the many rules and choices you'll confront wisely and confidently. When you've worked hard all your life, you deserve many comfortable, active, and financially secure golden years.

CHAPTER TEN

Finding Financial Pros You Can Trust

How to Pick a Broker or Financial Planner—and Still Control Your Own Finances

We've talked a lot so far about taking (back) control of your family's financial future. So it will probably come as no surprise when we say, "Your best financial planner is *you*." The fact is, no one knows better than you do what your family's needs are, how much risk you are comfortable with, what your total financial picture is. And certainly no one cares as much about protecting your family's financial security as you do. But that's not to say you don't need professional investment consultants to help you achieve your goals. Everyone could probably benefit from a little expert advice. Just make sure that you maintain control of your finances and that you fully understand every decision you make.

How do you get good financial advice and assistance? In most cases, one of your first choices should be a stockbroker/investment consultant with a major Wall Street firm. These firms have the research and technical analysis to help you find the investments that meet your needs, the reputation to assure you of their integrity, and the deep pockets to correct a mistake when one occurs.

DOLANS' SMART MONEY TIP: Before you ever talk to a stockbroker, chances are very good that you will already have dealt with other financial professionals, such as bankers and insurance agents. Why not buy stocks, bonds, and mutual funds from them? Simply because we believe in using specialists. Bankers specialize in bank accounts and loans, insurance agents specialize in insurance protection, and neither one specializes in investments to the degree that we believe is necessary to succeed. Nowadays if you have a heart ailment you don't go to a general practitioner, you go to a heart specialist. We believe that as life gets more and more complicated during the years ahead, specialists for financial help will become even more important.

GETTING THE MOST FROM YOUR STOCKBROKER

Whether you need a discount broker or a full service broker depends upon your level of expertise. You should use a full service stockbroker from a major Wall Street firm or a respected regional firm to help you pick individual stocks if you have no good ideas of your own. A full service broker can also help you find good bonds with the proper quality and maturity, including tax-free bonds. The larger the firm, generally the larger the inventory of bonds and the better your chances of finding what *you* need.

"Hey, Dolans," you may be saying, "What's the deal? You actually like full service brokers!" In some cases, yes. Many people do not have the time, interest, or expertise to pick stocks and bonds themselves. So why not have an expert do it for you? We know many good full service brokers who have very loyal clients to show for their efforts. On the other hand, we hear from hundreds of callers every year who feel their broker has not taken good care of them. It's simply a question of finding a good broker, and then keeping in close touch with him or her so you know what's happening with your account.

In our opinion, you really ought to avoid buying insurance from a stockbroker. First of all, we don't think you should consider insurance an "investment." And a real stock expert might not be as good in insurance. Do your insurance business with an insurance professional.

CHOOSING A STOCKBROKER

How do you find a good stockbroker? Like almost anything else, a personal referral is the best. Ask someone you trust—someone who has had success in investing, and someone who has a similar profile to you in terms of age, family, income, and investment objectives.

You also want to check the integrity and safety (you know us!) of the brokerage firm. There are two easy steps you can take. First, call Weiss Research, at 800-289-9222, and for $15.00 get a financial safety rating on any national or regional and many local brokerage firms in the country. Next, call the National Association of Security Dealers (NASD), at 800-289-9999, to see if there have been any suits or complaints against the broker and what his or her status is. You can also call the North American Securities Administration Association, at 800-942-9022, which will refer you to a state official who can tell you if there are any complaints outstanding against the individual broker. To check out penny-stock brokers, call NASD, at 800-289-9999.

Most reputable brokerage firms are members of NASD and must abide by its rules. The NASD is there to protect you. Below is a list of all NASD field offices. Call the office nearest you for information about a specific brokerage house. (Of course, when you're talking about a big brokerage firm like Merrill Lynch or Paine Webber, you know they will have had some suits and complaints filed against them. It's inevitable.)

Executive Office
National Association of Securities
  Dealers, Inc.
1735 K. Street, N.W.
Washington, DC 20006-1506
202-728-8400

London Office
NASDAQ International, Ltd.
43 London Wall
London EC2M 5TB
United Kingdom
011-44-71-374-6969

Gordon S. Macklin Building
9513 Key West Avenue
Rockville, MD 20850-3389
301-590-6500

NASDAQ Data Center
80 Merritt Boulevard
Trumbull, CT 06611
203-385-4500

District 1
One Union Square
600 University, Suite
  1911
Seattle, WA 98101-3132
206-624-0790

District 2N
425 California Street, Room
  1400
San Francisco, CA 94104
415-781-3434

District 2S
300 S. Grand Avenue, 16th Floor
Los Angeles, CA 90071
213-627-2122

District 3
1401 17th Street, Suite 700
Denver, CO 80202
303-298-7234

District 4
12 Wyandotte Plaza
120 W. 12th Street, Suite 900
Kansas City, MO 64105
816-421-5700

District 5
Energy Centre
1100 Poydras Street, Suite 850
New Orleans, LA 70163
504-522-6527

District 6
Olympia & York Tower
1999 Bryan Street, Suite 1450
Dallas, TX 75201
214-969-75201

District 7
One Securities Centre, Suite 500
3490 Piedmont Road, N.E.
Atlanta, GA 30305
404-239-6100

District 8
1680 Three First National Plaza
70 W. Madison
Chicago, IL 60602
312-899-4400

District 9
1940 E. 6th Street, 5th Floor
Cleveland, OH 44114
216-694-4545

District 10
1735 K Street, N.W.
Washington, DC 20006-1506
202-728-8400

District 11
1818 Market Street, 14th
  Floor
Philadelphia, PA 19103
215-665-1180

District 12
NASD Financial Center
33 Whitehall Street
New York, NY 10004
212-858-4000

District 13
260 Franklin Street, 20th
  Floor
Boston, MA 02110
617-439-4404

QUESTIONS TO ASK YOUR STOCKBROKER

Once you've found a broker you think you might like doing business with, you want to ask him or her a few key questions. Remember, *you* are doing the interviewing!

1. How many years have you been in the business, and what professional credentials do you have?
2. What is your approach to investing?
3. What is your investing specialty: growth stocks, utilities, corporate bonds, options and futures?
4. Can you give me the names of some of your clients whom I may call?
5. Have you ever been reprimanded, disciplined, or censured by the SEC?
6. What is your basic fee structure?

Then there are questions to ask your broker about a particular investment before you buy, such as:

1. What can I expect from this investment in terms of capital gains and income?
2. What is the time frame for this investment and how long do I have to keep my money tied up?
3. What are the downsides, the risks of this investment—and is there any scenario under which I could lose all my money? 50 percent of my money?
4. How much will *you* make on this trade?
5. What are some investment alternatives with similar risks and potential—and why is this one better for me and my family?

WHAT HAPPENS WHEN YOU PLACE AN ORDER?

When you place an order to buy stock, your broker writes up the order, and it is punched into the computer at the branch office. It goes through to the floor of the exchange where that stock is traded and where the firm has a clerk at a computer terminal. That clerk sends your order to the professional who works for your firm on the floor. He goes to the specialist who is trading that stock, places your order, executes the trade—and the entire procedure reverses itself. It goes from the floor broker, to the firm's broker at the exchange, then back to your broker as a confirmation of the executed trade. The whole process should take no more than two minutes. If you place an order over the phone, it might take five minutes. And unless you specify a price or a ''limit order'' for execution (i.e., you say "I want to buy XYZ at $10"), then you're going to pay the price at which the stock is trading at the moment your order hits the floor and is executed. It is called a "market" order.

Your order will be executed before you send money (unless you are using money already in your account with that broker). You have five business days to pay up the cost of the stock plus commission and service charge. If you buy the stock on a Tuesday, you must have remitted your check by the following Tuesday. If you don't send a check, you can be sued. If you open the newspaper and see that the stock dropped 10 points right after you purchased it, you can't call back and say, "I changed my mind." There is no changing your mind. You own it, period. All your broker can do is to sell you out of the stock immediately, then you owe the difference between what you bought it for and what the firm had to sell it for, minus a commission for both the purchase and the sale.

HOW BROKERS MAKE MONEY

It's important to understand right off the bat that a broker's best interest is not necessarily your best interest. He charges a commission when you trade (buy and sell); the higher the commission and the more often you trade, the more money he makes. You make money when you sell an investment that goes up in price or that pays you a dividend—preferably both. Knowing where a broker makes his money will help you be a more informed consumer.

Typically, brokerage firms charge the highest commissions for the most complex investments (usually a good sign that you shouldn't buy them). For instance, a Treasury bond involves a commission of 1 percent or less, whereas a blue chip stock might cost you a commission of 2 to 3 percent. By the way, we're talking here about "round lots." Round lots are orders of 100 shares, and most brokers prefer you to trade in these 100-share increments. Your commission will be much higher if you try to buy fewer than 100 shares (so-called "odd lots").

As we go up the ladder of complexity, the rates get steeper. Thinly traded stocks might run you a 3 to 4 percent commission, and limited partnerships could involve commissions of 8, 9, or even 10 percent!

Your individual broker gets about one-third of the commission; the brokerage firm gets the rest. And these days, firms are also charging more and more "nuisance fees" for things like annual account maintenance, postage and handling, inactive accounts, transfers to another firm, and so on. Forewarned is forearmed!

Another little bit of info to be aware of. Stock commissions are added on top of the stock price, while bond commissions are usually included in the bond price. It doesn't mean you don't pay a commission to buy a bond; it's just expressed differently.

DOLANS' SMART MONEY TIP: Since bond commissions are usually built into the price of the bond, it's a lot harder to comparison shop. Your best bet: Call around to four or five brokers and ask the price for the same bond—maturity, issuer, face value. That's the only way to really know what commission you're paying. The higher the bond's yield, the lower the built-in commission is.

SHOULD YOU USE A DISCOUNT BROKER?

What about discount brokers? If you use a discount broker, you can pay a commission that's 50 to 70 percent less than that of a full service broker. What you won't get, however, is any advice or guidance. That's fine, if you don't need any help.

If you simply want to execute a trade, then shop for the best commission you can find. Call and say, "I have 100 shares of this stock and I'd like to sell it. What will you charge me to do it?" Do that with three to six of the discount brokers you have identified in your area. Whoever gives you the lowest quote gets your trade that day. Don't forget, even discount brokers vary in terms of commissions. Generally speaking, the firms that offer more services charge higher commissions.

This assumes that you have the shares in your name and in your possession and that you're ready to sell them. If you've got them at a full service broker in the firm's name, then you have to sell them through that firm. Otherwise you have to wait a good 30 days to get the stock certificates issued in your name, and you may not want to wait.

What about paying no commission? Sounds good to us! More than 150 companies listed on the New York Stock Exchange offer "DRIPs"— dividend reinvestment plans. These plans allow you to automatically invest your dividends from a stock you already own in more shares of that stock at no commission. Such plans also allow you to invest cash directly through the company and buy even more shares commission free. For help finding a listing of participating companies, see Chapter Four.

HOW DO YOU CHANGE BROKERS?

Suppose you're unhappy with your current stockbroker and you want to switch. What now? Unfortunately, it can be very difficult. In fact, that's why people often wind up having accounts all over town—because they changed brokers several times but never got their old accounts moved to the new firm. This is also one reason why we believe that buying in-house proprietary products doesn't make sense. If you're with a broker at Merrill who sells you a Merrill Lynch in-house mutual fund and who then moves to Paine Webber, Paine Webber will not take those funds. So now you are either going to have to find a new broker at Merrill, have an inactive account (with a fee, naturally), or sell out of those funds, no matter what the price, before you can transfer those funds to the new firm. And that's not to mention the fact that there are very few in-house products with decent track records.

Another detail in transferring from one firm to another is your stock certificates. If the certificates are in your name, they're easy to move. If they are in the street name (the brokerage firm's name), it's not as easy. Some brokerage firms charge you to change certificates into your own name. Whenever you can, buy the stock in your own name if you think you are not going to stay with the firm. It doesn't cost any more to buy it that way. If you're a "buy and hold" investor (a long-term investor), some firms may also hit you with a fee for leaving stock in an account and not buying and selling each year. If you hold the certificates in your possession, you won't get hit with this "inactive account" fee.

If you're going to change brokers, locate the broker and the firm to which you want to transfer your account. Do that first. The new firm will contact the previous firm and set up the transfer; you'll have to fill out forms at both firms. But you've got to keep after both sides—your old broker and your new broker—especially the new brokerage if it's a busy firm and you're not going to do an immediate big trade. And certainly the firm you're trying to leave is going to do all it can to hang on to your money. Many people think they have to sell everything—liquidate—in order to move, but that's not true. As we said, you have to liquidate any in-house funds. But as far as stocks, bonds, money markets, anything of that nature, if you've got the certificates of ownership in your name and in your possession, then it is merely a matter of saying to the old firm, "Close my account and please write me a check for my cash balance."

If the certificates are in the old firm's name, a visit almost always works better than a phone call. Go in and you say to your old broker, "I'm moving to Paine Webber. I want everything transferred to this new account number." That should be all it takes. But every couple of days call and ask your new broker if the transfer has been completed. The certificates would remain in the new firm's "street name."

SECRETS YOUR BROKER WILL NEVER TELL YOU

While there are plenty of honest, helpful stockbrokers, there are a few things you just shouldn't hold your breath waiting to hear even from them. Some of our favorites:

1. If you ever suspect that you didn't get the price you should have gotten when you bought or sold a stock, ask to see *Fitch's Time and Sales*. It will show you every trade on the day you placed an order, with the time and price. If you know at what time you placed your order, you may catch your broker dead to rights with not executing it at the proper price. Moreover, he'll probably faint from shock when you ask to see *Fitch's*.

2. Brokers are never going to volunteer to most people the fact that they can give you discounts on trades. You can't do one trade every three years and expect your broker to give you a discount. But if you do a lot of business with that broker, you have every right to say, "Hey, look, can I do another 500 shares of XYZ, and why don't you give me a 25 percent (or more) discount off the commission?"

3. Your broker will probably never tell you to buy a Treasury security because the commission is so low, yet Treasuries are one of the most important elements in a sensible portfolio.

4. Your broker may not tell you about "break" points. These are discounts on mutual fund commissions for large trades. Usually the first break point is at $25,000. If you put $20,000 into the fund, you may have to pay 8½ percent commission. But if you put $25,001 into the fund, the commission may be 7 percent.

5. Your broker may not tell you if the stock is coming out of the firm's inventory. Why would you care? Well, because if it's coming out of the firm's inventory, you may be overpaying for it.

6. If you're trying to change brokers, there are certain rules that dictate how long the firm can take to make the change. The average person doesn't even know that such a rule exists.

PROTECTING YOURSELF FROM BROKER ABUSE

One of the most common questions we get is what to do when you feel your broker has done you wrong. Unfortunately, there are no guarantees on Wall Street, and losing money is one of the risks you take. But for the purposes of our discussion, broker abuse includes things like inappropriate recommendations for your age, financial situation, or goals, overtrading (or "churning"), misrepresentation, lack of full disclosure, and unauthorized trades. Remember, the statute of limitations on investment complaints is, generally speaking, six years.

The first line of defense is you. Read your brokerage statement as soon as you get it. You may catch an unauthorized trade or find something that needs clarification right on the statement. If you just throw it in a drawer, it could be months before you see what's going on. The closer the contact you keep with your broker, your account, and your investments, the further away you'll stay from broker abuse (probably). Churning, for example, almost always happens when a client gives "discretion" to a broker; i.e., you turn over the decision-making authority to buy and sell to your broker. *Don't grant discretionary powers to your financial consultant.*

DOLAN'S SMART MONEY TIP: One possible sign of churning (overtrading for excessive commissions) is when you see more and more trades in your account done over the counter (OTC). Another sign is when the total value of trades made in your account in a year equals more than four times your total assets.

The more carefully you watch your account, the less chance your broker will be inclined to take advantage of you. But if you do feel you've been the victim of abuse, take your complaint through the chain of command as follows: First, go to the broker and see if there has been a misunderstanding or whether something can be worked out. When the broker says no, go to the branch manager. After the branch manager has told you that he monitors all his brokers and there is nothing that the broker has done that was out of line, you then write the director of compliance at the main headquarters of the firm.

Every once in a while, there has been such grievous misuse of your account that the compliance department responds and says it would like to work out a deal with you. That happens about one half of 1 percent of the time. The other 99.5 percent of the time, you are going to get a letter saying that the account has been inspected thoroughly and there was absolutely nothing wrong with what the broker did. And that's when you call the National Association of Securities Dealers (NASD). If your complaint involves an amount under $10,000, it's considered a "small claims" situation. Contact the NASD in your region of the country (see pages 239–240), and it will send you a sheet with guidelines on how to proceed in an arbitration hearing. If it is over $10,000, then you need to find a lawyer who is expert in securities litigation and who will go to arbitration on your behalf.

Unfortunately, you've got to go through that chain to get to arbitration to resolve a dispute. It's very frustrating, and don't expect people along the line to side with you. If they do, you probably still should get yourself a lawyer, because if they are that quick to agree, they're going to try to settle for less than what you deserve. The bottom line: If they offer you a settlement, get a lawyer; if they don't offer you a settlement, get a lawyer. That's about the size of it. To learn more, pick up *Investor Beware*, by John Lawrence Allen (Wiley & Sons, $19.95).

SHOULD YOU USE A FINANCIAL PLANNER INSTEAD?

Another popular option for obtaining investment expertise is to work with a financial planner who may or may not work at a brokerage firm. In theory, a financial planner will take a look at your total picture, project what that picture might possibly look like in the future, and how you and your family are going to get from here to there. That makes a lot of sense. But in practice we've found it usually doesn't work that way. Too many financial planners sell totally inappropriate insurance products as "a way to become wealthy." You know we believe that insurance should be bought as protection, not an investment, so we take issue with financial planners on this point. Perhaps the problem stems from the fact that the financial planning industry was created by the insurance industry.

Also, in some cases financial planners do not have at their fingertips the type of references and research that the brokerage industry has available. Many financial planners are only product pushers. Just because somebody has taken a correspondence course doesn't necessarily mean that he or she is going to be better or more knowledgeable than a broker.

We believe you will be better off with a specialist than a jack-of-all-trades. As we said earlier, no one can be expert in all financial fields. So if you go with a financial planner, look for a team—with a tax expert, an insurance expert, an estate-planning expert, an investments expert. One planner cannot do it all. If he tells you he can, walk away. But a financial planning "team" may be just what the doctor ordered.

FINDING A FINANCIAL PLANNER YOU CAN TRUST

Another serious concern we have about the whole financial planning industry is that there aren't enough people at the SEC to police them. We read a study in *Money* magazine recently that said it would take 30 years for the current staff of the SEC to check out the 25,000 financial planners and investment advisory firms registered with the SEC. You're basically on your own.

Since there isn't a handy-dandy 800 number you can call up (as there is with brokerage firms) to see if a financial planner has been indicted or investigated, you can only go with referrals. If the planner will not give you a half dozen of his clients with whom you may speak, vote with your feet! If he will not tell you what a plan looks like before you pay him anything, walk away. Understand what a financial planner does, the fee involved, how it's calculated, and whether it's worth it.

The International Association of Financial Planners will give you a list of the planners in your area by zip code, but there's no quality control. Anybody who pays the fee can be a member of the club. So your best bet is to go with a referral. If you can't get a reliable referral, you'll have to do some comparison shopping on your own. For a place to start, you can contact:

- American Institute of Certified Public Accountants' Personal Financial Planning Division, at 800-862-4272, for a free list of planners in your state
- Institute of Certified Financial Planners, at 800-282-7526, for three planners in your area

- International Association for Financial Planning, at 800-945-4237, for five planners in your area
- National Association of Personal Financial Advisors, at 800-366-2732, for fee-only planners in your area

This last option is, in many cases, our favorite choice because the members of this association are all "fee-only" financial planners. Let us explain exactly what that means.

THREE TYPES OF FINANCIAL PLANNERS

Financial planners basically come in three varieties: fee only, fee plus commission, and commission only. We would prefer that most people use a fee-only planner because with that arrangement the planner doesn't have a vested interest in what you buy, meaning, he or she is less likely to suggest the highest-commission choices. In some cases a fee-only planner will give you no-commission product recommendations. That's the ultimate—you've gotten a look-see at your entire financial picture and you've been given no-commission ways to fund those objectives. The only problem with the fee-only arrangement is that after you pay the fee, all you have is a plan. You still have to implement it. We've found most people don't get around to doing that. The fee can be by the hour or a flat fee—typically anywhere from $75 to $200 per hour or a flat fee of $2,000 to $5,000, depending on the size of your portfolio.

Fee-plus-commission planners manage to hit you two ways. They hit you with the fee first and then they turn around and implement what they suggested and hit you with the commissions. Basically, you're paying for what a broker could do for you and then you've added a fee into it. This doesn't mean all fee-plus-commission planners are bad; it's merely a warning to be hesitant.

With commission-only planners, the more you spend on commissions, the more they make. So what do you think unscrupulous financial planners are going to recommend? After all, that's the only way they make any money! Plus, because they are "financial planners," they can talk you into disclosing everything about your financial situation and possibly capture influence over more of your assets.

It's a good sign when a financial planner makes recommendations that don't have a price tag attached, such as: "Well, you really ought to buy a few U.S. Savings Bonds.'' If he makes recommendations that come without commissions attached, then you may be dealing with somebody who can do you some good.

No matter how you pay, it's important that you feel comfortable with an individual planner.

TEN QUESTIONS TO ASK A FINANCIAL PLANNER—BEFORE YOU HAND OVER YOUR MONEY

As we said before, the best way to find a financial planner is by referral. Once you've found one you think you can work with (the chemistry feels good!), here's what you want to ask:

1. *"What kind of products do you specialize in?"* If you want to build up a stock portfolio and the planner doesn't or can't sell individual stocks, then you're not getting the benefit of that person's expertise—and you're not getting the investment help you want and need.

2. *"Where do you get your financial advice?"* This is a surprise question for most planners, which means you'll probably get an honest answer. What you want to hear is that he or she gets info from a variety of resources, including professional publications, personal contacts in the industry, and institutional research. If the planner has access only to the same financial information as you, what's the advantage of dealing with him?

3. *"How long have you been in business?"* You want a minimum of three to five years. And that means five years as a financial planner, not five years as an insurance agent and two months as a financial planner.

4. *"Are you independent, affiliated with an individual financial planning firm, or a Certified Financial Planner at a Wall Street firm?"* This will give you an idea of the resources behind the planner, and the assets you can tap if your account is mishandled. A CFP should also be a Registered Investment Adviser (with the SEC).

5. *"May I see a profit and loss statement from your company?"* You want to see if the company is solvent. This is particularly important with a small firm.

6. *"Do you or your company have any sort of malpractice insurance policy?"* With a financial planner, you have the option of suing in case of malpractice, but it won't do you any good if the company has no assets.

7. *"Will you fully disclose in advance all commissions and fees you will receive from me and the products you sell to me?"* You want to know where this planner's bread is buttered before you take his or her advice.

8. *"Have you ever had any complaints or lawsuits filed against you?"* Then check it out for yourself, by calling your state securities commission and the SEC, at 202-272-7450.

9. *"How many clients do you have and can I talk to some of them?"* This should be a number of clients that indicates experience and trust, but not so many that you'll get lost in the shuffle. Between 40 and 60 is a good range. Call three or four of them and ask what their experience has been, how they've been treated, and how (whether?) their financial situation has improved. If a planner won't give you references, walk out!

10. *"How often will we meet, and may I call you at any time to talk about my account?"* You want a regular, formal meeting to review your account, its progress and its holdings, perhaps once a quarter. You also want to be able to contact your planner easily when you have a question or concern.

Above all, make sure you understand what you're getting for your money; then determine whether it's worth the money you're being asked to spend.

DOLANS' SMART MONEY TIP: Don't do business with the first financial planner you speak to—not before talking to two or three others to compare services, style, experience, and costs. You'll be more comfortable and more confident that you've made a wise choice. It's taken you years to accumulate your assets. Isn't it worth a few hours of research to pick the planner who will help you manage them?

FIVE INVESTMENT "BAD DEALS" TO AVOID AT ANY COST

No matter from whom you are buying investments, here are five "bad deals" we urge you to avoid:

1. *Penny stocks.* A penny stock is any stock selling for less than $5 per share. For one thing, most big brokerage firms will not allow you to buy and sell stocks for under $5. Even more important, stocks selling for under $5 per share generally are extremely risky, thinly traded, and volatile. In our opinion, they're just not worth the risk.

2. *Limited partnerships.* Limited partnerships are pools of investors' money used to acquire real estate, purchase oil and gas ventures, fund movie projects, or buy equipment to lease out. The proceeds are invested by a general partner, who is supposed to know a particular investment area. You are a limited partner in that your liability is limited to the amount you invest. The lack of liquidity makes even a good limited partnership seem like a ball and chain. Statistically there have been very few good ones. If you find yourself stuck in a limited partnership, the following companies *may* (and it's a big *may*) be able to find a buyer for your investment. But in many cases, you'll get only cents on the dollar. And be sure to talk with your tax professional about that pesky IRS term *recapture.*

Liquidity Fund	800-833-3360
Partnership Securities Exchange	800-736-9797
	415-763-5555 (in California)
Raymond James & Associates	800-237-4240
Chicago Partnership Board	800-272-6273

The American Association of Limited Partners has a very good booklet entitled *Examining the Health of Your Partnership,* available for $5.00, postpaid, by calling 800-342-2257. Annual membership in the AALP is $29.00 and includes a free copy of the pamphlet.

3. *CMOs.* Collateralized Mortgage Obligations (or, as we like to call them, Collateralized *Moron* Obligations) are pools of mortgages, usually backed by government agencies. When interest rates start moving up again, CMOs are going to be a total nightmare.

4. *Commodity funds.* Commodities are such things as soy beans, orange juice, pork bellies, gold and silver, oil, natural gas, and other staples that are grown or mined. A commodity fund offers professional management and diversification as a mutual fund does, but the underlying assets—the commodities—are extremely volatile, due to weather, disasters, and strikes. Most people don't understand them, and most commodity funds have not performed well. Even those that have had a reasonable performance are extremely volatile and probably too risky for most investors.

5. *New issues of closed-end funds.* They tell you these are no-load, but the broker's commission is built in. As soon as the new-issue phase is complete, the fund almost always drops to a discount, that is, below the initial offering price.

GETTING HELP FROM OTHER FINANCIAL PROS

Other financial pros you may want to consider are an insurance adviser and a tax adviser. We talk more about both areas in our tax and insurance chapters but, again, your best source of information is from referrals. Talk to people you respect. Ask, "Who do you use?" "Do you like your tax guy?" "Have they saved you money?" "Have they made you money?"

For a tax expert, you may want to consider using a member of the National Association of Enrolled Agents. To qualify, members must pass all four parts of a comprehensive, four-day IRS exam or have worked on taxes for the IRS for at least five years in a row. Call 800-424-4330 for a list of members in your area.

You may also want to call the local chapter of the American Institute of Certified Public Accountants for information relating to finding a CPA in your area.

What should you ask a tax consultant? Here are a few key questions to help you find an expert to suit your needs:

What's your experience, background, and training?
How long have you been practicing?
What type of ongoing training do you have, and how often?
How many returns have you prepared each year for the past five
    years?
How much will you charge me, given a brief description of my fi-
    nancial situation?
How will we communicate and how long do you need to prepare my
    return?
Will you represent me before the IRS in case I'm audited?

Remember, before you sign anything, even if it's been prepared by a world-class accountant, read it *yourself!*

BE A GOOD SHEPHERD

There are good brokers, planners, and tax and insurance people out there. The really good ones are smart enough to do their best and make money for themselves, too. The bad ones make their money despite your possible losses. But the fact is that not one of them—good, bad, or indifferent—cares about your money the way you do. So if you are looking for professional help from any of these people, in any area, and don't monitor it yourself, you are inevitably asking for trouble. It may be a very scary thing, but *the ultimate responsibility is your own—period!*

Maybe the reason you're hiring and paying a professional is so that you don't have to do the work. Fine. But the reality is that you have to keep an eye on what's going on. You don't have to check the papers every day; you don't have to be an investment expert. But you do need to keep track of what's happening with your account. You must know what you own, what price you paid, your profits and losses. And you must keep a watchful eye on your long-term goals and periodically check your progress.

If you can't or won't keep the overall control of your finances yourself, you shouldn't do business with any of these people.

CHAPTER ELEVEN

Creative Estate Planning

How to Protect Your Assets During Your Lifetime . . . and After Your Death

"Estate planning?" Count me out! I don't have much, so forget the estate-planning techniques, Dolans! I don't need any of these fancy, hot-shot, lawyer-driven strategies to take care of my few assets."

We hear that a lot. But wait a minute. These days, millions of Americans have a net worth of $600,000 or more, which includes a home (plus a vacation home, if you're lucky), a life insurance policy, a company benefits plan, investments, furnishings, etc. If you don't mind paying up to a 55 percent tax on all your "stuff" when you die, then forget estate planning. But if preserving your assets for your benefit and your family's while you're alive as well as minimizing estate taxes and facilitating the transfer of your assets to your heirs is important to you, then let's talk about estate planning.

If you need further incentive, see the table below. No federal taxes are owed on the first $600,000 of an estate, but once you go over $600,000, here's what you face—as this book goes to press:

Assets in an estate	get taxed at this rate
$600,001–$750,000	37%
$750,001–$1,000,000	39%
$1,000,001–$1,250,000	41%
$1,250,001–$1,500,000	43%
$1,500,001–$2,000,000	45%

Assets in an estate	get taxed at this rate
$2,000,001–$2,500,000	49%
$2,500,001–$10,000,000	50%
$10,000,000–$18,340,000	55%
$18,340,001 and higher	50%

It's hard to think of anything people hate talking about more than death. Yet if you're concerned about your family, you want to be sure to provide for and protect them after you're gone. And that's what estate planning is all about.

A lot of our listeners, viewers, and newsletter subscribers assume estate planning advice doesn't apply to them, because they think it is only for the very wealthy, the "fat cats." "I don't have an estate, so why am I worried about planning for it?" But estate planning goes beyond protecting what you have. It is really a way to take care of yourself and your loved ones if you become disabled, to pass on to your loved ones whatever you have after you die, and to save every tax dollar, attorney fee, and court cost possible.

In the next 20 years, a total of $6.8 trillion in the United States is going to pass from one generation to another. It's the largest transfer of wealth in the history of the world. And the transfer will only get bigger as the decades go by. Believe us, the IRS has its greedy eyes on this money, and it will do everything it can cook up to take as much from—and leave as little for—your heirs as it possibly can. So it's up to you (with our help, of course) to protect your family and make sure they get to keep and enjoy all the assets you worked so hard to build. It's important to understand that estate planning is not to be used solely to save taxes. If estate taxes are already due, there's no way to avoid them. But planning ahead can lighten the load.

Today's "blended" families have rendered the issues of asset ownership and protection even more vexing and challenging. Second marriages, children from previous marriages, adopted children, and single-parent households have further complicated proper estate planning. Moreover, rumblings from Washington that the current administration is interested in increasing estate taxes has angered and confused many taxpayers, many of whom are confronting the need for estate planning for the first time and have no idea where to begin.

Let's start with a few basics. First of all, the will. Generally speaking, a will is a set of written instructions, enforceable by law, that directs how a person's property will be disposed of at death.

We strongly believe that *everyone* should draw up a will. Without one, your state will impose its own version of your "last will and testament" that might be vastly different from what you intended. But we don't believe that wills are viable interstate estate planning tools. We are more mobile as a society than ever. We move for a better job, to live closer to our kids or our parents, to retire to a warmer climate, etc. And wills are insufficient when your estate straddles state lines. Trusts, which we'll discuss in a minute, are much better.

THE PROBLEMS OF PROBATE

One major problem with wills is that they must go through probate, a legal process that is public, time-consuming, expensive, and puts too much control in the hands of the legal system. Probate is primarily aimed at paying creditors and then distributing assets to your heirs. It is designed to make sure your heirs don't inherit your assets and leave your creditors holding the (empty) bag. The probate court examines your will (if you have one), your assets and your debts, and makes sure your creditors are paid off. Probate costs are approximately 5 percent of your estate, but the nasty surprise is that this 5 percent comes off the top, without accounting for debts. For instance, if your estate includes a $1 million home on which you still owe $800,000, your heirs must pay 5 percent of $1 million, or $50,000, even though their net asset is really only $200,000. In effect, 5 percent has turned into 25 percent.

Although it may take months and even years to distribute the assets of an estate in probate, your estate generally has only nine months from the time of your death to settle up with any creditors and the IRS. In countless cases of large estates with few liquid assets, heirs wind up selling the home, the cars, the boats, the land, what have you, at "distressed sale" prices—to pay off the IRS.

But before we give the IRS a really bad rap (who, us?), let's be fair. Federal estate tax law allows you to do two things:

1. You can pass an unlimited amount to your spouse, tax free (but watch out when the second spouse dies!), and

2. You can pass up to $600,000 to nonspouse heirs, tax free, before federal estate taxes kick in.

Now the bad news: Your estate will be valued at the going market rate. For example, your home will be assessed at current market value, not what you paid for it 30, 40, or 50 years ago. The same goes for all your other assets. So, although your assets may have cost you a lot less to buy, they are taxed at today's prices. Also, any gifts to family and friends during your lifetime that exceed your $10,000 per year gift-tax exclusion will be deducted from your $600,000 lifetime estate-tax exclusion. During your lifetime, you can give $10,000 per year—$20,000 from you and your spouse—to each child, grandchild, or other loved one without causing you or them to owe any taxes on the gift. (A little later we'll talk about how to take advantage of this tax-free gift to lower your estate taxes!)

One bit of relief: Your heirs will not have to pay capital gains taxes on top of federal estate taxes on your home when they sell it. This is called a "stepped-up basis," and it states that once the owner of an asset dies, the clock is reset on the value of that asset. So, if your son inherits your $250,000 home (meaning the house is worth $250,000 when he inherits it, regardless of what you paid for it originally), he will pay capital gains taxes only on the amount over $250,000 when and if he ever sells that home. Even if your estate doesn't actually pay estate taxes because your estate was valued at less than $600,000, your son still gets this "step up" in cost basis.

We think, in general, that many people would be far better off considering setting up a trust, either revocable or irrevocable, rather than depending solely on a will. Often a will and a trust work very well together.

Trusts differ from wills in that:

- Trusts avoid probate, and, if properly set up, minimize federal estate taxes.
- You may benefit from the assets in your trust while you are alive.
- A trust, with your successor trustee taking over if you become incompetent, is much more flexible than a will. The successor trustee can manage your assets to care for you. Don't forget, assets covered by a will do not pass to your heirs until you die. Suppose you don't die, but are unable to care for yourself!

A revocable living trust is an estate-planning tool designed to preserve and administer property. It's flexible and can be changed at any time. Trusts can help minimize estate taxes and help you distribute your property the way you want.

THE GREAT BENEFITS OF A REVOCABLE LIVING TRUST

We especially like properly set up revocable living trusts for a number of reasons. Revocable living trusts:

- Create one vehicle to handle all your assets
- Avoid probate and preserve privacy
- Are easy to create and maintain
- Are valid in every state
- Provide easy distribution of your assets at death
- Take care of you during your lifetime
- Are easily changed during your lifetime
- Are difficult to contest.

You can be the trustee of your own trust; if you're married, your spouse can be the trustee with you. Usually your trust is set up to pay you income while you're living, but you transfer "ownership" of the assets into the name of the trust. Your instructions for what will happen to you and your estate should you become disabled or die are all part of the trust documents. You can change those instructions at any time. (We'll talk about the value of a living trust during your lifetime in a moment.) When people think trusts, they think loss of control. But with a revocable living trust, you have complete control. You've given the instructions you want followed, you've named the beneficiaries, and you can change all that at any time.

The great estate-planning benefit of a living trust is that the assets in the trust do not go through probate. Thus you avoid the costs, legal fees, and court-filing fees associated with probate; you avoid the years it takes to get an estate through the probate process (your heirs can get the assets right away); and you avoid the publicity of probate (since probate is a court proceeding, everything is a matter of public record). However, a living trust does not allow your heirs to escape estate taxes. They still have to pay. Also, any income from the trust assets during your lifetime is still taxable, and you must report it on your yearly income tax returns.

A revocable living trust also allows you to dictate specifically how your assets are to be dispersed. This can avoid a lot of ugly family disputes, since instructions in trusts are much less subject to revisions by the court than are those in wills.

Of course, if you don't put your property in your trust, it doesn't do you any good. That's a surprisingly common mistake. Folks set up a trust, then never get around to transferring title and ownership of their assets, or they transfer what they have at the moment but forget to add things over time. Remember, whatever is not in the trust is going straight to probate.

If you want the instructions in the trust to apply to all your assets, make sure you have your attorney draft a "pour-over" will to accompany your trust. A pour-over will automatically includes in your trust everything you own that isn't already in your trust when you die. *Note:* This will not allow those assets to escape probate. If you owned them when you die, they go to probate. But this will allow your instructions within the trust to apply to those assets as well. Again, your real goal is to have all your assets already inside the trust before you die.

Some states do not permit the trustee and the beneficiary to be the same person. It's an old doctrine called the doctrine of merger, which says that if the trustee and the beneficiary and the maker of the trust are all the same person, you don't really have a trust. This can easily be avoided by a lawyer who understands estate planning. The best way to set up a living trust is to name yourself as trustor (maker of the trust) and trustee (manager of the trust) and then name your kids or other trusted relatives as "successor trustees" and "beneficiaries."

No matter what type of trust you set up, another pitfall is naming an unknown or untrustworthy trustee. You don't want to name anyone with a potential conflict of interest, such as your stockbroker or insurance agent. How could they resist a little trading here and there to generate some commissions? Most people name a family member, but this too can cause heartache. We hate to say it, but plenty of kids have run off with their brothers' and sisters' inheritance, or invested it in their latest business scheme, or lost it in a nasty divorce. Choose your trustee with care. And be as clear and specific as you possibly can be in your instructions when you set up the trust; that way there may be less for the kids and grandkids to fight over.

DOUBLING YOUR $600,000 LIFETIME EXCLUSION!

We noted earlier that you can leave at death, or during your lifetime, up to $600,000 free of federal estate taxes and gift taxes. And you can pass to your spouse an unlimited amount of money, as it stands now. That's called the unlimited marital deduction. But pay close attention here. When you die, if your spouse gets everything, then she or he can pass on only $600,000 to your heirs federal estate-tax free when she or he dies.

Here's how a living trust can preserve both $600,000 exclusions, so you can leave up to $1.2 million estate-tax free. Construct your living trust with two subtrusts (sometimes called an A-B trust). While both spouses are alive, the trust remains as a single whole. Upon the first spouse's death, the trust automatically divides into two. One is a marital trust and is for the surviving spouse, and the other is a family trust for your heirs; $600,000 will go into the family trust and the rest into the marital trust. The family trust includes $600,000, so it passes tax free to your heirs, although the surviving spouse can take income from this trust if needed. And your spouse gets the rest, also estate-tax free, because of the unlimited marital exemption. Then when the second spouse dies, that spouse can also pass on $600,000 to your heirs estate-tax free.

DOLANS' SAFETY WARNING: There are two pitfalls to watch out for. 1) If the trust states that the surviving spouse can revoke both halves of the split trust after the first spouse's death, that power invalidates the $600,000 exemption on the family subtrust. After all, if the surviving spouse can change the rules and get all the money after the first spouse dies, there's been no real split. 2) Make sure title for all assets has been transferred into the trust's name. Any assets still officially owned by individuals go straight to probate.

AVOIDING ESTATE TAXES ON LIFE INSURANCE

Did you know that life insurance, although income-tax free to the recipient, is not estate-tax free? That's right. If you are the owner of the policy, it is included in your estate when you die. If you make your living trust the beneficiary of insurance proceeds, you can avoid probate on the proceeds, but your estate still has to pay federal estate taxes, not to mention the state inheritance taxes levied by some states.

People often buy life insurance to help pay federal estate taxes. However, if the life insurance purchased for that reason is itself subject to federal estate taxes—listen to this!—as much as 55 percent of the proceeds will be lost in taxes.

Here's how a special kind of trust can, partially or totally, pay estate taxes due on your death. You set up an irrevocable life insurance trust (ILIT), sometimes called a "wealth transfer trust." Don't let your eyes glaze over! This strategy could save you big bucks. If an ILIT is created properly, it is the owner and beneficiary of your life insurance policy. You cannot be the trustee, nor should your spouse be named trustee. Most people name a trusted financial adviser. Because ILITs don't die, any life insurance proceeds that are collected by the trust are not subject to income tax or federal estate tax. But what must you give up for this benefit?

ILITs are irrevocable. That means that once it is signed, it cannot be changed unless a court approves the change—and that isn't so easy. By using a good estate-planning attorney, however, the adverse effects of irrevocability can be minimized. The good news is that by using an ILIT, you can control how the life insurance proceeds are used by your heirs. In addition, by keeping the proceeds in a trust for your family, they are free from the claims of their creditors or divorce courts in almost all situations. Given our litigious society and the number of divorces, this benefit is significant.

Each time a life insurance premium is paid into an ILIT, it is really a gift to the beneficiaries of the ILIT. Because an ILIT is a separate and distinct entity, it is really a gift with strings attached. That means you control the gift, but it may be subject to gift tax. However, an ILIT can be set up in such a way that the gifts qualify for the $10,000 annual exclusion for gifts. This means that if the ILIT has three children as beneficiaries, a total of $30,000 worth of gifts by the husband and $30,000 worth of gifts by the wife can be made. That will buy a lot of insurance!

Furthermore, if $10,000 worth of premiums buys $1 million worth of life insurance, then that $10,000 has created $1 million worth of wealth that is free of federal estate-tax! (That is why the ILIT is sometimes called a wealth transfer trust.)

For married couples, if proper planning has been done, the federal estate tax is not due until both spouses die. Which spouse should be insured? There is no sure way to know which spouse will die first, so insurance companies have developed a type of life insurance called "second-to-die insurance." It pays only after both spouses pass away.

The great benefit of this type of life insurance is that it is much less expensive than purchasing a separate policy on each spouse.

Irrevocable life insurance trusts are important planning tools. If used when planning with a good estate-planning attorney and a good life insurance agent, an ILIT is one of the best ways available to save on your federal estate taxes.

ANOTHER WAY FOR INSURANCE TO COVER ESTATE TAXES

Many folks buy life insurance policies specifically so their heirs can use the proceeds to pay estate taxes, without realizing that the policy is itself subject to estate taxes! A better way is for the children or grandchildren to buy the policy on the parents (or grandparents). That way, the kids can still be the beneficiaries, but the policy is not considered part of the parents' estate when they die. But, remember, you have given up some control. There is no trust involved that can ensure the proceeds are used the way you want!

DOLANS' SMART MONEY TIP: In fact, the parents or grandparents can still pay for the policy by giving up to $10,000 per year, per spouse, to each child to go toward covering the premiums. Of course, you want to impress upon the children the importance of using the gift to pay the premiums, and not for a new convertible.

Remember, there's no good reason for spouses to own policies on each other. They get an unlimited estate-tax exemption when the first spouse dies, so they have gained no estate-tax advantage in doing so. Better to have the kids own the policies.

What if you already own a life insurance policy that you want to transfer into a trust? You can "give" it to the trust, but you may encounter a gift tax if the gift is valued at more than your $10,000 per year maximum. Consult your insurance agent to determine the value of the gift.

RETIREMENT PLANS WITHIN AN ESTATE

IRAs and other retirement plans are included in your estate for estate-tax purposes, and they can also present income tax problems for your heirs.

A spouse can treat inherited IRAs as his or her own. But for nonspouses, the general rule is that IRA proceeds must be distributed to the heirs and taxed within five years of the death. If you've already started taking benefits, they must continue on your schedule. However, your heirs can choose to take them based on their own life expectancy, as long as they start taking money within a year of the account holder's death. And they cannot recalculate their life expectancy later, nor can they combine the inherited IRA with other IRAs they own—no rollovers allowed.

If your IRA or retirement plan is especially large, another booby prize awaits: Your heirs may get hit with a 15 percent surtax on top of regular income taxes for annual withdrawals that exceed $150,000 (or lump sums over $750,000). If your account is that big, consider taking money out while you're still alive and putting it into an irrevocable trust. Your kids thus escape both probate and estate taxes, and they may even escape the 15 percent surtax.

GIFTS THAT BYPASS UNCLE SAM

Back in the good old days, the Rockefellers and the Mellons used to pass their millions from grandparent to grandchildren and completely avoid federal estate taxes. As you can imagine, Congress didn't like that idea much, so they put a stop to it, sort of. Current law now allows everyone to pass up to $1 million tax free if they can skip a generation. But if you try to skip a generation for more than $1 million, then you pay a penalty tax—not only estate tax, but a 55 percent penalty tax on top of that.

Here's how to leave more than $1 million (we should be so lucky). Take your $1 million and give it to your grandchildren to spend on premiums for an insurance policy on your life, which could be a $100 million policy. Have the grandchildren own the policy and name them as the beneficiaries. Technically they've been given $1 million, which is generation skipping tax free, but really they get $100 million. However, you will have to pay federal gift taxes on the $1 million to the extent that it exceeds your $600,000 lifetime exclusion.

LIFE ESTATE FOR SMALLER ESTATES

For all of us who *don't* have Rockefeller-size estates, here's another estate-planning tool you might consider to shelter your assets.

First, a warning!! We can't tell you how many times an older couple or surviving spouse has called us and said that a well-meaning relative, lawyer, or CPA has counseled them to give their home away to their child or children to protect their assets. True, with certain restrictions that gift of a home does prevent Medicaid from seizing the home. (As we'll discuss later, Medicaid can't seize the home from the spouse, but it can lay claim to it in an estate, once both spouses have died.) But here's the rub! If you give your home to your kids (or anyone), while you are still alive, their cost basis for tax purposes is your basis, typically what you originally paid for the house. So, if you originally paid $40,000 for the house and the kids turn around and sell it for $200,000, they owe taxes on $160,000 of gain—regardless of what the home was worth when you gave it to them!

Here's a better way to go, especially if your estate is under $600,000. It's called a life estate. With a life estate, you can give your home to your kids (or anyone), live in it for the rest of your life, *and* give the heirs (your kids or whomever) a big tax break. What's more, it costs you very little to do so. A life estate lets you (the owner) continue living in your home for the rest of your life. How? By setting up a lifetime tenancy that expires at your death. At that time, the home belongs to your heirs, and the tax advantage accrues to them.

Here's an example we ran across recently. Mary is a 60-year-old widow with two adult children, Ben and Amy. Mary's $250,000 estate consists of her home, presently valued at $150,000, and other assets. Mary would love for her kids to get the home when she dies, but she is concerned that her major asset, her home, might have to be sold to pay nursing home expenses if she needs such care in the future. Rather than giving the home to the kids now and giving them a future tax problem, Mary can give Ben and Amy the "remainder interest" in her home (they will receive it at her death) while she retains a life estate.

Here are the benefits Mary and her kids enjoy:

- The home avoids the potentially expensive and time-consuming probate process.
- The life estate is easy and relatively inexpensive ($100–$250) to set up. All it takes is a real estate attorney to prepare a deed that transfers the remainder interest to Ben and Amy while Mary retains a life estate.
- Mary may live in the home for the rest of her life. Even if her

kids sell their remainder interest, Mary's right to live in the home for the rest of her life is unaffected. (Mary's also still responsible for the maintenance and upkeep of the property.)

• Thirty months after the transfer, the value of the remainder interest in the home is no longer considered Mary's asset, which means it cannot be tapped to pay her health care. Should Mary need expensive medical treatment and/or a nursing home stay, she won't have to sell her home to pay for it.

• When Mary dies, the children's "cost basis" is "stepped up" to its value on the date of Mary's death, *not* its value when she bought it.

The gift of the home to her kids immediately reduces Mary's $600,000 lifetime gift exclusion by $150,000. And the value of the home at Mary's death will be included in her gross estate for estate-tax purposes. Which is why this strategy is especially appropriate for families with estates of $600,000 or less. You preserve the home for your family, protect it from catastrophic health-care costs, and avoid a tax nightmare for your kids. And, by staying under the $600,000 estate-tax exemption limit, you avoid estate taxes as well!

QUALIFIED PERSONAL RESIDENCE TRUST FOR LARGER ESTATES

If you have an estate worth more than $600,000, you may want to protect your home with another strategy called a qualified personal residence trust. With this kind of trust, the IRS allows you to give away your house but to continue to live in it for a certain period of time after you've given it away. For example, say I'm going to give away my house, but for 10 years I continue to live in it. And after 10 years, I either move or I continue to live in it, and pay reasonable market-rate rent and expenses.

The advantage of using a qualified personal residence trust is this: You get the growth of the house's value out of your estate. Let's say you have a $500,000 house and in 10 years you want to give it to your children. In 10 years, given the erosive power of inflation, $500,000 might only buy a $150,000 house. So estate law says you've made a gift of $150,000. Your $600,000 lifetime estate-tax exclusion is docked for only $150,000.

Yet when the house goes to your kids it could be worth $600,000 or more.

The time period can be five years, eight years, any specific pre-agreed time. And you must live out the term of the agreement, or the trust is canceled and the property reverts to your estate (which is why we don't all make 99-year trusts!). When the trust period is over, the kids own the house. The trust is irrevocable, so don't set it up lightly.

CUTTING YOUR TAXES BY GIVING AWAY YOUR HOME

If you want to give away your house for a tax deduction, give the remainder interest to charity. Here's how it works: You say, "My wife and I are going to continue living in our house, but after our deaths the house is going to go to the United Way." You then calculate your life expectancy and figure out the future value of the house, as we described above. You can take an income tax deduction currently for that future gift to charity. This allows you to give away your house to charity, live in it all your life and the life of your wife or your husband, and still get a tax deduction. It's called a split gift with charity.

There are limits to how much in charitable contributions you can deduct from your income taxes each year. If the value of the deduction exceeds that limit, you can spread it out over the next five years. If you are charitably minded, get together with your tax adviser and explore the different ways you can "gift and deduct," especially the charitable remainder trust, which is another way to make gifts to charity while benefiting you and your family while you're alive.

ESTATE PROTECTION WHILE YOU'RE LIVING

We've talked about the use of trusts and other strategies for smart estate planning after you die. Now let's talk about estate planning for your lifetime. We're referring specifically to how to take care of your family and your assets should you become disabled. According to insurance morbidity tables, most people are six times more likely to become disabled in the next year than to die. And if you become mentally disabled, you go to probate court. That's right, probate while you're still alive. It's called a guardianship or a conservatorship.

Can a will take care of you during your lifetime? No. A will only applies after you've died. In the event that you may become mentally disabled, you can set up what is called a durable power of attorney, naming someone to act on your behalf (not just a power of attorney, because it terminates upon disability of the principal). Or you can set up a trust, naming a successor trustee who would take over if you became disabled. We prefer a trust, because you can specify your instructions, and they must be followed whether you become disabled or die.

A LIVING WILL

You might also want to consider writing a "living will," also called a physician's directive. A living will is used to specify your wishes for your own future in case you become unable to speak for yourself. If, for example, you're terminally ill, the living will can state your wish to refuse any medical treatment that artificially prolongs your life.

The reason for a living will is not necessarily to benefit you, the patient; it's for your survivors. It takes the pressure off of them. The worst thing that you can do is not give them any instructions. They now have to make a life and death decision, perhaps not knowing what you would have wanted. Why not tell them, so they don't have to wonder if they made the right decision?

Some states also allow you to set up a "health care proxy" or "health care durable power of attorney," which gives someone else the right to make medical decisions for you if you become incapacitated. The distinction between these arrangements and a living will has become blurred, since "medical" decisions cannot always be distinguished from "life-sustaining treatment" decisions.

PROTECTING YOUR ASSETS WHEN YOU BECOME ILL

There's been a great deal of attention directed lately toward skyrocketing health-care costs, particularly nursing home and long-term care costs. How do you protect your assets from the expense of catastrophic illness and nursing homes? Medicare, which is a hospital insurance plan and a medical insurance plan, will pay only for *skilled* nursing home care that is required after a hospital stay—and even then will pay for only the first

20 days. Medicaid, which is able to pick up nursing home costs, kicks in only after you have impoverished yourself. You must spend down your assets first. Medicaid is basically medical welfare.

Let's talk about a couple of estate-planning techniques to avoid that. An awful lot of people believe the most important thing to do is to give their house to their kids. Then, they figure, Medicaid can't attach it as one of their assets. In fact, current rules say your home is not attachable as a Medicaid asset. Basically Medicaid has divided assets into two groups: countable and noncountable. Countable assets are those that you must spend down before Medicaid will pay for your care. They include: cash over $2,000, stocks, bonds, IRAs, Keoghs, CDs, Treasury notes, bonds, and bills, savings bonds, investment property, vacation homes, second vehicles, and everything else except those considered noncountable. Noncountable assets you can hang onto while still receiving Medicaid include: your primary residence, up to $2,000 cash (in most states), a car, personal jewelry, a prepaid funeral, household effects, a burial account, and term life insurance (because it has no cash surrender value). Note: Noncountable assets vary by state; check with your state welfare department.

MAKING COUNTABLE ASSETS NONCOUNTABLE

Your estate-planning goal is to turn countable assets into noncountable assets, so the government cannot force you to spend or liquidate them in order to receive Medicaid. Assets can be protected from the government by giving them away, holding them in a Medicaid trust, and holding them in certain types of joint accounts. Just as with federal estate taxes, a revocable trust will not protect you. The only kind of trust that will protect your assets is an irrevocable trust that prevents the trustee from giving you the money. In other words, if the trustee of your irrevocable trust can pay you a monthly income, that income must be used to pay for care before Medicaid will pay. Similarly, if the trustee can give you some or all of the assets, those assets must be spent before Medicaid will pay. In fact, even if the trustee refuses to give you the assets, you still cannot get Medicaid until you personally pay an amount equal to the value of those assets in trust.

DOLANS' SMART MONEY TIP: An irrevocable trust that does not allow the trustee (who is not you) to give you the assets or the income but does allow the trustee to distribute income to a third-party beneficiary (again, not you) will protect your assets and your income within the trust.

PROTECTING SPOUSES FROM RUNNING OUT OF MONEY

Fortunately Congress did heed the cry of those spouses who were becoming impoverished and literally thrown out onto the street before their infirm spouses could qualify for Medicaid. At that point, the spouse was left with nothing. So in 1988, Congress passed the Spousal Impoverishment Act, which allows the at-home spouse to keep half of the total amount of assets, valued on the day the spouse went into the nursing home or hospital. That half share may not be less than $13,296 nor more than $66,480 (indexed for inflation). Again, dollar amounts may vary from one state to another. Note that the half share is based on the value of your total assets on the day of hospitalization, not on the day you apply for Medicaid. In fact, by the time you apply for Medicaid, the at-home spouse's "half" will probably be significantly more than half of what's left.

As for income, most states require the patient to contribute all of his or her income toward health-care expenses before Medicaid will pay. The at-home spouse can keep all of his or her own income, but one of the sick or disabled spouse's. The only exception is that the at-home spouse is permitted to keep at least $856, but no more than $1,662 from total joint annual income.

PROTECTING YOUR ASSETS WITHOUT A TRUST

What if you don't have a trust? Can't you just give away your assets to your kids, so they get the money and you don't spend the "inheritance" on health care? This is where the 30-month rule becomes important. Any countable asset transferred within 30 months of applying for Medicaid doesn't count as a transfer. So you won't be allowed to get Medicaid until you spend the amount equal to the value of the transfer, even if you really don't own those assets anymore.

Of course, if you beat the 30-month rule, you're fine. (You may have given your kids a future capital gains tax nightmare, though; see the discussion of life estates on pages 264–266.) The loophole in the 30-month rule is this: You *can* transfer noncountable assets at any time, even within 30 months, without penalty. You can also spend countable assets to acquire noncountable assets, even during the 30-month period. If, for example, you believe you may need Medicaid within the next 30 months, review the two lists and see if you can help out your spouse or kids by buying some noncountable assets with countable funds. As long as you pay fair market value, you're OK. You can pay off loans, too.

There may even be another loophole. You can (yes, you can) argue with Medicaid and win. For instance, if you gave away a countable asset within 30 months of applying for Medicaid but had a good reason, you may be able to get Medicaid anyway. Most states will accept your argument if you can show that you were in good health when you made the transfer and had no reason to expect that you'd be in a nursing home within 30 months; if you had, at that time, enough countable assets to cover your reasonably expected health-care costs; if you had already established a pattern of giving away assets for estate-planning purposes or, say, helping your kids pay for college; or if you can show you were not aware of the rules at the time.

All of this assumes you want to receive Medicaid. Maybe you'd rather spend your own money for care in your old age, even if there may be little or nothing left for your heirs. We think that's a real consideration, and one only you can answer for yourself.

THE DANGERS OF JOINT OWNERSHIP

In estate planning, both for sickness and death, owning an asset jointly with someone else can get you tangled in an awful spool of red tape. Most joint accounts and joint ownerships are ''or'' accounts, meaning either owner can withdraw the money or liquidate the asset without the other's signature or permission. For Medicaid purposes, you're better off with ''and'' accounts, which require both parties to agree to the withdrawal or sale. Unlike a trust, assets in an ''and'' account are usually not accessible for Medicaid purposes if the other owner refuses (remember, with a trust, it didn't matter if the trustees refused). Of course, the co-owner doesn't have access to the asset either, because he or she needs the patient's signature; once the patient signs, the asset is ''countable'' for the purpose of qualifying for Medicaid.

PROTECTING YOUR HOME FROM MEDICAID AFTER YOUR DEATH

A bit earlier, we said that your home was a noncountable asset, meaning the government can't force your spouse to sell it to pay for your health care before Medicaid kicks in. However, what Medicaid will often do is place a lien on your home after both you and your spouse have died. The government has told states that they can actually take your home before you die, if you are single, in a nursing home, and cannot show that you will be coming home within six months. But most states allow your home to remain noncountable, even if no one is living there, until you and your spouse have died.

If your spouse is living in the home and you die on Medicaid, the government will be waiting for your spouse to die so it can seize the house to pay for the care you got (ghoulish, isn't it?). But you can transfer your half of the house to your spouse, making her or him the sole owner, while you're in the nursing home, even while you're receiving Medicaid. Your spouse can transfer that house to anyone else, and then Medicaid can't get it.

DOLANS' SAFETY WARNING: Don't transfer the house directly from your name to your kids, if you are the patient. This will disqualify you from Medicaid benefits for 30 months, or until you spend what the house was worth. Make the transfer via the at-home spouse. You could also have your spouse (or you, if you have 30 months to plan ahead) transfer the house into a trust. This will avoid the lien after death as well, since the house is not owned by either spouse.

WHAT DOESN'T WORK?

We've named quite a few estate-planning techniques that don't work in this chapter. Let's summarize here so you don't fall prey to any of them.

1. Buying life insurance to pay for estate taxes but owning the policy in your own name. Any policies you own are included in your estate when you die; they raise the value of your estate and are subject to estate taxes of up to 55 percent.

2. A living trust to escape estate taxes. Remember, revocable trusts escape probate, but not estate taxes in excess of $600,000 if you are single or $1.2 million if you are married.

3. Setting up a trust that you don't transfer any assets into. Easy mistake to make. You build the nest, then don't put any eggs into it!

4. A "constitutional trust." There are salesmen going around saying that if you put everything in this type of irrevocable trust, you'll never have to pay income or federal estate taxes. That's a big scam. It doesn't work. The IRS will just kill you in terms of taxes. Stay away from these.

5. Do-it-yourself estate-planning and will kits. This is akin to performing your own appendectomy. If you've worked a lifetime for $100,000 or $200,000 or $1 million of assets, doesn't it make sense to spend a few thousand to protect it? Go to a professional and get your affairs handled properly. You'll save much more than you spend. In fact, you may want to look for an "elder law" specialist. More and more attorneys are specializing in this huge and complex field. Just be sure you get good references, and find someone with good experience in this area of the law.

6. Not doing anything. Thousands of Americans die each year without leaving any instructions, any will, any trust arrangement. This puts all their loved ones in a terrible position, and subjects their inheritance to the maximum burden from the IRS and others.

Yes, it's difficult to think about these questions, difficult to discuss them with those you love, difficult to make the necessary arrangements we've covered in this chapter. But the ultimate act of love is for you to sit down and talk to those you love about what you want for yourself should you become sick, and what you want for them after your death. It may be the hardest thing you ever do as a family, but it will be one of the most important gifts you can leave your family once you're gone.

Although we have covered a lot of estate-planning ground in this chapter, we have just scratched the surface. The extra effort you make to learn about basic estate-planning techniques will, in our opinion, pay handsome dividends for you and your family—now and after you have passed away.

For further information, we recommend you read:

- *Protect Your Estate,* by Esperti and Peterson (McGraw Hill, $14.95)
- *Loving Trust,* by Esperti and Peterson (Penguin Books, $14.00)
- *How to Protect Your Life Savings from Catastrophic Illness and Nursing Homes,* by Harley Gordon (Financial Planning Institute, $19.95; 800-955-2626)

CHAPTER TWELVE

The Tax Man Cometh

How to Pay Less and Exercise Your Rights as a Taxpayer

You've heard Mark Twain's famous saying "In this world nothing is certain but death and taxes!" Well, at our house we have another saying that tags that one . . . "and I'm certainly not going to rush into either one!"

Unfortunately, Mark Twain was right—taxes are unavoidable. But, with a little help from us, you can cut your tax bill down to the bone, avoid an audit, survive an audit if you face one, and master the blizzard of forms and rules so that you get the best of the IRS (and not the other way around). As with so many other money subjects, it's what you don't know that kills you. When you understand a little about your rights and the IRS's limitations (it does have limitations!), you don't have to be pushed around—and you won't pay a nickel more in taxes than you absolutely have to pay.

PAYING LESS

Of course, the first question most people ask about taxes is, "How can I pay less?" First, you want to maximize your deductions so that your taxable income is as low as possible (not your income, mind you, just the money on which you must pay taxes). Then you want to take advantage of some little-known tricks and quirks in the tax laws that can save you time and money. Are you with us? OK, let's get cracking!

ELEVEN COMMONLY OVERLOOKED TAX DEDUCTIONS YOU SHOULD KNOW ABOUT

Tax deductions are an endangered species. For years Congress has targeted them with a "seek and destroy" mission; every new congressional session begins by considering ways to get more of your money. The reason? Eliminating tax deductions allows Congress to increase your total tax hit without increasing the tax rate. Naturally, when you enjoy fewer tax deductions, the percentage of income on which you pay taxes increases.

Despite the congressional annual tax deduction hunting trip, there still are many deductions left to bag. The obvious ones are mortgage interest, state and local taxes, and charitable contributions. That's right, you can deduct from your taxable income the money you spend on mortgage interest (up to $1.1 million on your primary residence and a secondary residence, combined), state taxes, local taxes, and charitable contributions. We expect that Congress will attack these as well, but for the time being they are safe and available and you should claim them.

In addition to these well-known deductions, we have uncovered some little-known expenses that most of you can claim but probably overlook. Why pay more than you have to? These deductions are perfectly legitimate and will reduce your already too-heavy tax burden.

1. *This book is tax deductible!* That's right. The tax law allows a deduction for any expenses you incur to preserve assets and earn income. (See Tax Code section 212.) The entire purpose of this book is to illustrate how you can keep more of what you earn and become a more astute financial consumer. Take advantage—deduct this book.

2. *Fighting the IRS is tax deductible.* Who would believe it? Most folks cave in and pay the IRS, believing it's easier than fighting. But how many citizens would fight an obvious injustice if they knew they could deduct the fees and costs incurred in the fight? Tax Code section 212(3) allows a deduction for fees and costs incurred when defending an IRS matter, such as audits or a tax collection claim. Now you really have a reason to fight back!

3. *Investment expenses are tax deductible.* Under Tax Code section 212(1), expenses you incur to manage your investment portfolio are tax deductible. This includes investment counsel you pay for in the form of newsletters, magazines, or other publications, and fees paid to management consultants and investment advisers. It does include commissions (fees). Commissions (fees) are added to the purchase price and deducted

from sales proceeds. It also includes some legal fees for estate planning. But this does *not* include travel expenses to an investment conference . . . so much for that seminar in Hawaii!

4. *Job-hunting expenses are tax deductible.* Many Americans are in transition regarding their careers. Either they are changing jobs by choice or somebody has made the decision for them. In either event, you can lessen the blow of job hunting by deducting some of the expenses. Money spent on meals, transportation, mileage, lodging, etc., is deductible. Keep a log of your expenses to ensure they will not be attacked by the IRS. The log should record the date, amount, place incurred, and purpose of the expense.

5. *Your résumé is tax deductible.* You can't get hired without a résumé! The expenses of résumé production can be high, especially if you need numerous copies or often change your résumé. Also, the costs of mailing that résumé are tax deductible. Deducting the costs of typing, producing, and mailing your résumé can make changing jobs a bit less taxing.

6. *Charitable contributions of cash are tax deductible.* This is an area of great confusion. The IRS says you cannot deduct cash charitable contributions. Many so-called tax experts say you're entitled to a minimum amount as a cash contribution, say $100 to $200. Neither is correct. You are entitled to deduct every nickel made in cash contributions, provided you can prove the deduction. How do you prove a cash contribution? Simple. Keep a contemporaneous log of your contributions. The log should show the date, the amount contributed, and to whom.

DOLANS' SMART MONEY TIP: Make your log airtight by having it notarized at the end of each month. When signed under penalty of perjury in the presence of a notary, your log becomes a sworn statement akin to courtroom testimony.

7. *Fees for prepaying mortgage notes are tax deductible.* Did you get stuck with any penalties or fees for prepaying a mortgage or other loan? Deduct them! The IRS long ago ruled that fees for prepaying mortgage notes or installment contracts are deductible. (See IRS Revenue Rulings 57-198 and 73-137.)

8. *Union dues are tax deductible.* Union dues are costs you must incur to remain employed. Years ago the IRS issued a ruling holding union dues to be entirely deductible. (See IRS Revenue Ruling 72-463.)

9. *Mortgage points are tax deductible.* There has been a lot of con-

fusion over this issue for a long time. At one point, the IRS referred to mortgage points as a "fee" for obtaining the mortgage, and consequently not currently deductible. However, the rule now reads that when the points are based upon a percentage of the loan, they are deductible. You can deduct 100 percent of the points for an original mortgage on your principal residence, but you must amortize points paid on a refinanced mortgage or on any mortgage on your second home over the life of the loan. (See *IRS Publication 545, Interest Expenses.*)

10. *Local license fees can be tax deductible.* When license fees meet certain criteria, they are tax deductible. The fee for your driver's license may actually be tax deductible. Specifically, you can deduct fees that are: a) value-added taxes based upon a percentage of total value; b) imposed on an annual basis; and c) imposed on personal property. (See Tax Code section 164.)

11. *Educational expenses can be deductible.* Fees and costs for reeducating yourself can be tax deductible. They are deductible when you will improve your skills as a result of the education. These are the criteria you must demonstrate to deduct educational costs: a) The education cannot train you for a new trade or business; b) you currently meet the minimum requirements to retain your employment; and c) the course will improve your skills, or you are required by law or your employer to receive the training.

HOW TO CLAIM DEDUCTIONS

Once you've discovered these deductions, you should know that they can be claimed in one of two ways. First, if you own your own small business and the expenses are directly related to the operation of your business, you should claim them as business expenses. Business-expense deductions are claimed on Schedule C, Profit or Loss from Business.

Take full advantage of Schedule C deductions whenever possible. Not only will you reduce your income taxes by deducting on Schedule C, but you decrease your Social Security tax burden as well. And at 15.3 percent of business profit, the Social Security tax is no small matter.

If you are not self-employed, your deductions must be claimed on Schedule A, Itemized Deductions. There is a line for tax payments, charitable contributions, and miscellaneous deductions, in addition to other general categories. Business-related expenses fall into the category of miscellaneous deductions. Use Form 2106 to itemize the deductions. Unless your deductions fall plainly into one of the categories listed on Schedule A, claim them under miscellaneous deductions.

MAKE SURE YOUR DEDUCTIONS ARE AIRTIGHT

The IRS makes a good living every year nitpicking your deductions. In fact, the average face-to-face audit nets the agency an additional $5,900! That's over and above what you already paid in taxes.

You've probably been told a hundred times that the key to surviving a tax audit is to "keep good records." The best systems are the simplest. Don't try to become an accountant if you aren't one. The key is to set up a simple bookkeeping entry system that allows you to record your expenses by category as they occur. This is referred to as a log or ledger system. As the expense occurs, enter the date, the amount, and purpose of the expense. As suggested earlier, have your log entries notarized on a regular basis, perhaps monthly. This transforms your records into sworn statements. That carries a lot of extra weight when you are questioned by the IRS.

Our "Straight Talk" tax consultant, Dan Pilla, has created a system that we feel is among the best available. The system, based upon Dan's 15 years of experience solving IRS audit problems, will show you how to avoid them in the first place. It's effective because it's simple and because it's based squarely on what the IRS requires in a bookkeeping system. Dan's system is described in his book *Stairway to Freedom: A Complete Taxpayer Protection System* (Winning Publications, Inc., $39.95; 800-553-6458).

THE ONE FORM THE IRS DOES NOT WANT YOU TO KNOW ABOUT

Generally, the IRS is trying to cram some form or other down your throat. It usually happens just after Christmas, at which time the agency mails tax return preparation kits to about 113 million American homes. But of all the thousands of pages of forms, there is one that the IRS has been hiding for years. This one will never show up in your mailbox. In fact, the IRS denies the form even exists! It refuses to make the form public or explain how it is used. Even when asked point blank, the IRS lies about it. "What kind of form is this?" you are probably asking. "If they don't want me to know about it, I bet I'm gonna love it." Yes, you will.

The "secret" form is IRS Form 1127. It is entitled Application for Extension of Time for Payment of Tax. You read that correctly: application for extension of time to *pay taxes*. You probably know you can get an extension for filing your return (Form 4868), but we doubt you ever heard of getting an extension for *paying* your income taxes. See pages 281 and 282 for the form that doesn't exist!

In 1990, the IRS penalized 8.3 million citizens for not paying their taxes on time. The agency collected about $1.2 billion in failure-to-pay penalties and interest on the penalties from those citizens. The sad truth is it all could have been avoided if those citizens knew of their right to file Form 1127. You see, when a properly completed Form 1127 is filed and approved by the IRS, you can obtain up to six additional months to pay the tax due, without further penalties.

The form must be filed on or before the due date of the tax to be effective. For income taxes, you must therefore file the 1127 by April 15. A word of caution, however. The extension is not automatic. It must be approved by the IRS to be effective. In order to win the extension, you must show that:

1. You exercised ordinary business care and prudence in providing for your taxes, but due to no fault of your own you were unable to pay the correct amount.
2. You will experience undue hardship if forced to pay the tax by the due date. An undue hardship is more than just inconvenience. It is the kind of hardship that may cause serious financial repercussions, such as inability to provide living expenses for your family.
3. You must show that you are unable to borrow the money.
4. You must provide security to the IRS to ensure they can collect what is owed. The security can take the form of a tax lien in favor of the IRS for the amount due.

Form 1127 is an extremely simple document. In fact, it is one of the simplest tax forms in existence. Yet to prevail in your application, you must attach supplemental information to prove you meet the four criteria outlined above. You must also provide a financial statement (Form

Form 1127
(Rev. 5-92)

Department of the Treasury
Internal Revenue Service

APPLICATION FOR EXTENSION OF TIME FOR PAYMENT OF TAX

(Please read conditions on back before completing this form)

Please Type or Print	Taxpayer's Name (include Spouse if this is for a joint return)	Social Security Number or Employer Identification Number
	Present Address	
		Spouse's Social Security Number if this is for a Joint Return
	City, Town or Post Office, State, and Zip Code	

District Director of Internal Revenue at _____
(Enter City and State where IRS Office is located)

I request an extension from _____ , 19 _____ , to _____ , 19 _____ ,
(Enter Due Date of Return)

to pay tax of $ _____ for the year ended _____ , 19_____ .

This extension is necessary because *(If more space is needed, please attach a separate sheet):* _____

_____

_____

_____

I can not borrow to pay the tax because: _____

_____

_____

To show the need for the extension, I am attaching: (1) a statement of my assets and liabilities at the end of last month (showing book and market values of assets and whether securities are listed or unlisted); and (2) an itemized list of money I received and spent for 3 months before the date the tax is due.

I propose to secure this liability as follows:

_____

_____

Under penalties of perjury, I declare that I have examined this application, including any accompanying schedules and statements, and to the best of my knowledge and belief it is true, correct, and complete.

_____ _____
SIGNATURE (BOTH SIGNATURES IF THIS IS FOR A JOINT RETURN)   (DATE)

The District Director will let you know whether the extension is approved or denied and will tell you the form of bond, if necessary. However, the Director cannot consider an application if it is filed after the due date of the return. A list of approved surety companies will be sent to you upon request.

(The following will be filled in by the IRS.)

This application is   ☐ approved   for the following reasons:
                      ☐ denied

_____

_____

Interest _____   Date of assessment _____   Identifying no. _____

Penalty _____   _____   _____
                            (SIGNATURE)   (DATE)

(over)   Form **1127** (Rev. 5-92)

CONDITIONS UNDER WHICH EXTENSIONS FOR PAYMENTS MAY BE GRANTED UNDER SECTION 6161 OF THE INTERNAL REVENUE CODE

The District Director may approve an extension for payment of your tax if you show that it will cause you undue hardship to pay it on the date it is due. Your application must be filed with the District Director on or before the date payment is due.

If you are asking to pay the amount you owe in installments, rather than to delay making any payments, do not complete this form. Instead, contact your local IRS office, or call 1-800-829-1040. However, if you owe a deficiency (an amount owed after your return is examined), you can discuss an installment agreement with the person who examines your return when you agree to the deficiency.

1. **Undue hardship.**—This means more than inconvenience. You must show that you will have substantial financial loss if you pay your tax on the date it is due. (This loss could be caused by selling property at a sacrifice price.) You must show that you do not have enough cash, above necessary working capital, to pay the tax. In determining cash available, include anything you can convert into cash, and use current market prices. Also, show that you can not borrow to pay the tax, except under terms that will cause you severe loss and hardship.

2. **Limits.**—As a general rule, an extension to pay income or gift tax on a return is limited to 6 months from the date payment is due. An extension may be granted for more than 6 months if you are abroad.

An extension to pay a deficiency (an amount you owe after an examination of your return) in income or gift tax is limited to 18 months from the date payment is due and, in exceptional cases, up to another 12 months.

No extension is granted to pay a deficiency caused by negligence, intentional disregard of rules and regulations, or fraud with intent to evade tax.

3. **Interest.**—Interest is charged at the underpayment rate in Code section 6621(a)(2).

4. **Security.**—Security satisfactory to the District Director is required to get an extension. This assures that the risk to the Government is no greater at the end of the extension than at the beginning. The kind of security, such as bond, notice of lien, mortgage, pledge, deed of trust of specific property or general assets, personal surety, or other, will depend on the circumstances in each case. Ordinarily, when you receive approval of your application, deposit with the District Director any collateral that was agreed upon for security. No collateral is required if you have no assets.

5. **Due date of payment for which extension is granted.**—Before the extension runs out, pay the tax for which the extension is granted (without notice and demand from the District Director).

6. **Filing requirements.**—If you need an extension to pay tax, submit an application with supporting documents on or before the date the tax is due. File the application with the District Director (Attn: Chief, Special Procedures function) where you maintain your legal residence or principal place of business. If, however, the tax will be paid to the Assistant Commissioner (International), file the application with that office. If you need an extension to pay estate tax, file Form 4768, Application for Extension of Time to File U.S. Estate Tax Return and/or Pay Estate Tax.

Form 1127 (Rev. 5-92)

*U.S. GPO: 1992-312-711/61562

433-A) and a list of your income and expenses for the last three months. Sound difficult? Not really. It involves some legwork, but think of the penalty money you'll save if the application is granted.

If the IRS grants your Form 1127, you win six additional months to pay the tax, free of penalties! However interest still accrues on the unpaid tax amount.

RED FLAG DEDUCTIONS—FILE WITH CARE

There is no single word that strikes as much fear in the heart of a taxpayer as "audit." We've had listeners of our radio show call us with a freshly received audit notice in their hands, on the verge of tears. What to do? "An ounce of prevention . . ." as they say. In other words, avoid the audit in the first place. For starters, let's cover some "red flag" deductions—items on a tax return that tend to raise eyebrows at the IRS. The biggest red flags are:

- Abnormally high deductions. The average medical deduction claimed by tax filers is about 12 percent of gross income; the average charitable contributions claimed as a deduction is about 5 percent of gross income; the average interest deduction (such as for your mortgage) is 15 percent.
- Home office deduction. It may be perfectly justified, and provable, but the IRS is more likely to question this one than most others, and 1993 has seen tougher home office deduction regulation.
- Travel and entertainment deductions.
- Using your car for business.
- Income on limited partnerships and other tax shelters.
- Donations of appreciated property (as opposed to cash) to charity.

In all cases, your best defense is to keep careful and complete records and receipts.

AUDIT-PROOF YOUR RETURN

Next, there's another form the IRS doesn't like to talk about: IRS Form 8275, Disclosure Statement. The Disclosure Statement is a means to make your income tax return penalty-proof and audit-proof. It allows a taxpayer to provide proof to the IRS, at the time of filing the return, regarding any potential "red flag" item on the return. By filing Form 8275, you put the IRS on notice of the potential problem area. You also provide all the facts and circumstances justifying your claim to the item.

Submitting Form 8275 with your return accomplishes two important things. First, you eliminate the prospect of being called in for an audit over the issue. After all, the audit is the means used to ascertain your reasons for making a claim. With Form 8275, you've already given all your reasons—and copies of documentary proof—with the return itself. The IRS will have all it needs right in front of it. No need for you to be dragged in for an audit.

Second, and perhaps more important, should the IRS determine you're not entitled to claim the particular item as a deduction, you avoid penalties when full disclosure of all facts is made on the return with Form 8275. This is critical, given the IRS's love affair with penalty assessments.

"Why draw attention to the red flags in my return—won't that simply trigger an audit?" you might be wondering. The truth is the form itself does not trigger an audit. But if your return does contain some red flags, you are virtually assured it will trigger a face-to-face examination without Form 8275. With the form and supporting documentation, there is no need for face-to-face scrutiny. The supporting material is there, and all the IRS must do is pass on the merits of your claim. Of course, if it disallows the deduction, you have the right to appeal the decision. Meanwhile, you've avoided penalties and interest payments mounting up.

THE STATUTES OF LIMITATIONS

"Can I ever stop worrying?" "Can they audit every return I've ever filed?" We hear these questions a lot from our radio show listeners and we want to provide an authoritative answer. You can stop worrying. There are definitive statutes of limitations that govern the IRS's ability to assess and collect taxes. To better protect yourself, you should know what those statutes are.

Limiting a Tax Audit

The IRS's ability to audit a tax return is governed by what is known as the Assessment Statute of Limitations. That law provides that the IRS has just three years from the date a return is filed during which to make an assessment of taxes regarding that return. An assessment is the IRS's formal determination that you owe money. For example, if you filed your 1980 federal income tax return on April 15, 1990, the IRS could no longer audit the return after April 15, 1993 (three years from the date of filing).

Watch out for the exceptions to this rule. The most common exception is when the taxpayer agrees to extend the ASED (Assessment Statute Expiration Date). That is done by voluntarily signing IRS Form 872, Assessment of Statute Waiver. Often, when the ASED is imminent, an IRS auditor will ask you to sign this form without explaining the full impact of your actions. *Don't sign it.* You cannot be forced to sign and you will not lose your right to appeal if you do not.

Another exception to the general three-year rule is when 25 percent of gross income or more is omitted from the return. If that happens, the ASED grows to six years from the date the return is filed. Another exception is when fraud is alleged by the IRS. When fraud is raised as an issue, there is no time limit for the IRS. If the IRS raises fraud in connection with its dealings with you, you should immediately terminate any conference or discussion. You cannot be forced to make statements when the issue involves fraud, and we strongly recommend you seek experienced tax counsel to assist with such a serious matter.

Limiting the IRS's Ability to Collect

You will be happy to know that the IRS cannot chase you for the rest of your life if you owe taxes. Their right to collect is governed by the Collection Statute of Limitations. Effective November 5, 1990, the IRS has just 10 years in which to collect a tax, beginning from the date of assessment. To determine the deadline, count forward 10 years from the date of assessment (the date on which the IRS officially records a tax deficiency as a debt on its books; not the date you file a return nor the date the IRS issued a notice). The assessment date is commonly shown on the face of a tax lien. That alone is the governing date for purposes of determining the deadline.

As you might imagine, there are circumstances in which the deadline can be extended. The most common way is by voluntary consent of the taxpayer. IRS Form 900, Tax Collection Waiver, is used to extend the deadline. Often IRS agents will persuade you to sign a Form 900 by threatening lien or levy if you do not. We recommend you consult experienced tax counsel before you sign any such form.

DEFENDING YOURSELF IN A TAX AUDIT

Even if you are conservative in your tax filing and scrupulous in your record keeping, you could still be called in for an audit. A certain percentage of audits are simply picked by lottery. If your number comes up, you get audited.

Audits are scary experiences, and that's just the way the IRS likes it. The more afraid you are, the more likely you'll just pay up with no questions asked. But you don't have to be the loser in an audit. The following tips will give you plenty of ammunition for use in an audit, if you are unlucky enough to be selected.

1. *Don't assume you're wrong.* Just because you were chosen for an audit doesn't mean you made a mistake on your return. Quite the contrary. Your return was selected largely on the basis of a computer program that scans returns looking for the most likely candidates. The audit is your opportunity to prove you filed your return correctly.

2. *Be prepared to prove your claims.* The crux of every audit can be boiled down to just one word—proof. If you use a tax preparer, ask him to go with you or to represent you. If you or your tax preparer can prove the accuracy of the claims made on your return, you will leave the audit no poorer than when you left. If you can't, well . . .

3. *Don't be bullied.* Tax auditors are trained to be bullies. They push you around and try to make you believe that their word is gospel and they hold all the cards. Don't buy it! *Tax auditors are the least powerful of all IRS employees.* You cannot be forced into an audit for which you are ill-prepared, and you cannot be forced to accept any findings with which you disagree.

You may (and should) request a reasonable amount of time to organize your income and expense records. Again, don't be bullied!

4. *Ask questions until you understand everything.* Never agree with a tax auditor if you do not understand all the issues and points of discussion. You have the right to know the basis for all proposals, and you have the right to provide any additional information that may help you.

5. *Don't volunteer additional information.* Cooperate, yes; answer questions, yes. But don't provide added info the auditor never asked about in the first place. Be brief, to the point, and direct. No chatting required—this is not a cocktail party!

6. *Everything is negotiable.* Few people realize it, but an audit is not unlike any other negotiation. The only difference is that the auditor does

not want you to believe you are involved in one. He would prefer that you believe his word is final and that you must pay what he says you owe. One important key to dealing successfully with an auditor is to make him understand you are aware of, and willing to use, your right of appeal.

7. *Never sign when you don't agree.* Tax auditors will push for a signature when the audit is complete. The form they want signed is IRS Form 870 Waiver. If you sign it, you thereby consent to assessment of the tax. Stated more simply, you agree to allow the IRS to begin collecting what the auditor says you owe. You cannot be forced to sign the form. Contrary to the rantings of most auditors, it will not "go badly" for you if you refuse.

USING YOUR RIGHT OF APPEAL

A tax auditor can make no final decision disallowing any of your deductions. He can merely make recommendations. If you disagree, you have three options. You should be prepared to employ all three:

- Ask for more time to present additional information (30-day extensions are given without much fuss)
- Ask for a meeting with the auditor's supervisor
- Appeal the decision to the IRS Appeals Division.

An appeal is made by drafting a document known as a protest letter. You have 30 days from the date of the auditor's notice disallowing deductions in which to submit the letter (again, you should have no trouble getting a 30-day extension on this deadline). Your protest letter should explain what you disagree with and why. Be sure to ask for a meeting with a representative of the Appeals Division. This division is set up to mediate disputed audit cases; frankly, taxpayers fare much better there than before the tax auditors. *IRS Publication 5 Appeals Rights,* explains more about the right of appeal and drafting the protest letter.

DOLANS' SMART MONEY TIP: As soon as you get a notice from your auditor with which you disagree, request—in writing—copies of the auditor's work papers. Direct your request to the District Director's Disclosure Officer. The more you know about how the auditor reached his conclusions, the better armed you'll be to defend your position.

And remember, the Appeals Division is not interested in losing in court. So make it clear in your protest letter that you are fully prepared to go to court to defend yourself. In and of itself, this can be a powerful negotiating chip.

YOUR RIGHTS AS A TAXPAYER

Actually, your right to appeal is just one of your rights under the IRS code. Don't hold your breath waiting for the IRS to tell you this, but your rights go way beyond just "the right to remain silent"! They are rights that every citizen should be prepared to put to use if the need ever arises. These rights can assure you that you will never become a tax collection statistic. Here are some of your most important rights.

1. *The right to say "no" to a tax auditor.* Does the idea of saying "no" to an IRS auditor terrify you? It shouldn't. The tax auditor never has any final authority over you in an audit. However, as much as the auditor may huff and puff, you have the right to challenge his or her decision. IRS statistics tell us taxpayers win their cases about 64 percent of the time.

2. *The right to eliminate penalties.* One of the most common problems taxpayers face is IRS penalties. The IRS has a penalty for every day of the week. In fact, it has penalties for every hour of every day of the week. There are more than 150 different penalties contained in the tax law, and the IRS can find one to hit you with at every turn. Each penalty is subject to cancellation, however. The IRS generally "forgets" to tell you that (surprise, surprise). All penalties can be canceled when the taxpayer can show he acted reasonably and in good faith and not in an effort to deceive or mislead the IRS. In most cases, a simple letter of explanation setting out all the appropriate facts will do the job.

3. *The right to a correspondence audit.* Do you dread the thought of facing the IRS in an audit? Do you crumble under pressure or when faced by an authority figure? Are you afraid you'll say something stupid or incorrect to an auditor? Our advice is simple. Don't go to the audit!

We're not telling you to hop the first plane to the Bahamas, but we are saying you have the right to a *correspondence audit*, which is nothing more than conducting your audit through the mail. You avoid the stress of a face-to-face meeting, the hassle, the inconvenience and expense of taking time off work, and the possibility you will say something that can be misconstrued by the auditor. The correspondence audit involves submitting copies of your documentation to the agent via mail, together with letters of explanation on any legitimate question.

4. *The right to an installment agreement.* Things can get ugly fast when you owe the IRS money. Notices make it clear the IRS wants the money now—all of it. Unfortunately, the agency doesn't always explain your right to an installment agreement. If you can't pay in full, you should promptly take advantage of the installment agreement. Get a copy of IRS Form 433-A, The Financial Statement. Complete it fully and accurately and submit it to the collection agent. The 433-A lists your income and expenses, assets and liabilities. From the statement, you can negotiate a reasonable installment payment based upon your ability to pay.

5. *The right to challenge notices.* The IRS mails tens of millions of notices each year. They are almost always demands for more money. The good news is that you can challenge and cancel those notices if you disagree and act promptly (see page 291).

6. *Using the Problems Resolution Office.* One of the most frustrating aspects of dealing with a huge, often uncaring bureaucracy such as the IRS is that it can be difficult to get even the most obvious errors corrected. If you are ever backed into a corner by the agency and no one seems willing or able to help, contact the Problems Resolution Office (PRO). The PRO was set up in 1988 to assist citizens whose problems seem to fall through the gaping cracks in the floor of the IRS's "We care" department. Simple problems, such as account statements and case status, can be handled with a phone call. Pressing problems such as improper statement demands or wage and bank levies should be addressed in writing with Form 911, Application for Taxpayers' Assistance Order. For the phone number of the PRO office nearest you, call the IRS, at 800-829-3676, and order *IRS Publication 1320, Operation Link.* Or look for the number in your phone book, under U.S. Government, Treasury Department, Internal Revenue Service, Problems Resolution Office.

LICKING THE IRS WITH A POSTAGE STAMP

The IRS collects billions of dollars every year just by sending bills in the mail. The bills include notices of changes made to your account, demands for payment of interest and penalties, and computerized audits. Take heart! The IRS can alter your account only with your permission. That's right. You have the right to challenge these notices. When you do, the IRS must cancel them! Let us examine a few of the most common notices and how to cancel them.

1. *Notice of unreported income.* Information returns, such as W-2s (which report the money you earn from an employer) and 1099s (which report the money you earn elsewhere, such as bank account interest or dividends), flood into IRS service centers by the hundreds of millions. In 1992, the IRS processed about 1.2 billion information returns. When they hit the service center, the IRS cross-checks information returns with all tax returns filed, looking for unreported income. Once the cross-checking process is complete, millions of notices are sent to taxpayers, claiming they failed to report all their income and demanding the additional tax payments now due, plus interest and penalty. It may sound like a good idea to catch the "cheaters," but the problem is that about half of all such notices mailed by the IRS are dead wrong!

When you receive a notice with which you don't agree, speak up! You have 60 days in which to respond—in writing—challenging the demand. Your letter should explain that you do not agree with the IRS's computations, showing them why with documentation, and that you demand the tax be canceled. When you react this way, the IRS usually has no choice but to cancel the tax.

2. *The tax return nonfiler.* In addition to unreported income, the IRS uses information returns to track down people who don't file any tax return at all. If the agency discovers a "nonfiler," an appropriate notice is mailed. But, again, about 50 percent of such notices are simply wrong. So don't panic. Respond in writing within 60 days and include a photocopy of your return. Your letter should contain the firm, direct statement that you did indeed file. On the photocopy of your return, write in big red letters the words "Photocopy—Do NOT Process." This will prevent the service center from processing the copy as an original filing, resulting in double-billing. Who needs that?

3. *Errors on your return.* IRS computer programs check all tax returns for math errors and mechanical errors. A math error is just as it suggests: an error in addition, subtraction, etc. A mechanical error occurs when an entry is not placed on the proper line or is not carried correctly from one form to another. When such errors are found, the IRS corrects the return and mails a bill to the citizen. Unfortunately—you guessed it—it is wrong about half the time.

Once again, you can challenge the bill in writing within 60 days of the date on the notice. Your response should use clear, pointed language. Explain that you disagree with the agency's determination and demand that the tax be canceled.

4. *Notices from out-of-the blue.* In addition to each of the specific notices we have already mentioned, the IRS has been known to create notices that demand additional taxes for no real reason. As hard as that may be to imagine, the IRS does mail notices to taxpayers that allege a mistake but that do not explain what that mistake was. We often wonder whether any mistake exists at all. Most people just pay the bill rather than make any effort to question it. In fact, it seems the IRS has figured out that any bill for $589 or less will just be paid by taxpayers rather than questioned. If you don't owe, don't pay! Write back, within 60 days, and demand that the tax be canceled.

HOW NOT TO PAY PENALTIES AND INTEREST CHARGES

Billions in penalties are charged every year and most taxpayers simply pay the bill. If they only knew of their right to demand cancellation of those penalties, we know the vast majority would save themselves hundreds of dollars.

When are you most likely to face penalties? We've already talked about unreported income, and of course the IRS will demand that you pay not only the tax on the unreported income, but also a 20 percent penalty (20 percent of the amount you didn't report). Here are two more penalty triggers—and some advice on how to avoid paying any penalties:

Underpaying Your Estimated Taxes

When you are self-employed or your employer does not withhold your taxes (and send them to the IRS for you), you must pay estimated taxes each quarter. How much tax should you pay? Either 90 percent of what you will owe, or (generally) 100 percent of what you paid the previous year. But what happens when you get to the end of the year (or, more likely, April 15 of the following year) and realize you didn't pay enough? The IRS slaps you with a penalty based on current interest rates. You can avoid penalties if your income came in unevenly during the year (use

Form 2210), or if underpayment was due to some disaster, casualty, or other unusual circumstance.

Late Filing

Every American adult knows that tax returns are due by April 15. If you file late (without an approved extension), the IRS will hit you with a 5 percent penalty for every month you are late, up to a maximum of 25 percent. The penalty for *paying* your taxes late is 0.5 percent per month, also capped at 25 percent. During any month in which you incur both penalties, you get a "break"—you only get charged 4.5 percent per month. Thanks a lot.

But you may be able to avoid these penalties altogether, with one of these 10 reasons:

1. You filed by April 15 but sent your return to the wrong IRS office.
2. You got your return to the post office in time (by midnight on April 15) and have a certified mail receipt to prove it.
3. You filed late because of serious illness or a death in the family.
4. You filed late because you were out of the country unavoidably.
5. You applied for the necessary IRS forms in advance but did not receive them in time.
6. You went to an IRS office for help (before April 15), but no IRS representative could meet with you.
7. You relied on wrong information provided by an IRS worker or in an IRS publication (yes, there are mistakes in these, too).
8. Your professional tax adviser incorrectly advised you.
9. Your records were destroyed by flood or fire in your home or in your office.
10. For reasons beyond your control, you were unable to obtain the necessary records to determine how much you owed.

When demanding cancellation of any penalty, you should always make your request in writing. Each penalty provision of the tax code contains a good-faith, reasonable-cause provision. It means simply that the penalty does not apply if you made a reasonable effort to comply with the law. As you might imagine, penalties are designed to punish those who make no effort to comply with the law or who deliberately and intentionally fail to comply. They are not designed to be used when you make an innocent mistake or honest oversight. Your letter demanding cancellation should set out facts that allow the IRS to conclude that you acted in good faith and on reasonable cause. You should expressly point out that you never deliberately set out to break the law.

Sometimes the most crushing aspect of the tax bill can be the added interest charge. If you could earn that kind of return on your investments, you'd never have to work again! If any of us charged those kinds of rates, we'd be behind bars! The IRS doesn't like to explain, however, that interest can be canceled. The 1988 Taxpayer's Bill of Rights Act guarantees us the right to cancel interest assessments under certain circumstances. Three conditions lead to cancellation of interest:

- When the interest was incurred because of an error made by the IRS,
- When the interest was incurred because of a delay caused exclusively by the IRS, or
- When the interest is demanded on money that was sent to you by the IRS completely in error.

To cancel interest, write a letter to the IRS and mail it to the service center that issued the bill. The letter must show that the interest was assessed because of one of the three conditions listed above. Be specific and demand cancellation.

DOLANS' SMART MONEY TIP: All correspondence with the IRS, including your tax return, should be done through certified mail, with return receipt requested. This way you have tangible proof that your letter or return was both mailed by you and received by the IRS.

THE TAX FORMS BLIZZARD

We've already talked about a few of the most important IRS forms, but there are literally thousands of tax forms, instructions, and publications produced and distributed by the IRS every year. It is not humanly possible to read every form and publication (even if you wanted to), but here are a few that might be worthy of your attention:

Publication 1, Your Rights as a Taxpayer. Written by command of the Taxpayer's Bill of Rights Act, it describes some of your rights as a taxpayer, including the right to a correspondence audit and to challenge the decision of a tax auditor. It is not a complete statement of your rights, but it's a good start.

Publication 5, Appeals Rights. This document describes in detail your right of appeal, the manner in which the appeal is made, the role of the Appeals Division, and how to draft a written protest letter.

Publication 17, Your Federal Income Tax. This lengthy booklet explains in detail much of what the average person should know about the IRS, tax return filings, and basic tax law procedure.

Publication 334, Tax Guide for Small Business. This publication explains the rights and obligations one faces as a small business owner. Of particular interest is a description of the various forms that small businesses are responsible to file, particularly those involving employees.

Publication 586A, Tax Collection Process, Income Tax. This document describes the manner in which the IRS collects delinquent income taxes. It tells you what potential problems the IRS can cause when you owe taxes, and it explains your right to an installment agreement.

Publication 594, Tax Collection Process, Employment Tax. This publication explains just how the IRS will attempt to collect delinquent employment taxes. If you employ others in your business, you should read this document.

Publication 908, Taxes and Bankruptcy. This describes the effect of bankruptcy on federal income tax debts and the other aspects of discharge of indebtedness. While not a complete guide to bankruptcy, it does reveal one of the best-kept tax secrets in the country: Federal income taxes are dischargeable in bankruptcy!

Publication 910, Guide to Free Tax Services. The IRS provides a number of free services to the public, including tax tips and general information on a host of specific areas. This document itemizes the services available and tells you how to access them.

Circular E, Employers' Guide to Withholding. This booklet provides details on how to handle the tax obligations of your employees. It tells you how to handle withholding taxes, how to make timely deposits, and how to prepare Forms W-2 and W-3. It also provides the tables needed to accurately withhold and pay over income and FICA withholding taxes taken from your employees' paychecks.

DOLANS' SAFETY WARNING: We have found that IRS publications do contain errors. Whether this is deliberate or inadvertent, we can only guess. But we strongly recommend that if you rely on any statements made in an IRS publication, be sure to keep a complete copy of the publication in your tax return file. If you are later called to account for the error, you can prove you relied upon IRS statements, thereby avoiding interest and penalties!

All IRS forms and publications discussed in this chapter are available by contacting the IRS's Distribution Center. A list of the locations is shown below.

How to Get IRS Forms and Publications

You can order tax forms and publications from the IRS Forms Distribution Center for your state at the address below. Or, if you prefer, you can photocopy tax forms from reproducible copies kept at participating public libraries. In addition, many of these libraries have reference sets of IRS publications that you can read or copy.

If you are located in:	*Send to "Forms Distribution Center" for your state*
Alaska, Arizona, California, Colorado, Hawaii, Idaho, Montana, Nevada, New Mexico, Oregon, Utah, Washington, Wyoming	Western Area Distribution Center Rancho Cordova, CA 95743-0001
Alabama, Arkansas, Illinois, Indiana, Iowa, Kansas, Kentucky, Louisiana, Michigan, Minnesota, Mississippi, Missouri,Nebraska, North Dakota, Ohio, Oklahoma, South Dakota, Tennessee, Texas, Wisconsin	Central Area Distribution Center P.O. Box 9903 Bloomington, IL 61799

Connecticut, Delaware, District of Columbia, Florida, Georgia, Maine, Maryland, Massachusetts, New Hampshire, New Jersey, New York, North Carolina, Pennsylvania, Rhode Island, South Carolina, Vermont, Virginia, West Virginia

Eastern Area Distribution Center P.O. Box 85074 Richmond, VA 23261-5074

Foreign Addresses—Taxpayers with mailing addresses in foreign countries should send their requests for forms and publications to Forms Distribution Center, P.O. Box 25866, Richmond, VA 23289; or Forms Distribution Center, Rancho Cordova, CA 95743-0001, whichever is closer.

Puerto Rico—Forms Distribution Center, P.O. Box 25866, Richmond, VA 23289

Virgin Islands—V.I. Bureau of Internal Revenue, Lockharts Garden, No. 1A, Charlotte Amalie, St. Thomas, VI 00802

THE TAX COLLECTION PROCESS—A FEW IRS "CANS AND CAN'TS"

Most people believe the power of the IRS is unlimited. While the agency certainly does possess awesome powers, they are not unlimited. Your own power is greatly enhanced if you know just a little about how the system works.

The IRS Can:

File a lien against your property. If you owe money and don't pay, expect a lien to be filed. The lien records the fact that the IRS claims an interest in your property. You will be unable to sell or transfer the property until the lien is released.

Levy bank accounts and payroll checks. The IRS can reach into your bank account and paycheck—without a court order. This is an awesome power that, if unchecked, can lead to devastating consequences.

Seize assets such as homes and autos. The worse IRS-induced nightmare involves seized assets such as homes, businesses, and autos. Certainly the IRS has the power to do such things, and this should never be taken lightly.

Now for some good news.

The IRS Can't:

Assess taxes against you without providing notice. In all cases the IRS must inform you of its intent to assess taxes against you. Prior to assessing the tax, it must afford you an opportunity to appeal the decision. While the appeal is pending, you cannot be forced to pay any of the tax and the IRS can take no legal action to collect.

Levy your pay without providing notice. The law requires that the IRS provide at least 30-day notice of its intent to levy your wages or salary. If the IRS fails to provide the notice, any collection action taken is improper. You can use the 30-day period to straighten out misunderstandings or gain assistance from the Problems Resolution Office.

Seize your home without prior supervisory approval. One of the main points of argument for the passage of the Taxpayer's Bill of Rights Act was the IRS's sometimes ruthless action of seizing a person's principal residence. The Bill of Rights Act says the IRS cannot seize your principal residence unless this action is approved by a manager of no less stature than a District Director, the highest-level manager in an IRS district, which generally encompasses an entire state.

Levy 100 percent of your weekly or monthly pay. At one time business as usual for the IRS was to levy a person's entire weekly or monthly salary, leaving nothing with which to pay bills or feed the family. The IRS can no longer legally do such a thing. Income necessary to pay basic living expenses is exempt from levy.

Refuse to remove a lien once the tax is paid. Another infamous IRS practice came to an end with the Taxpayer's Bill of Rights Act—the habit of refusing to remove tax liens once the bill was paid. The IRS must now release the lien when asked to do so, provided the tax is paid in full or legally uncollectible.

DOLANS' SMART MONEY TIP: One of the very best books on cutting taxes and taking advantage of your taxpayer rights is Dan Pilla's 44 *Ways to Lick the IRS with a Postage Stamp* (Winning Publications, Inc., $14.95 postpaid; 800-553-6458).

CUTTING YOUR TAXES TO THE BONE

After all is said and done, wouldn't you love to pay less in taxes? Who wouldn't? We'd like to close this chapter with 15 more ways to reduce your taxes. Consult your tax adviser for a more detailed explanation of each of them.

1. When you take out a mortgage to buy your home, you can deduct the points you pay on that year's tax return, as long as they are calculated as a percentage of the mortgage (as most are). Points paid on refinancing or on a second-home mortgage are deductible over the term of the loan.

2. When you sell your home, you do not have to pay taxes on the gain as long as you buy or build a home of equal or greater value within two years. Consult your tax professional for more details.

3. If you sell your home and you help the buyer pay points, you can reduce the profit you claim on the sale by the amount you pay in points.

4. If you are over 55, you can realize a profit of as much as $125,000 on the sale of your home without paying taxes on it. A few catches: You can use this exemption only once in both your and your spouse's lifetime. So make the most of it. Don't use it if you are going to turn around and buy a house for close to the same amount of money. Use #2 (above) in that case. Save the $125,000 exemption for when you are selling your home, realizing a big profit, and not planning on buying another home, or for when you are planning on buying a much less expensive home.

5. Some home improvements qualify as medical expense deductions. Two of the most popular: a ground-floor bathroom for a person who cannot climb stairs for health reasons and an air conditioner or filter for people with serious allergies.

6. When you sell your home, you can also reduce your ''profit'' by deducting certain selling expenses, such as your real estate agent's commission, attorney's fees, notary fees, title search, and transfer fees or stamp taxes.

7. If you own a second home, you can rent it out for less than 14 days and the rental income is tax free. You also get full benefit of mortgage interest deductions and property tax deductions.

8. On the flip side, if the home is rented, *you* can use it for up to 14 days and still may be able to get full rental deductions.

9. When you move, you can deduct your moving expenses even if you don't have a job when you arrive. However, two conditions must be fulfilled: The location of the job you eventually land must be at least 35 miles farther from your old home than your old job was, and you must work at the new job for at least 39 weeks of the first 12 months after the move.

10. If your employer pays for or provides child day-care services under an official, company-wide plan, as much as $5,000 ($2,500 if you are married and filing separately) is tax free, with a few restrictions. The $5,000 exclusion can be taken through a total employer-provided dependent-care assistance program and/or through an employee contributory program in a "cafeteria" plan.

11. Your dependent children can receive up to $600 of investment income tax free. That means you can invest $5,000 to $10,000 in your child's name without paying taxes on the income, depending on the yield. Also, the first $3,400 of wages your child earns is tax free.

12. Any U.S. Savings Bonds issued after December 31, 1989, provide tax-free income if the bonds are redeemed to pay for higher education (like your kids' college tuition), with certain earnings and ownership restrictions.

13. You can earn up to $70,000 working abroad and pay no income taxes on the money, with certain restrictions.

14. If you work late at night, occasional reimbursement from your employer for transportation or meals on account of overtime is also tax free. And if you need a place to stay to do your job, such as a home for a cleric or a suite for a hotel manager, the value of the lodgings is not taxable, as long as you have accepted the accommodations as a condition of employment.

15. Finally, here's a smart money tip for making the most of your miscellaneous deductions: Bunch them in even years. For any expenses you pay annually, defer them at the end of odd years (like 1993, 1995, etc.) and pay them in January of 1994 or 1996. At the end of the even years, accelerate payments you might have made in January, and make them in December instead. The result may be that you can deduct more of your expenses. For example, if your annual miscellaneous deductions total $1,500, you never hit your $2,000 limit and hence can never deduct them. But by bunching them in every other year, you can pay $3,000 in

the even years and deduct $1,000 from your taxable income. You pay the same amount, but now some of the money is tax deductible.

We hope you feel a little better about your tax situation, now that we've reviewed how to pay less and control more. If you do have a run-in with people at the IRS, remember: You're paying their salary with your tax dollars, so you have every reason to exercise the full extent of your taxpayer rights.

CHAPTER THIRTEEN

Does It Still Make Sense to Invest in Real Estate?

How to Find the Best Deals Available for Rental or Resale

Ever since the end of World War II, real estate has been a great investment. You almost couldn't help but make money. The cost of real estate,
fueled by inflation, outpaced almost all other investments, and you didn't
have to do a thing to make your profits. Just buy a property and wait. But
that situation began to unravel in 1986 with the Tax Reform Act passed
by Congress. Tax deductions people had depended on for years vanished
and loopholes were sewn shut. Now you must be actively involved in the
management of a property to take advantage of most tax credits. "Passive
investors" are very limited in the deductions they can take.

Furthermore, as the 1980s progressed, hundreds of thousands of square
feet of office and retail space was built that went beyond any realistic
estimates of the demand for such space. Many experts now estimate that
certain metropolitan areas, such as New York City, Los Angeles, and
Dallas, have enough commercial space to supply the cities' needs for the
next 20 years without a single additional building being built.

Does that mean the boom is over? Is the investment opportunity once
held forth by real estate gone forever? Not entirely. What it does mean is
that you must be very selective, very careful, and very knowledgeable
when you buy real estate, either as a place to live or as an investment.

In this chapter, we'll discuss real estate investments and strategies that
our listeners and viewers most often ask about. This discussion is by *no*

means meant to be all-inclusive in nature, but rather a primer. At the end of the chapter, we list several excellent books that deal in detail with each of the topics we discuss in general. They supply plenty of information and homework for the potential real estate investor.

THE BEST SINGLE REAL ESTATE INVESTMENT

The single best real estate investment you and your family can make has always been your home. What else serves the double duty of fulfilling a basic need and potentially making you money over time? Nothing else— not your car, not your food, not your clothes, not your appliances or business equipment—will be worth more after five or ten years of use. Only your home.

Of course, there are no guarantees. It's possible (although unlikely) that your home could be worth less five years from now than it is today. Just ask the folks who bought houses in Texas and Louisiana in the mid-1980s! But for most of us, our homes will appreciate in value over the years.

BUYING REAL ESTATE FOR PROFIT

We talked in Chapter One about buying a home—how to shop smart and spend wisely, how to negotiate, finance, and insure your home. We stressed the importance of buying something comfortably within your price range, and something that fits your needs. Now let's turn our attention to some guidelines for buying real estate other than your home.

> DOLANS' SMART MONEY TIP: Investing in real estate is not for everyone. If you don't have cash, if you don't have some fixer-upper skills (and the time to practice them), if you don't have any interest in being a landlord, or if you want to get rich quick— then investing in real estate is not for you.

LANDLORDS AND HANDYMEN

Even if you don't have a lot of cash with which to invest, you can still make money in real estate beyond the equity you build up in your home.

Two of our favorite ways to turn real estate into an investment without a big infusion of cash are rentals and fixer-uppers.

When you own a house and rent it out, you enjoy some nifty tax advantages. You can deduct expenses for upkeep and repair, real estate taxes, mortgage interest, and insurance; you can deduct one trip per year to visit the property; and you can deduct the depreciation of the property on your tax return, taking off 3.5 percent of its cost the first year and 3.6 percent every year after that. Best of all, if your expenses exceed the income from the rental property, you can deduct the loss from your regular income up to $25,000 a year, with certain income restrictions.

If your total annual income is more than $150,000, you cannot deduct rental losses until the house is sold. Also, as you depreciate your property, your capital gains go up when you sell. For example, if you start with a $150,000 home and over the years depreciate it by 20 percent, your capital gains when you sell will be based on a cost basis of $120,000 ($150,000 − 20%, or $30,000), not $150,000.

You can buy a rental property for less than you'd spend on your own home. When you're shopping for rental property, you're not looking for a home for your family; you're looking for an investment. It doesn't matter whether or not you would live there, it simple matters whether someone else will and if you can make some money renting it.

You don't want a showplace; you want positive cash flow. That means you want property that you can rent out for more than you are paying on expenses. Thus, if you pay $600 per month on mortgage, taxes, and other expenses, and you can rent out the home for $650, you have positive cash flow of $50 per month, or $600 per year. If you paid $6,000 as a down payment for this house, you are now earning 10 percent of your money, plus tax benefits!

Of course, as an owner you are responsible for repairs and upkeep, so you want a home (and a tenant) that will require a minimum of both. You are also the person your tenant will call at 11 P.M. on Christmas Eve when the furnace goes out, or when the toilet overflows and floods the basement. Evaluate carefully whether or not this is the kind of investment you want. This is what the IRS means by an *active* real estate investor. An active investor is someone who owns at least 10 percent of the rental property and makes management decisions; choosing contractors to fix problems is allowed. To make use of the aforementioned tax benefits you must fit the IRS definition of an active investor.

If you're really not interested in playing landlord, here's another opportunity for you. Buy a fixer-upper at a distressed price, put in some sweat equity, and then sell it quickly. If you are handy, you can make some significant cosmetic improvements for a small amount of money, and then sell the home for much more than you paid.

In fact, you can buy a fixer-upper as an investment without a lot of cash—if you find a partner. Many real estate investors will be happy to supply the cash for the down payment and the mortgage payments while you hold the property, if you do the work. Of course, it's in everybody's interest to sell the property as soon as possible, and that's not as easy as it once was. So you must choose your fixer-upper carefully and investigate the resale values in the neighborhood, as well as how long the average home in that neighborhood stays on the market.

DOLANS' RULE OF THUMB: Here's a neat way to tell whether a potential rental property would really be a good investment. Divide the price of the property (the price you would pay to buy it) by the current gross annual rental revenue. No wishful thinking here—use the actual rental figure. Any property selling for more than seven times gross annual rental will probably result in negative cash flow. Most experienced investors won't pay more than five or six times the gross annual rental.

DOLANS' SMART MONEY TIP: Real estate markets have changed dramatically over the past four years, so don't rely on old information. Information on your "comps" (comparable sales with which to compare your property) should be no more than six months old, when possible, and don't depend on tax assessments as an index of values.

DISTRESSED PROPERTIES AND FORECLOSURES

If you're looking for a great deal on a property, you must look for a "motivated" seller, one who is anxious to get rid of the house in a hurry and who thus may be willing to sell at far below market value. This is particularly true if the owner has a great deal of equity in the home and doesn't need to get full price.

What motivates sellers to sell at a discount? Estate sales usually produce great bargains. The heirs want to sell quickly to pay off estate taxes or to resolve a dispute over who should inherit what. Divorce and remarriage often produce bargain sales, with two people splitting up and selling the home they lived in together or two people getting together and consolidating two households into one. And often owners of rental property get tired of playing landlord and want out immediately.

Another way to purchase a home for less than its true market value is to buy foreclosure property. This can often save you 15 percent to 25 percent or more on your total price (not to mention your monthly mortgage payments). What's the catch? In many cases, buyers are required to come up with a good percentage (if not all) of the purchase price in cash. If you have some ready cash, however, you can often scoop up a great deal.

Foreclosure property is not necessarily property in bad shape or in an undesirable location. Many foreclosures are not based on financial distress at all. Often the owners are a divorcing couple who cannot agree on a price or division of property, and who wind up having the bank foreclose on the home because neither side will pay the mortgage.

Your best bet is to approach the owners before an auction takes place. You can find their names at the local courthouse, in the newspapers, or through a foreclosure listing service like Foreclosure Research of America (301-590-1177). Go to the owners and offer to make up the back payments that are due the bank; also offer to give them some cash to help them relocate and start over. Rather than taking their chances at an auction, where almost all properties go back to the bank and the owners get nothing for whatever equity they thought they had, many owners would rather deal with you and at least get some cash and avoid the embarrassment of a public auction.

But don't get the idea that buying a foreclosure is a surefire, no-problem money-maker. A foreclosed property might not have been heated for the past six months and the water may have been left on. Squatters may be living in the property. Title may only be a quit claim deed instead of a special or general warranty deed. The former owners may have one year in which to reclaim the property; it's called the right of equity redemption. And there are a lot more problems that can occur. We won't list them all, but you can see that this is not a simple way to big profits.

BUYING AT AUCTION

If you have a large amount of cash readily available, you may want to investigate buying property at auction. There are two types of auctions:

forced and voluntary. Most forced auctions are conducted either by lenders who have foreclosed on properties, by the bankruptcy courts, or by the IRS for nonpayment of taxes. Most require the bidder to pay cash at the time of the auction for the full amount of the bid. Some states allow you to pay 10 percent at auction and the rest within a few days. Many auctions will not even let you in the door before the auction begins unless you have a certified check for a certain minimum amount of money.

Nowadays, there is so much interest in auctions that many of these end up selling at current market prices. Auctions can also end up being just another way to unload foreclosed and distressed properties that include the pitfalls we just mentioned.

Auctions are very risky for the novice investor, since you frequently have to wait to gain possession of the property (and sometimes the property can be damaged while you are seeking possession through the courts). Sometimes you cannot inspect the property thoroughly (or even get inside) prior to auction, and you don't have the right to change your mind after bidding. There are even some instances we've heard of where the bidder made a large deposit but couldn't arrange the financing within the time limit and had to forfeit the entire deposit! We much prefer the strategy of approaching the owners before the property goes to auction.

If you are an experienced buyer and you're looking for a bargain (who isn't?), check your local newspaper for a listing of available FHA properties. These are homes that HUD has acquired at foreclosure and wants to get off its books. The newspaper listing will include the ''asking price'' and the deadline for bids on the property. Once you've found a property you're interested in, you and your real estate agent must submit a HUD contract with your bid and a deposit of $500. Your real estate agent can contact HUD the following week to find out whether or not you've made the winning bid. If you have, HUD gives you 60 days to arrange financing and close the sale. For more information, contact HUD at 800-336-4582.

Voluntary auctions are usually not as treacherous as forced auctions, often because you are dealing with a less sophisticated seller. These most often occur in an estate sale. The problem here is that you often simply don't get a good deal. Auction fever takes hold, and the price gets bid up beyond fair market value.

DOLANS' SMART MONEY TIP: Rather than buying at auction, you'd probably be better off approaching a bank directly. Banks are forced to take back about 90 percent of the properties on which they foreclose. Very few sell at auction to home buyers or investors. The banks then have to sell these properties themselves and maintain them until they are sold, which involves property taxes, upkeep, etc.—a costly proposition. So obviously banks like to get rid of this drain. If you go to a bank or savings and loan directly and inquire about their REO (real estate owned) property, you may be able to find a great bargain. Bankers are often very "motivated" sellers and may even be willing to finance the deal!

BUYING REHABS FOR INCOME AND PROFIT

While many real estate tax breaks have been wiped off the books, the government still offers some tax incentives for investors in rehabilitation property, which basically includes property that is old and in disrepair. Uncle Sam tries to offer a little encouragement to intrepid investors willing to spend money on renovations.

There are two types of tax credits for rehabs: the 10 percent credit on nonresidential buildings built before 1936, and the 20 percent credit on "certified historic structures." With the 10 percent credit, you get a tax credit for 10 cents of every dollar spent on renovations. If you spend $50,000 on renovations, you can deduct $5,000, as long as your annual adjusted gross income is less than $200,000. The maximum rehab deduction is $7,000 per year, but you can carry forward any unused deductions into future years. And you can use excess rehab tax credits to offset passive income, not just active income. If you actively manage the property, you can deduct losses of up to $25,000 per year as well. Active income is derived from hands-on management of the property as defined on page 303. If you do not meet the criteria outlined there, you are considered a passive investor receiving passive income, which has a different tax treatment.

To qualify for the 10 percent credit, you must keep at least 50 percent of the existing external walls as external walls and keep at least 75 percent of the existing external walls as either internal or external walls, and keep at least 75 percent of the existing structural framework in place.

To qualify for the 20 percent credit, the property must be recognized as historic by the Department of Interior's National Register of Historic

Places, or be located in a certified historic district. Your plans for renovation and reconstruction must be approved by the National Park Service,
and then the completed work must pass an inspection. There are often
local historic renovation rules and guidelines you must follow as well, so
check these out with the local historic society before you begin sand-
blasting.

While tax credits are great, there are two real reasons to invest in
rehabs: because you love historic restoration, and because you can make
some money doing it. The gains you'll make on restoring and reselling or
leasing the property should eventually dwarf the tax benefits.

FINANCING THAT FIXER-UPPER

Even if your renovation project can't boast that George Washington once
slept there, you can get some help financing that fixer-upper. HUD's
203(k) program allows you to roll your mortgage payments and repair
expenses into a single loan. By applying for a loan from a HUD-approved
lender, and providing a set of plans and specifications for repairs and
reconstruction, you're on your way. HUD must inspect the home to
evaluate the likely appreciation; it must approve the plans and make sure
that the repairs are done correctly and the costs are reasonable. Once
approved, your loan includes a "repair escrow," which is basically a line
of credit you can draw on to pay for repairs and renovations. There are no
income limits, and the interest rates on the loans tend to be pretty competitive with conventional mortgages. For more information, call 813-
228-2501.

Another approach to look into after you've purchased the property is to
borrow money under HUD's Title I program. You may be able to get as
much as $25,000 for repairs.

For publications, call the HUD Homebuyer Hotline at 800-767-4483.

NO-MONEY-DOWN STRATEGIES

The only real estate investment we know of that you can enter with little
or no money down and with a degree of safety is your home. Through a
VA or FHA loan, you can buy a home with no down payment up through
one of 5 percent, and the government guarantees your loan to the lender.

In other words, if you default the government agency steps in and pays. The VA and the FHA set maximum mortgage limits on guaranteed, no-money-down mortgages, and they vary by region.

Even if you can't qualify for a VA or it's hard to find an FHA loan, you can often get one by assuming an existing loan from a motivated seller. With older VA and FHA loans, you don't even have to go through the qualification process for the loan, although more recent loans require it.

Another way to buy a property with no money down is for the seller to "take back" a second mortgage for the down payment. With this kind of arrangement, you make payments directly to the seller, who in effect becomes a "bank." But a word of caution with this strategy. If you're thinking of buying a house in this manner, you may be better off not doing it and waiting until you can save enough money to make the down payment yourself. It's tough enough making one mortgage payment, let alone two!

REITS AND RELPS

Apart from buying real estate—either to live in, to immediately resell (flip), to rent out as an investment, or to fix up and sell—there are several other real estate investments you may want to consider.

Two involve investment "pools," where you join other investors and buy a group of properties. With a Real Estate Limited Partnership (RELP), you and other investors get together for a certain length of time, buy residential, commercial, or mixed-use properties, and split the income while you are landlords and the profits when you sell. With a real estate investment trust (REIT), you buy shares of stock in a real estate company, which you can sell at any time. REITs are more liquid than RELPs, hence less risky. The trade-off is that, when a RELP works, you can make a lot more money than with a REIT. But the track record of publicly sold RELPs is sketchy at best. It is difficult for the average investor to find the good ones among all the bad.

If you decide a RELP is really for you, proceed with caution! In addition to checking out the strength of the properties, you should also check out the track record of the general partner (that's the manager of the partnership). You want to be sure he or she (or they) has extensive (more than five years) experience with the same type of real estate that's in this limited partnership. And remember, this is a long-term commitment.

We prefer REITs, which trade on the open market and can be bought and sold easily. REITs can be great income investments, because they are required to distribute at least 95 percent of their earnings to their shareholders. But not any old REIT will do—and don't be dazzled by promises of double-digit income! Before you invest in a REIT, make sure it boasts the following: debt that does not exceed 20 percent of assets; a consistent track record of improved earnings and dividends; diversification across many different geographic locations and types of properties; and income-producing properties with positive cash flow.

Note: There are really three different types of REITs: equity REITs, mortgage REITs, and hybrid REITs that are combinations of the two. Equity REITs give you participation in both current income from the properties and capital appreciation from sales of the properties; mortgage REITs are lending pools that offer good current income but limited capital appreciation. The hybrid REIT combines the two.

HELPING SOMEONE PAY THEIR TAXES

Another interesting way to make money in real estate without owning a home is to invest in tax lien certificates, which are available in 39 of the 50 states. With tax lien certificates, you effectively help a home owner pay his unpaid taxes. For paying these taxes (state or federal), you earn a high rate of interest on your investment (generally over 10 percent annualized). The delinquent taxpayers must buy back the certificates from you before the specified term ends, rather than having the IRS foreclose on their homes. If they manage to pay you back on time (and the vast majority do), they must pay you principal plus the guaranteed interest. If the home owner doesn't buy back the certificates, you can convert the certificates into a real estate investment by foreclosing on the actual property. The foreclosure is conducted by the state with the state's full power. This allows you to own the property or sell it to the highest bidder. Call your county clerk and ask which office handles tax lien certificates. Then visit that office in person and ask how to proceed.

But tax lien certificates are not a "no fail" investment in real estate. If you don't have time to research the properties and talk with municipalities about the procedure and the properties, you're limiting your chances for success. It's also important to understand that tax liens are not liquid. Once you buy in, you're in for the duration. There are no monthly or quarterly dividends along the way either. Principal and interest are paid in one lump sum at the conclusion. If you're looking for current income, this is not the investment for you. Your money is inaccessible until the lien is paid off or the state forecloses on the property and resells it.

The rates on tax liens can vary widely, too. In most states tax liens are auctioned off with people bidding against one another for the rate of interest and the penalty to be paid to you by the delinquent taxpayer. The rule of thumb to remember here, as with any investment: the higher the rate, the riskier the property.

DISCOUNTED MORTGAGES

Many home buyers wind up paying monthly mortgage checks to a different bank than the one they applied to for their original mortgage. That's because lenders often sell mortgages in order to free up cash before the 30 years involved in the loan are up. You can play with the big boys here by buying mortgages yourself. Banks, savings and loans, mortgage companies, and credit unions may be willing to sell you a mortgage at a discount, just to get the cash now, rather than later.

Many sellers offer second mortgages to buyers who cannot come up with enough money for a down payment or who cannot qualify for a big enough mortgage. You can step in and buy these second mortgages from sellers for a nice profit. First, if the private, second-mortgage holder is ready to quit the lender business and get his cash, he will probably be willing to sell the mortgage at a discount. Say he lent $15,000; you may be able to buy it for $10,000 or $12,000. Then you start collecting the interest payments from the borrower. But, don't forget, you're getting interest on the full amount of the mortgage, not your discounted price, which effectively raises your rate of return.

Suppose you want to originate second mortgages; in other words, you want to lend the money yourself. How do you find borrowers? One easy way is to place an ad in your local paper. Simply state that you have money available for second mortgages, and that your interest rate will be 1 to 2 percentage points higher than the going fixed-rate mortgage. You will become a lender, just like a bank, and collect interest from the borrower. But obviously, as a lender, you must be careful to screen borrowers and your collateral (the property). Make sure these bases are covered before you write a check.

LOOKING BEFORE YOU LEAP

When you buy real estate as an investment, you want to view it with a slightly different eye than when you buy a home. Yes, you want a great location, solid construction, flying colors on a home inspection, and—of course—a great price! But you also want this deal to be a money-maker, not a financial black hole.

So do your homework. Check out the appreciation in real estate values for the neighborhood each year over the past 10 years. Drive around and look at the upkeep of lots, yards, cars in driveways, paint, chimneys. Find out what the going rent is for a home in that neighborhood (a quick look in the classified section of the local paper and a Saturday drive should be all you need). If you're looking at commercial space, find out what the vacancy rate is in the area, both by driving around and noting "for lease" signs, and by talking with a commercial real estate agent. If you're really adventurous, respond to some of the "for lease" signs as a prospective tenant, and see how eager (or even desperate) the owners are. Location is still the buzzword in real estate. The more convenient your rental property is to services like public transportation, schools, churches, markets, and downtown, the better (providing the neighborhood is safe and well maintained). A quiet cul-de-sac two blocks off the main thoroughfare is pretty hard to beat.

Again, for most of us the single best (and only) real estate investment worth making is our home. For those with the time and interest to dabble in investment real estate, the boom may be over, but there are still some "deals" available. Just proceed carefully. It's all too easy to catch "real estate fever," and that could be damaging to your family's financial health.

You Can Do It!

Now that wasn't so bad, was it? Look at all the ground we've just covered together. Your family has to be in better financial shape, even if you use just a fraction of this information. But that's the wonderful thing about getting your money act together. Even if you never buy a stock that triples in value overnight, you can still increase the money in the old family cookie jar just by not throwing it away. Found money can be just as helpful in funding your child's college education or securing a financially fit retirement as investing in things that go up in value. Ben Franklin said it best: "A penny saved is a penny earned."

The whole trick to this money thing is to trust yourself and your own instincts. Yes, financial folks would love to have you dependent on them forever. But you don't have to hang on their every word. Even when their advice is good, it's still biased. All you have to do is save a little something regularly and beat inflation, so that your buying power stays the same from year to year. You don't have to beat inflation by 10 percent, either. When you try to go for the home run instead of a single or, if you're real lucky, a double, you run a much bigger chance of striking out. We don't want any homer hitters on our family team. Just aim to always make it to first base. Even a properly stroked bunt can do that.

Unless you start saving now, you're going to retire a lot poorer than your parents, or you'll find yourself putting off that retirement to a much later date. Neither really strikes us as being a good alternative. So let's get cracking!

Here are a few tips to get you started:

1. Start by saving $10 a month. No, you won't get rich, but you will get into a savings mode. Once you flex your savings muscle you'll start to like it. And, surprise of surprises, as the monthly $10 starts to grow, you'll find yourself wanting to save more and more.

2. Don't worry about where to invest this $10 a month. Just accumulate the money. If you can only handle a bank account as an investment choice to begin with, use the bank account. There'll be plenty of time later to venture into better alternatives, like the investments we talk about in Chapter Four. Don't let your discomfort with better investments cause you to not save. We do believe that all those "experts" yelling at you to do better with your investments are scaring you away from saving in the first place. Put cotton in your ears and save away!

3. Make full use of 401(k)s, IRAs, 403(b)s, SEPs, and Keoghs, whatever option you have access to. Once again, don't avoid these tax-deferred chances to build wealth just because you have to make investment choices. For starters, put the money in a safe, uncomplicated choices and then make it your first priority to study the other options.

And that's really all it's going to take. Yes, it's really just that simple: Three steps to financial independence. Once you've mastered the investment options in your tax-deferred accounts, you've mastered the choices for all your investments. The choices work the same whether tax deferred or not.

One last piece of advice. Even financial pros need sources of aid to turn to. So before we close, we want to give you a list of places to go to for help when you need a specific question answered. We use these very same sources ourselves.

Checking the safety of your bank: Veribanc, (800-44-BANKS; $10.00 for the first bank, $5.00 for each additional bank.

Credit troubles and budgeting help: National Foundation for Consumer Credit (800-388-CCCS); they'll give you the address of the office nearest you (free).

Low-rate/no-fee credit cards: Bankcard Holders of America (800-553-8025); $4.00 for a current list; list of secured cards also available.

Questions concerning FDIC insurance on bank accounts: FDIC Consumer Hotline (800-934-3342); the service is free.

Latest mortgage rates in your area: HSH Associates (800-UPDATES); $18.00 for your local lenders. FHA-HUD Home Buyers Hotline (800-767-4483); the service is free.

Mutual fund information: Investment Company Institute (202-293-7700); free publications.

Answers to insurance questions: National Consumer Insurance Hotline (800-942-4242); the service is free.

Information about franchise opportunities: International Franchise Association (202-628-8000); $20.00 for Franchise Opportunities Handbook.

Information about pensions: Pension Rights Center (202-296-3778); booklets at various prices.

Social Security information: Social Security Administration (800-772-1213).

Tax information: IRS (800-829-1040); the service is free.

Tax forms: IRS (800-829-FORM); the service is free.

Checking the safety of an insurance company: Weiss Research (800-289-9222); $15.00 per company.

Checking the disciplinary history of a stockbroker or brokerage firm: National Association of Securities Dealers (800-289-9999); the service is free.

Checking the disciplinary history of a commodities broker or firm: National Futures Association (800-676-4NFA); the service is free.

So there you are: three easy steps to financial freedom and our list of important phone numbers to keep handy. You're all ready to start, and we know you're motivated because you've read this book!

Our last words of encouragement: Do it! There's nothing standing in your way. You and your family will have a wonderful time together, a time of saving, planning ahead, and prospering. We know you can do it!

Acknowledgments

Thanks to our friends and fellow investment professionals whose continuing support of our many activities is very much appreciated: Steve Pennacchio, Renno Peterson, Kal Chany, Remar Sutton, Marc Eisenson, Dan Pilla, Peter Miller, Ted Thomas, John Allen, Ernie Kessler, Jim and Christine Lynch, Martin Shenkman, John Lucht, Ken Weber, Martin Weiss, Warren Heller, Art Kaufman, Bob Basso, Martin Yate and Harley Gordon.

Special thanks to our friend Marji Grant Ross for her invaluable assistance with this book.

Index

About the Authors

Ken and Daria Dolan, America's first family of finance, combine more than thirty years of experience in excess of 100 different areas of personal finance. Both began their careers as account executives of major New York Stock Exchange member firms. Among other positions held on Wall Street, Ken served as Vice-Chairman of a prominent international investment banking firm and Daria was a senior executive of a financial services consulting firm.

The Dolans host a daily national radio "money" call-in show on the WOR Radio Network which airs on nearly 100 radio stations across America.

In addition to co-hosting "Smart Money with the Dolans" on CNBC-TV for four years, they have appeared on numerous television shows such as "Wall Street Week," The NBC Nightly News with Tom Brokaw, "The Sally Jessy Raphael Show," "The Joan Rivers Show," "The Home Show," and many more.

The Dolans write a monthly column for *Money* magazine, author an award-winning newsletter *STRAIGHT TALK On Your Money* and are among the lecture circuit's most sought-after speakers.

The Dolans have been married for 22 years and are the parents of a daughter, Meredith.

Daria Dolan is a member of the Board of Trustees of Pine Manor College in Chestnut Hill, Massachusetts.